Economic and Monetary Union Macroeconomic Policies

Economic and Monetary Union Macroeconomic Policies

Current Practices and Alternatives

Philip Arestis
University of Cambridge

Malcolm Sawyer
University of Leeds

palgrave
macmillan

Softcover reprint of the hardcover 1st edition 2013 978-0-230-23222-8

First published 2013 by
PALGRAVE MACMILLAN

Palgrave Macmillan in the UK is an imprint of Macmillan Publishers Limited, registered in England, company number 785998, of Houndmills, Basingstoke, Hampshire RG21 6XS.

Palgrave Macmillan in the US is a division of St Martin's Press LLC, 175 Fifth Avenue, New York, NY 10010.

Palgrave Macmillan is the global academic imprint of the above companies and has companies and representatives throughout the world.

Palgrave® and Macmillan® are registered trademarks in the United States, the United Kingdom, Europe and other countries

ISBN 978-1-349-31257-3 ISBN 978-1-137-31789-6 (eBook)
DOI 10.1057/9781137317896

This book is printed on paper suitable for recycling and made from fully managed and sustained forest sources. Logging, pulping and manufacturing processes are expected to conform to the environmental regulations of the country of origin.

A catalogue record for this book is available from the British Library.

A catalog record for this book is available from the Library of Congress.

Contents

List of Figure

List of Tables

1
Introduction

1.1 General considerations

It was only during 2011 that the possibility of some form of break-up of the Economic and Monetary Union (hereafter EMU, and alternatively referred to as the euro area or euro zone) with one or more members leaving, especially Greece, became a matter of serious political debate. Although some analysts and commentators had from the outset expressed doubts on the long-term sustainability of a currency union, which was not based on political union, or indeed economic integration, the experience of the first decade or so appeared to indicate that there was no cause for concern over the long-term future of the euro (see, however, Arestis and Sawyer, 2003a, 2006a, 2006c, 2012a). But, as will be argued below, problems were bubbling under the surface, which were placing strains on the monetary union; these came to the fore as the 'great recession' unfolded, and became clearly obvious as the euro crisis emerged (Arestis and Sawyer, 2012a). The economic performance of the euro area as a whole had, since its formation, been relatively weak (as evidenced below) but not disastrously so, and indeed some of the smaller economies had experienced faster growth (than before the formation of the euro). Inflation and nominal interest rates were lower in many countries as compared with previous experience. There were signs of emerging problems given the persistence of inflationary differentials between member countries, leaving some, notably the southern European countries, in situations of deteriorating competitiveness. The current account imbalances between countries were tending to grow, with substantial capital flows from the surplus countries (mainly northern European, and Germany in particular) to deficit countries (mainly southern European, with Greece and Portugal most seriously affected), and the associated build-up of debts.

The macroeconomic policy framework within which the euro area operated has been subjected to a great deal of criticism from a range of perspectives. From a broadly Keynesian perspective it was the deflationary fiscal policy with limits on national budget deficits enshrined in the Stability and Growth Pact (SGP) that became the focus of intense criticism. But the conditions of the SGP have been breached frequently, notably by Germany and France in the first instance followed by many others. The global financial crisis starting in 2007, and intensifying in 2008[1] with the resultant sharp downturns in economic activity, helped to reveal many of the underlying issues of the euro area. The limits on budget deficits had to be suspended to cope with the sharpness of the downturn. The institutional settings of an independent central bank and the nature of its relationships with national governments (as fiscal authorities) hampered responses to the financial crisis, and later made it more difficult for national governments to fund their budget deficits.

One theme of this book is that the present (2011–13) crisis of the EMU was 'an accident waiting to happen' and comes from the interaction of the pressures imposed by the financial crisis with the design of the EMU, and that an economically successful single currency would require major changes in the design of EMU. In chapters 7 and 9 we consider the design changes, which are seen as required for a sustainable single currency consistent with economic prosperity. In this context, design changes may be something of a euphemism – in our view the changes required for a efficiently functioning monetary union involve substantial moves towards what would in effect be a political union, and a complete change in the dominant economic and political ideology which governs the present EMU.

This book seeks to decipher the type of economic analysis underlying the macroeconomic policies of the EMU in terms of its theoretical and economic policy framework. It argues that the challenges to the EMU's macroeconomic policies lie in their lack of potential to achieve full employment and low inflation in the euro area. It is concluded that these policies as they currently operate have not performed satisfactorily since the inception of the EMU and that furthermore they are unlikely to operate any better in the future; indeed, they are unlikely to save the EMU from continuing crisis. The ways in which the policy framework lies at the heart of the present crisis of the EMU are set out. The book presents some alternatives, which are based on a different theoretical framework, and proposes different institutional arrangements and policies, and which would therefore amount to substantial moves towards a de facto political union.

The EMU was founded in January 1999, simultaneously with the European Central Bank (ECB), and also the European System of Central Banks (ESCB), which includes the central banks of all EU member countries;[2] with the launch of the single currency (euro) first being introduced as a virtual currency. The euro was established for financial transactions with the exchange rates between those national currencies, which were to be absorbed by the euro, being fixed to six significant figures. At the beginning of 2002 the euro replaced the component national currencies for all transactions for 12 countries, namely Austria, Belgium, Finland, France, Germany, Greece, Ireland, Italy, Luxembourg, the Netherlands, Portugal and Spain. This meant that three countries of the then 15 members of the European Union (hereafter EU-15), namely Denmark, Sweden and the United Kingdom, did not join the euro at this time.

The European Union (hereafter EU) expanded in May 2004 with the admittance of ten new member countries, eight from Central and Eastern Europe countries (CEEC) (the Czech Republic, Estonia, Hungary, Latvia, Lithuania, Poland, Slovenia and Slovakia) plus Cyprus and Malta. There was a subsequent expansion with Bulgaria and Romania joining in January 2007, and Croatia joined in mid-2013. Of the new (2004) member states, five have since adopted the euro, namely Slovenia (2007), Cyprus and Malta (2008), Slovakia (2009) and Estonia (2011). In this book our main focus concerns the general issues surrounding the euro and its operation. However, in assessing the economic performance of the countries adopting the euro we focus on the initial 12 members, and we refer to the countries which have adopted the euro as the euro area. When we provide figures on economic performance of the euro area, unless otherwise stated, they refer to the initial 12 members.

In Arestis, Brown and Sawyer (2001) we described the build-up to the formation of the euro, tracing back the various threads leading to the launch of the euro back to at least 1970. In this book we pick up that story again but we move on from there in a significant way.

1.2 Developments in euro area governance

The Maastricht Treaty (formally, the Treaty on European Union, or TEU) was notable for establishing the 'convergence criteria' for a nation's membership of the Economic and Monetary Union. The nature of these convergence criteria in terms of what they included and what they excluded, and their importance, are evaluated in the next chapter. We argue that those 'convergence criteria', through the omission of any reference to current account imbalances, to convergence or divergence of business cycles, and the level of unemployment, stored up future problems for the EMU – and it is clear from recent events that they have indeed caused serious problems.

The Stability and Growth Pact (SGP) has, in principle, been the pact governing the operation of the EMU and of national governments within EMU on the fiscal front, though the limits on budget deficits and government debt set out in the SGP have been broken frequently, especially by the powerful EMU member countries. The macroeconomic model, which underpins the SGP, is considered in chapter 3 and the monetary and fiscal policies associated with the SGP are subjected to critical examination in chapters 4 and 5, respectively. The fiscal policy of the SGP was somewhat modified in 2005 with some loosening of the restraints on budget deficits, but there had been no substantial changes until 2011, when measures such as the 'six pack' and then the 'fiscal compact' were introduced (embodied in the Treaty on Stability, Coordination and Governance, TSCG) and these are discussed in some detail in chapter 5. The 'fiscal compact' continues many of the features of the SGP with some tightening of the deficit targets and the 'excessive deficit procedure' as well as the intention of stricter surveillance of national deficit positions.

The activities, operations and policies of the Economic and Monetary Union (EMU) and the member countries have been under the direction of a series of treaties usually referred to by the name of the city where the treaty was formulated or signed. Successive treaties have built heavily on their predecessor, although on each occasion significant changes were also involved. The Maastricht Treaty was notable for establishing the 'convergence criteria' for a nation's membership of the Economic and Monetary Union (as set out in chapter 2 below). The Treaty of Amsterdam amended the Treaty of the European Union, the treaties establishing the European Communities and certain related acts, which was signed on 2 October 1997, and entered into force on 1 May 1999. The Treaty of Amsterdam provided a greater emphasis on citizenship and the rights of individuals and some increased powers for the European Parliament. It also contained the beginnings of a common foreign and security policy (CFSP), reinforced in the later Treaty of Lisbon and the reform of the institutions in the run-up to enlargement. The present treaty, labelled the Treaty of Lisbon, was signed in Lisbon by the EU member states on 13 December 2007, and entered into force on 1 December 2009. The Treaty of Lisbon itself followed an ill-fated attempt to introduce a European Constitution. A European Convention, under the chair of Giscard D'Estaing, the then President of France, had been established in 2003 to draw up what was then termed a European Constitution, or the Constitutional Treaty. After a period of consultation, a draft European Constitution was presented for confirmation by nations. The treaty introducing the Constitution was signed on 29 October 2004 by representatives of the then 25 EU member states. The draft constitution ran to some 300 pages covering the full gamut of political, social and economic issues. In debates and discussion over the draft Constitution, a great deal of attention was paid to the relationship between the European Union and the member states and the democratic structures (or lack thereof) within the EU. It was later ratified by 18 member states, which included referenda endorsing it in Spain and Luxembourg. However, the rejection of the document by French and Dutch voters in May and June 2005 brought the ratification process to an end.

In the event, the changes associated with the Treaty of Lisbon were matters such as the creation of a President of the European Union, changes to qualified majority voting and establishment of a Foreign Minister. The parts of the Treaty of Lisbon, which have particular relevance for economic policies, were by and large a 'cut and paste' job from the preceding treaty. The Treaty of Lisbon can in many respects be seen as a European Constitution in that the treaty sets out the legal framework within which the European Union operates. In that light there are two significant features for the future development of economic policies. The first is that economic policies are indeed embedded in the treaty. Hence, for example, an 'independent' central bank with its operations based on the objective of price stability is contained within the treaty. As we will argue below, this means that a set of economic policies, which were thought suitable at the time of the treaty, are set down 'in stone'. This leads to the second feature, namely that the Treaty of Lisbon, and hence economic policies and their structures, can only be changed with the unanimous support of all member countries.

A recent important further shift has been the Treaty on Stability, Coordination and Governance in the Economic and Monetary Union (TSCG),[3] which is an intergovernmental agreement signed during 2012 to which we will give much attention below. This treaty is particularly significant for this book as it encompasses the 'fiscal compact' as well as calls for 'structural reforms', as will be discussed below. It is also significant in that it is an agreement amongst most, but not all, member countries with the UK and the Czech Republic as notable absentees. As such, it sets out a mechanism by which governance can be changed without unanimity of member countries by the use of a Treaty amongst a range of countries.

1.3 The economic philosophy of EMU

In this introductory chapter we seek to elaborate the nature of the economic philosophy which is embedded in the treaty and then to specifically consider the macroeconomic policies that are in the treaty and the problems which arise from them.

We begin with the question as to whether the Treaty of Lisbon can be reasonably described as being neo-liberal in nature. Neo-liberalism involves a focus on the role and extension of trade and markets, international trade without political impediments and private property. This is not to argue that there is a fully coherent policy agenda, and that all policies can fit into a specific policy agenda. It is rather to ask whether the Treaty of Lisbon confirms in place a framework, which is essentially neo-liberal and points to further developments in the neo-liberal direction. As will be seen later there are 'ratchet' effects – there is encouragement within the treaty for liberalisation but once liberalisation has occurred there is no provision for deliberalisation if necessary.

The neo-liberal agenda of the Treaty of Lisbon is well illustrated in view of several references to 'the principle of an open market economy with free competition' (e.g. Article 119), though many would question whether competition can ever be 'free'. But later there is reference to 'a highly competitive social market economy' (article 3), which in no way defines what is meant by a social market economy, though it is linked with 'aiming at full employment and social progress' without considering whether a market economy can ever generate full employment. By implication, there is no indication on which a range of activities will take place outside of the market, or whether the market is to control all of economic life.

For the purposes set out in Article 3 of the Treaty on European Union, 'the activities of the Member States and the Union shall include, as provided in the Treaties, the adoption of an economic policy which is based on the close coordination of Member States' economic policies, on the internal market and on the definition of common objectives, and conducted in accordance with the principle of an open market economy with free competition' (Article 119-1). It is also suggested that 'the definition and conduct of a single monetary policy and exchange-rate policy the primary objective of both of which shall be to maintain price stability and, without prejudice to this objective, to support the general economic policies in the Union, in accordance with the principle of an open market economy with free competition' (Article 119-2; see, also, Article 120).

The Treaty of Lisbon (and to a great extent its predecessors) laid down principles for economic policies (both micro- and macroeconomic ones) and various processes for the coordination of policies between the nation states (within the European Union). On this score, the Treaty of Lisbon states that 'The Member States shall coordinate their economic policies within the Union. To this end, the Council shall adopt measures, in particular broad guidelines for these policies. Specific provisions shall apply to those Member States whose currency is the euro. The Union shall take measures to ensure coordination of the employment policies of the Member States, in particular by defining guidelines for these policies' (Article 5). In the area of social policies it is a looser arrangement in that 'The Union may take initiatives to ensure coordination of Member States' social policies' (Article 5).

Within the EU, and this is reflected in successive treaties including the Lisbon Treaty, the assignment of a range of 'competencies' with regard to policy areas to the EU itself and others remaining with the member states.

In this section we briefly set out what the current position is with respect to those competencies and the related issue of subsidiarity. This is a prelude to subsequent discussion. In the economic sphere there were no proposed shifts of a similar magnitude. But our concern here is not centred on the relative powers of nation states and the EC per se. Our concern is rather twofold: (i) what is the nature of the coordination of economic decision-making which emerges? How far is the coordination in effect undertaken through a single central body (the extreme case being the European Central Bank, which could be said to coordinate interest rate policy across all members of the euro area through the imposition of a single interest rate and how far is the coordination undertaken by member states)? Then how effective is that coordination and does it meet the requirements needed for the successful operation of a single market and for the countries involved for the single currency? And (ii) in terms of the economic policies, pursued at the EU level and in terms of those policies, which are coordinated through actions of the member states, what is the 'model' which governs those policies? In any federation or federal state there are many issues of the relationship between the members and the centre.

A currency area is in general also a nation state, and hence the currency area is also a political union. A central feature of the EMU is that it is a currency union but not a political union. Within a political union, there are economic and social policies implemented at the level of the political union, and others that fall within the remit of local or regional government (often constrained by national policies). Hence, there are common policies across the political union, and in effect there is coordination of policies between constituent parts of the political union. There will, for example, be a structure of taxation, which will apply across the political union, as well as a structure and level of taxation that will vary at the local or regional level. Similarly, there will be national policies on the operation of labour markets, with possible significant variations at the regional level in a federal system (as in the USA, for example). In chapter 9 we visit the question as to whether a currency union has to be supported by a political union in order to operate successfully (which is not to say that political union always produces a prosperous currency union). A political union would entail, for example, substantial amounts of taxation raised at the central level, and the ability of the union to operate budget deficits and fiscal policy. Another element would be in effect the coordination of a range of economic policies, which would be set at the central level. The present policy coordination arrangements within the EMU and the EU can then be compared with those that would arise under a political union, and the question later discussed is whether the present forms of policy coordination help or hinder the operation of a single currency.

There are areas where although the implementation of policy lies in the hands of the national authorities, with strict guidelines (and the threat of penalties for non-compliance) laid down at the federal level. For the operation of the euro, it is the Stability and Growth Pact, with its limits on budget deficits of member governments, which provides the clearest example (and, as discussed below, despite many governments having broken the 3 per cent upper limit, no sanctions have actually been imposed). Another example relates to the provision of state aid (and thereby constrains the operation of national industrial policies and rescue of companies in financial difficulties) and is illustrative of the general neo-liberal stance of the EU. Examples are given in what follows: 'Save as otherwise provided in the Treaties, any aid granted by a Member State or through State resources in any form whatsoever which distorts or threatens to distort competition by favouring certain undertakings or the production of certain goods shall, in so far as it affects trade between Member States, be incompatible with the internal market' (Article 107-1; see also Article 108). It is also the case that 'Within the framework of the provisions set out below, restrictions on freedom to provide services within the Union shall be prohibited in respect of nationals of Member States who are established in a Member State other than that of the person for whom the services are intended' (Article 56). Also, 'The Member States shall endeavour to undertake the liberalisation of services beyond the extent required by the directives issued pursuant to Article 59(1), if their general economic situation and the situation of the economic sector concerned so permit. To this end, the Commission shall make recommendations to the Member States concerned' (Article 60). And, 'Undertakings entrusted with the operation of services of general economic interest or having the character of a revenue-producing monopoly shall be subject to the rules contained in the Treaties, in particular to the rules on competition, in so far as the application of such rules does not obstruct the performance, in law or in fact, of the particular tasks assigned to them. The development of trade must not be affected to such an extent as would be contrary to the interests of the Union' (Article 106-2).

The European Union has some elements of a federal economic structure with certain policies being centrally determined, others settled at the national level within a framework of coordination and others at the national level (for example, taxation). The Economic and Monetary Union, which started with 12 members (out of the then 15 members of the European Union), has now reached 17 (but now out of 27 members of the European Union). This has inevitably raised issues of a two-speed Europe with an inner core pursuing further integration and an outer core, some seeking to join EMU and others making sure they do not! These issues of two (or multi-speed) Europe have intensified in the aftermath of the economic crisis with pressures for further economic union, moves towards in effect political union, not to mention banking union. The EMU has one central authority (the European Central Bank, or ECB) and a set of fiscal policies (as further elaborated many times below) under the Stability and Growth Pact (SGP, and now also the 'fiscal compact'), which seek to impose a common set of budget policies on all members of EMU (with some overflow onto the budget positions of the other members of the EU). The attention in this book will be very much on the macroeconomic policies, which have these centralised features, albeit that fiscal and budget policies are operated by member national governments and the absence of an EMU-level fiscal policy is one of the shortcomings of the arrangements within EMU.[4] There are some fields of economic policies, which are centralised within the European Union; notably the Common Agriculture Policy (CAP) and competition policy, both of which date back to the founding of the European Union. But the EMU is a part of the EU and as such operates within the policy frameworks of the EU. The policies on the free movement of labour, the approach to industrial policy and the limitations on State Aid, employment and labour market policies and so on, are all relevant to the operations of a single currency area (and a single market).

In other areas of policy, the 'open method of coordination' (OMC) is in operation. This is described by the EU as 'a new framework' for cooperation between the member states, whose national policies can thus be directed towards certain common objectives. Under this intergovernmental method, the Member States are evaluated by one another (peer pressure), with the Commission's role being limited to surveillance. The European Parliament and the Court of Justice play virtually no part in the OMC process.

The open method of coordination takes place in areas, which fall within the competence of the Member States, such as employment, social protection, social inclusion, education, youth and training.

It is based principally on:

- jointly identifying and defining objectives to be achieved (adopted by the Council);
- jointly establishing measuring instruments (statistics, indicators, guidelines);
- benchmarking, that is, comparison of the member states' performance and exchange of best practices (monitored by the Commission).

Depending on the areas concerned, the OMC involves 'so-called 'soft law' measures which are binding on the Member States in varying degrees but which never take the form of directives, regulations or decisions' (http://europa.eu/legislation_summaries/glossary/open_method_coordination_en.htm; accessed April 2013).

The significance of these remarks for this book is rather obviously the Economic and Monetary Union is a part of, but not the whole, of the European Union. The policy coordination within the EMU has focused on macroeconomic coordination in the areas of monetary and fiscal policies, and has not been involved with other areas of coordination, such as price and wage determination, which are relevant for the successful operation of a currency union. Insofar as there is policy coordination which is relevant to the operation of the labour markets these lie with the European Union rather than EMU, and then come under the 'soft coordination' of the OMC approach.

1.3 Outline of the book

This book is concerned with macroeconomic policies and outcomes within the EMU. In doing so it attempts to throw light on a number of questions: the objectives of economic policy; the underlying 'model' of the policies; the nature of the imposed neo-liberal agenda; the shortcomings and design faults of the EMU project; and alternative policies for a better EMU.

The book comprises a total of ten chapters. Following this introduction (chapter 1) we discuss in chapter 2 the launch of the euro and the economic performance of the euro area both before and subsequent to the financial crisis and recession – what we label the 'great recession'. There is an analysis of the convergence criteria and the Stability and Growth Pact, followed by an examination of the economic performance of the euro area countries before and following the financial crisis. The first signs of the latter were apparent in August 2007 with the rise in the LIBOR rate, problems at PNB-Banque Paribas in France, and Northern Rock in the UK, and intensified in September 2008 with the collapse of Lehman Brothers; many other financial institutions in severe difficulties followed by major bailouts.

In chapter 3 we set out the theoretical underpinnings of macroeconomic policy within the EMU. The set of macroeconomic policies is closely related with the 'New Consensus Macroeconomics' and EMU can be seen as a crucial example of the application of this 'new consensus', although there are differences between the two in terms of the relevant policy implications. The following two chapters deal in some detail with monetary policy (chapter 4) and then fiscal policy in the EMU (chapter 5). We present a critique of the policy arrangements in those two domains. In chapter 4 we offer a critique of the establishment of a central bank, the European Central Bank (ECB), and the way it functions, especially the lack of a 'lender of last resort' policy dimension. The ECB pursues two types of policies: an economic policy and a monetary policy, both of which are of the 'one size fits all' approach. This is particularly problematic, we suggest, in the absence of other pan-EMU economic policies. In chapter 5 criticism is made of the implementation of the Stability and Growth Pact, what has come to be known as 'the fiscal pact', and its subsequent development, known as the 'fiscal compact'. This is undertaken along with the role of fiscal policy, which is considered to be totally ineffective by the creators of the SGP and the proponents of the 'New Consensus Macroeconomics' framework. Chapter 6 considers employment policies in the EU and how they impact on the euro area. Two important features dominate the discussion in this chapter. The first is the notion that labour markets and their institutions differ substantially and significantly across the member countries, which raises issues in terms of the operation of common macroeconomic policies. The second is that these differences in labour market institutions could lead to marked differences in economic performance, notably with regard to wage inflation and productivity trends. This raises the issue of possible differences in economic performance, which can generate divergences (or at least non-convergence) within the EMU.

Chapter 7 outlines the policies which we see as necessary for the achievement of full employment and low inflation. These policies are of general relevance and we apply them in the context of the EMU. We begin this chapter by considering what the objectives of economic policy should be, specifically in relation to macroeconomic policy, and how the instruments of economic policy can be used to achieve the stated objectives. We discuss the instruments of monetary policy and argue that monetary policy should be geared towards ensuring financial stability (rather than being so narrowly focused on inflation) and that additional tools of monetary policy should be developed to move away from sole reliance on the Central Bank's interest rate policy. In the case of fiscal policy we argue that this policy should be geared towards achieving a high level of economy activity and low unemployment. We also consider the required changes to the institutional arrangements to achieve the objectives suggested above.

Chapter 8 considers the future of the euro, especially in the light of its recent experience. It looks at whether or not the euro will survive under the current institutional arrangements, and if the expectation is that it will not do so what range of changes will be required for its survival. We discuss the extent to which Optimum Currency Area (OCA) considerations had any impact on the decision to introduce a single European currency or on the conditions governing which countries were to be members. The answer is that no such considerations were evident. We discuss the relevant OCA considerations before we move to issues that relate to the future of the euro. There is some discussion of fiscal policy and the European Central Bank from the point of view of monetary and financial policies, along with issues that relate to inflation and also current account deficits and competitiveness.

Chapter 9 discusses the issues of economic convergence and the needs for political integration if the euro is to survive. These issues have been touched on elsewhere in the book but this chapter elaborates further and fully on these two requirements. It demonstrates that the formation of the EMU, encompassing 17 politically independent countries, each with their own currencies prior to them joining the union, would be considerably influenced by considerations of economic convergence and political integration. Chapter 9 demonstrates that neither of these considerations had been influential in creating and shaping the EMU and the euro. Indeed, this chapter shows that in the absence of economic integration political union becomes paramount. Clearly, this is an argument based not on politics but purely on economic grounds that support the importance of developing pan-EMU economic policies, which, properly coordinated, could potentially drive the union to improved economic development. Finally. recent proposals in EMU towards what is termed fiscal union are examined and assessed.

2
The Launch of the Euro and Economic Performance

2.1 Introduction

We start by examining the formation of the Economic and Monetary Union (EMU), considering the 'convergence criteria' which in principle determine whether a European Union (EU) country could and should join the euro. These 'convergence criteria' continue to be applicable to potential members of EMU, though our focus here is on the application of those criteria to the initial membership of EMU. It is argued that there were some notable omissions from the criteria applied, and those omissions in effect stored up problems for the euro area, which came to prominence in the years after the financial crisis of the late 2000s.[1] This is followed by an overview of the macroeconomic performance in the euro area, which it is argued could be labelled lacklustre in the period preceding the financial crisis. In this overview we also point to the differences between the countries of the EMU, particularly with regard to inflation, competitiveness and the current account position, and indicate how those differences contributed significantly to the euro crisis.

The rest of this chapter proceeds as follows. After this short introduction, we discuss in section 2.2 the EMU convergence criteria and the Stability and Growth Pact (SGP). Section 2.3 assesses the economic performance of the euro area since its creation. Section 2.4 turns to the recent euro area crisis before some final comments are provided in section 2.5.

2.2. Convergence criteria and the Stability and Growth Pact

The Maastricht Treaty laid down criteria that should be met by those seeking to join the euro, and indeed countries meeting the criteria were obliged to join, though some countries secured opt-outs from that obligation. The convergence criteria are set in nominal terms (relating to inflation and interest rates, for example) with no mention of real convergence (in terms of, for example, output per head or unemployment rates) or even of the convergence of business cycles across countries. The criteria include a budget deficit and a government debt limit designed to establish 'fiscal responsibility' in the eyes of the financial markets but no underlying rationale was provided for the limits set down. The independence of the national central banks on an operational and political level was also on the list of these criteria. In terms of countries meeting the criteria, it must be said that with the exception of the inflation rate and the interest rate, they were not met as comfortably as it might have appeared initially. In fact a great deal of 'fudging' took place. In the event, 11 countries out of the then 15 member countries of the EU were deemed to have met both these criteria and joined the EMU (Greece was not included initially, but in January 2001 was deemed to have met the criteria and became a member of the EMU).[2] Denmark and the UK secured 'opt-outs' such that even when they satisfy the convergence criteria they are not obligated to join. Sweden voted against joining the euro in a referendum in 2003; and at the time of writing it does not satisfy the convergence criteria with regard to the independence of its central bank and membership of exchange rate mechanism.[3]

The convergence criteria to be applied to a country for membership of the EMU under the Maastricht Treaty are:

1. Average exchange rate not to deviate by more than 2.25 per cent from its central rate for the two years prior to membership;
2. Inflation rate not to exceed the average rate of inflation of the three community nations with the lowest inflation rate by 1.5 per cent;
3. Long-term interest rates not to exceed the average interest rate of the three countries with the lowest inflation rate by 2 per cent;
4. Government budget deficit not to exceed 3 per cent of its GDP;
5. Overall government debt not to exceed 60 per cent of its GDP.

It is also required that a country has adopted an 'independent central bank' – that is, a central bank with operational independence from the national government under which the central bank would adhere to the ECB's decisions on interest rates in pursuit of mainly the price stability objective; each national central bank adopts the interest rate as set by the ECB. The national central banks do, though, retain responsibility for the regulation of their domestic financial sector.

These convergence criteria are still relevant for non-EMU member countries within the EU in that if and when those criteria are met those countries are not only eligible but expected to adopt the euro. The themes within the 'convergence criteria' on limits on budget deficits and on monetary policy (with regard to the 'independence' of central banks) continue in the Stability and Growth Pact (hereafter SGP), which has governed the operations of the EMU, and will continue with the 'fiscal compact' (as discussed below in chapter 5).

The key features of the SGP are as follows: the first is the idea that national governments should aim for their budgets to be in balance or small surplus over the course of a business cycle and not to exceed 3 per cent of GDP in any given year; and the second is that the ECB acting independently use interest rate policy to achieve price stability. The nuances of these policies are discussed further in chapters 3 and 4 below. Under the 'fiscal compact' drawn up in late 2011 and coming into effect through Treaty on Stability, Coordination and Governance in the Economic and Monetary Union (also referred to as TSCG),[4] the requirements on the budget deficit limits were cast in terms of a balanced structural budget with significantly stronger penalties for a country not meeting those requirements (the issues over the 'fiscal compact' are discussed in detail in chapter 5).

The 'convergence criteria' are notable for what is included and what is excluded, and the messages that are conveyed by those omissions and commissions. The convergence of the rate of inflation rate and interest rate in a country with the average experiences of other potential members has a clear rationale in that under a currency union there is a single level of interest rate (as set by the central bank) and the clear expectation of similar rates of inflation across countries along with the operation of the 'law of one price' in a single market with a single currency. But there was no attempt to assess whether the inflationary conditions in potential member countries were similar, and that was significant in two respects. First, the inflation-targeting regime of the European Central Bank (ECB), if it is such a regime as discussed further below, rested on the linkage: interest rate → level of demand → inflation, and differences in the price and wage determination processes between countries would lead to different outcomes in terms of inflation resulting from a common interest rate. Thus, there would be a 'one size fits all' issue – as the change in inflation resulting from a change in interest rate would differ. Second, countries differed substantially in their inflationary experiences, expectations and attitudes to inflation (including the legendary German fear of inflation), which portended the continuation of differential rates of inflation between countries. The persistent difference in inflation rates means, of course, that one country's prices become higher relative to another country's prices and the former tends to lose competitiveness in international markets with consequent effects on the balance between exports and imports.

The convergence criteria also included a degree of stability of the country's exchange rate relative to other potential EMU countries prior to joining (albeit often within a +/–6 per cent band of variation), which again had a clear rationale as the exchange rate became fixed in a single currency. But no attention was given to the trade and current account positions of a potential entrant. This was highly significant as clearly the formation of a single currency, being the ultimate in fixing the nominal exchange rate between countries does not permit a 'no devaluation' option to adjust to a current account deficit (or revaluation for surplus). It is now readily apparent a change in the exchange rate of a country within a currency union can only be secured by internal deflation (or inflation in other member countries) or exit with the reintroduction of a national currency. The general proposition is that a trade deficit (relative to GDP) cannot be sustained indefinitely. It requires borrowing from overseas and hence willingness of foreigners to continue to lend, though experience suggests that a trade deficit can continue for a substantial period of time (many years). The borrowing to cover the trade deficit means rising debt and rising interest (and similar) payments on the debt, and then a tendency for the current account deficit to rise.[5] The creation of the single market, the removal of barriers to capital movement, the removal of exchange rate risk for borrowing between members of EMU all meant that it was rather easier for current account deficit countries to borrow to fund their deficits. The debts of the deficit countries built up in private and public hands, and those debts were predominantly owed to banks and other financial institutions in the surplus countries. The point to be made here is that this arose from a failure to consider current account imbalances at the time of formation of the euro and a failure to have any adjustment processes whereby those current account imbalances could be adjusted (or arrangements for the long-term funding of those imbalances).

The other notable omission from the establishment of the EMU and discussions leading up to its formation was any EMU-level fiscal policy involving a significant level of expenditure and taxation and ability to run budget deficits or surpluses. There is a European Union budget, amounting to just over 1 per cent of EU GDP, which is not only a relatively small budget but has to be balanced, and, of course, is an EU budget rather than an EMU one. This EU budget involves, through the structural funds and cohesion fund some transfers between countries broadly in the direction from richer to poorer countries. Within EMU there is no facility for direct or indirect fiscal transfers between countries. The significance of this lack of fiscal transfers is explored further below.

2.3 Economic performance

The euro was launched with much fanfare as a currency to rival the dollar; it was asserted that with the elimination of exchange rate risk and transactions cost would provide a boost to trade between the member countries and promote faster growth. In reviewing the economic performance of the euro area countries, we have two purposes. The first is to consider whether economic performance in terms of growth and unemployment improved and how that performance compares with other countries. The second is to highlight some of the features of differential economic performance between member countries which are related to the emergence of a euro crisis.

The following phases in the recent development and evolution of the Economic and Monetary Union and of the euro area are identified. 1992: the signing of the Maastricht Treaty took place; 1992–99: preparations for the euro and drive towards fulfilling the convergence criteria for membership were very active, along with the decision on membership, which took place in March 1998; 1999–2002: the exchange rates between EMU member countries were locked together, and euro was thereby brought in as a virtual currency; 2002: euro introduced as currency throughout the EMU region, and 2008 as the financial crisis gathers pace. In these discussions our view is limited to the 12 member countries, which were there at the launch of the euro as a 'real' currency in 2002.

In reporting on the economic performance of the euro area countries we present data relating to the four periods 1992–98, 1999–2001, and 2002–08, and then the period since 2008. Economic performance is here confined to the major macroeconomic variables of growth of GDP, unemployment, inflation and the current account of the balance of payments. The intention here is to describe the broad sweep of macroeconomic performance, and whilst we recognise the shortcomings of these variables (for example, GDP may not be a good measure of economic welfare, recorded unemployment may well understate the extent of actual unemployment) they serve our present purpose to provide the broad contours of economic performance. Some of these variables have been selected as they have been at the centre of attention for EMU policy makers, for example the rate of inflation and budget deficits. Other variables have been selected for the issues, which they raise on the operation of the EMU, for example, current account positions in the context of a fixed exchange rate regime (as EMU is for the countries participating), inflation rate differentials and changes in the effective real exchange rate between the member countries of EMU.

In evaluating the general macroeconomic performance some regard has to be given to the general world economic position. In the context of the euro area, this is important not only because inflation and growth in the rest of the world is likely to have a substantial impact on the euro area's economic performance but also since the proponents of the euro have often seen it as helping to strengthen the EU's economic standing.

The economic growth figures (Table 2.1) suggest a burst of growth around 1999–2001, but otherwise economic growth has been lacklustre, and it would be difficult to detect a faster growth effect coming from the formation of the euro. The major countries tended to grow slower than the smaller ones, notably Italy at below 1 per cent in the period 2002–08 and Germany at 1¼ per cent. The recession of 2009 is clearly evident, which struck all the EMU countries, with negative growth in all countries that year. The recovery in 2010 was sluggish with a number of countries with continuing negative growth, which continued in 2011 and 2012.

Table 2.1 Economic growth (average annual per cent)

	1981–91	1992–98	1999–2001	2002–08	2009	2010	2011	2012
Austria	2.6	2.26	2.53	2.10	-3.5	2.2	2.7	0.6
Belgium	2.2	1.84	2.67	2.03	-2.7	2.4	1.8	-0.1
Finland	2.2	2.33	3.77	3.06	-8.5	3.3	2.7	0.7
France	2.2	1.80	3.03	1.76	-3.1	1.6	1.7	0.2
Germany	2.8	1.65	2.27	1.26	-5.1	4.0	3.1	0.9
Greece	1.5	1.74	4.13	4.05	-3.1	-4.9	-7.1	-6.3
Ireland	3.5	6.68	8.73	4.43	-5.5	-0.8	1.4	0.5
Italy	2.5	1.39	2.47	0.90	-5.5	1.8	0.6	-2.2
Luxembourg	5.9	3.94	6.37	4.21	-4.1	2.9	1.7	0.6
Netherlands	2.5	2.84	3.50	1.84	-3.7	1.6	1.1	-0.9
Portugal	3.5	2.54	3.23	1.13	-2.9	1.4	-1.7	-3.1
Spain	3.2	2.35	4.43	2.89	-3.7	-0.3	0.4	-1.3
Euro Area*	2.5	1.86	2.93	1.73	-4.3	1.9	1.5	-0.4

Note: *Weighted average.
Figures for 2012 are forecast from OECD *Economic Outlook*, November 2012.
Source: OECD *Economic Outlook*, various issues.

Table 2.2 Unemployment (percentage of labour force)

	1992–98	1999–2002	2002–08	2007	2008	2009	2010	2011	2012**
Austria	5.37	4.83	5.30	4.4	3.8	4.8	4.4	4.1	4.8
Belgium	9.04	7.30	7.81	7.5	7.0	7.9	8.3	7.1	8.1
Finland	15.03	9.77	7.79	6.9	6.4	8.2	8.4	7.5	8.1
France	10.66	8.80	8.25	8.4	7.8	9.5	9.8	9.9	10.8
Germany	7.91	7.70	8.81	8.7	7.5	7.8	7.0	5.6	6.9
Greece	9.14	11.00	8.88	8.3	7.7	9.5	12.6	21.1	26.4
Ireland	12.81	4.60	4.86	4.6	6.3	11.8	13.7	14.7	14.1
Italy	10.73	10.17	7.36	6.1	6.8	7.8	8.4	9.3	11.6
Luxembourg	2.77	2.67	4.21	4.2	4.9	5.2	4.6	5.1	5.4
Netherlands	6.06	3.00	3.68	3.7	4.0	3.7	4.5	4.9	7.7
Portugal	6.47	4.13	7.15	8.9	8.5	10.6	12.0	14.6	15.7
Spain	17.60	11.03	9.86	8.3	11.4	18.0	20.1	23.2	26.3
Euro Area*	9.94	8.30	8.06	7.6	7.7	9.6	10.1	10.7	11.1

Notes: Figures refer to harmonised unemployment rates. * Weighted average. ** Economist (13 April 2013).

Source: Calculated from *OECD Economic Outlook*, 79 and 81, 92.

The figures relating to unemployment rates across the EMU countries are given in Table 2.2. Three features stand out. First, the disparities of unemployment rates between countries. These were particularly large during the 1990s, and then tended to narrow in the years before the crisis. The narrowing of the disparities could be largely attributed to the sharp falls in unemployment in Finland (where the rate had been particularly high as Finland was hit by the effects of the break-up of the Soviet Union), Ireland and Spain. By 2007, the latter two appeared to be the success stories of the EMU experience with the unemployment rate in that year having reached 4.6 per cent and 8.3 per cent respectively. But both had been built on unsustainable boom conditions in the housing and construction industry, and their unemployment rates soon rebounded sharply to reach the levels of the 1990s. Second, there was a general downward trend in the unemployment rates up to the financial crisis. This had been ascribed to the beneficial effects of the formation of the euro and of increased labour market flexibility. But the experiences of 2009 onwards should cast doubts on those views. Third, whilst the unemployment rate rose in all 12 countries between 2008 and 2009, the extent of the rises were sharply different, and reflected differences in the severity of the financial crisis and the policy responses. The figures of 2012 are very clear on this score.

Table 2.3 reports on the inflation experience. The figures for the first period 1992–98 mask the key feature of that period, namely that there was a downward trend in inflation: for the euro area as a whole falling

Table 2.3 Inflation rates (annual average)

	1992–98	1999–2001	2002–08	2009	2010	2011	2012
Austria	2.10	1.60	2.01	0.4	1.7	3.6	2.4
Belgium	1.80	2.07	2.19	0.0	2.3	3.5	2.6
Finland	1.73	2.30	1.51	1.6	1.7	3.3	3.1
France	1.76	1.40	2.19	0.1	1.7	2.3	2.2
Germany	1.10	1.30	1.87	0.2	1.2	2.5	2.1
Greece	7.52	2.90	3.47	1.3	4.7	3.1	1.0
Ireland	1.87	3.93	3.17	–1.7	–1.6	1.2	2.0
Italy	3.86	2.20	2.53	0.8	1.6	2.9	3.2
Luxembourg	1.20	2.40	3.04	0.0	2.8	3.7	2.8
Netherlands	1.86	3.13	2.10	1.0	0.9	2.5	2.8
Portugal	4.27	3.13	2.86	–0.9	1.4	3.6	2.7
Spain	3.57	2.83	3.46	–0.2	2.0	3.1	2.2
Euro Area*	2.28	1.87	2.36	0.3	1.6	2.7	2.4

Note: * Weighted average.
Figures for 2012 are forecast from OECD *Economic Outlook*, November 2012.
Source: *OECD Economic Outlook*, 79, 81, 92.

from over 3 per cent to 1.2 per cent in 1998 (the figure of 1.1 per cent for the following year marked the trough as far as inflation is concerned). The pressures to join the euro area lead not only to lower inflation but also to smaller differences in inflation between countries. In the period since 2002, there are two features of the inflation figures of particular note. First, the rate of inflation in the euro area averaged 2.4 per cent, and exceeded 2 per cent in each year, and the number 2 being significant here as 'below 2 per cent upper limit on inflation' is the inflation target, which the ECB has used to indicate 'price stability'. Whilst the ECB (2008) claimed in a tenth anniversary volume that 'we show that the euro has already brought several gains, including price stability and low interest rates' (p. 15), it is still the case that the price stability target has been persistently exceeded, albeit by a relatively small amount. The ECB (op. cit.) admits that much: 'While the ECB has been successful in maintaining a high degree of price stability in the euro area over now almost a full decade, average annual HICP inflation rates have remained elevated at levels that have persistently exceeded the upper limit of the ECB's definition of price stability since 2000' (p. 62).[6] The possibility for the use of monetary policy to target inflation and thereby achieve price stability is discussed at length in chapter 3.

Second, the differences in the inflationary experiences between member countries since 2002 are both noticeable and significant. A convergence of inflation rates had been achieved by 1998 as required by the convergence criteria as a number of countries pursued deflationary policies seeking to ensure that their inflation record was consistent with euro area membership. The differences in inflation rates across member countries, which have re-emerged since 2002, are significant in two respects. First, the euro in effect set the nominal exchange rates between member countries: the value of say the French franc and the German mark was fixed first prior to the formation of the euro, and then in effect continued by the adoption of the euro. But although the nominal exchange rate between the two countries is fixed, the real exchange rate between France and Germany varies as the prices in those two countries vary (and specifically as the prices of traded goods vary). The extent of trade between euro area countries is, of course, extensive with on average of two-thirds of a country's international trade being with a fellow EU member and one-third with other countries. Data from Eurostat indicate that for the EU-27 the share of exports to non-EU members rose from 31.2 per cent in 2003 to 35.7 per cent in 2011, and the corresponding figures for imports being 35.4 per cent and 38.6 per cent. The cumulated price changes since 2002 would suggest that the real exchange rate between, for example, Germany and Spain changed by the order of 12 per cent: in Germany the cumulated price increase was 14 per cent while in Spain it was 27 per cent (using the contrast between Finland and Greece would give a slightly larger difference).

The differences in the inflation experience raise significant issues for monetary policy. It is clearly the case that a monetary union has to have a single monetary policy, and as such monetary policy faces the 'one size fits all' problem – a single policy across a monetary union cannot be fully appropriate for all areas within the monetary union, an issue to which we return below. Further, the single policy interest rate set by the ECB translates into different real interest rates, and to some degree (at least from the perspective of the 'new consensus macroeconomics', on which more below) perverse ways: with a common nominal interest rate within the EMU a country with high inflation rate would have a relatively low real interest rate, when the approach to monetary policy adopted by the ECB and others would point to a higher real interest rate in a high inflation environment.

Table 2.4 illustrates the changing competitiveness of EMU countries based on relative unit labour costs (where an increase in the index indicates a deterioration in competitive position). For the euro area as a whole, competitiveness tended to deteriorate during much of the 2000s (as the value of the euro tended to rise against the dollar), and

Table 2.4 Relative unit labour costs (2005 = 100)

	1994-98	1999-2001	2002-08	2009	2010	2011	2012
Austria	109.9	101.8	100.2	102.4	99.7	99	98.3
Belgium	94.7	93.4	100.5	105	100.7	101.9	100
Finland	97.3	96.5	98.3	105.1	97.7	97	94.2
France	96.6	92.2	99.4	101.9	99.2	99.3	96.6
Germany	93.5	104.3	98.7	96	90.8	90.2	88.2
Greece	81.0	85.1	98.4	109.2	103.4	98.2	87
Ireland	83.0	80.0	98.9	105.9	95.4	91.5	85.8
Italy	87.2	87.0	98.7	105.6	100.4	98.8	97.6
Luxembourg	95.5	92.3	99.7	109.6	108.6	110.4	110.5
Netherlands	90.6	90.9	100.1	103	98.1	97.4	93.3
Portugal	85.9	89.3	98.0	99.8	97.7	97.2	90.9
Spain	86.1	87.6	100.4	107.6	102.2	99.3	93.6
Euro Area*	98.6	88.8	98.5	104.4	94.9	93.2	87.6

Note: 'Competitiveness-weighted relative unit labour costs for the overall economy in dollar terms. Competitiveness weights take into account the structure of competition in both export and import markets of the goods sector of 49 countries. An increase in the index indicates a real effective appreciation and a corresponding deterioration of the competitive position' (OECD, *Economic Outlook*, 92, p. 249).
Figures for 2012 are forecast from OECD, *Economic Outlook*, November 2012.
Source: OECD *Economic Outlook*, 92, Annex Table 43.

has improved substantially since 2008. It is the changing competitiveness of individual countries in the context of a single currency (and hence fixed exchange rate between member countries). The changing competitiveness will partially reflect the changing exchange rate of the euro and partially differences in unit labour cost trends. Comparisons between countries would indicate that there have been rather large changes in their relative competitiveness, with consequent impacts on their current account positions.

The movement in the real effective exchange rate (reer) of EMU member countries is indicated in Table 2.5. The real exchange rate is the nominal exchange rate adjusted by the ratio of prices in trading partners to prices in country concerned; this indicates the reer of original member countries in 2002, 2007 and 2010 with the level in 1999 set equal to 100. The movement in the reer will reflect inflation differentials, movements in the euro's value relative to other currencies and differences in trade patterns between member countries. The depreciation of the German reer (not surprisingly along with Austria) and the appreciation of the Irish, Spanish and Italian reer are particularly noticeable coming from differences in their inflation experience. These changes in the reer are taken relative to

Table 2.5 Real effective exchange rate (1999 = 100)

	2002	2007	2010	2011
Austria	93.72	95.55	95.73	95.44
Belgium	98.77	102.79	106.01	107.76
Finland	97.09	101.96	105.87	106.33
France	98.35	105.89	107.28	107.98
Germany	92.07	90.13	87.73	87.90
Greece	99.64	102.56	109.36	107.30
Ireland	100.84	124.25	120.63	115.77
Italy	99.13	111.62	113.73	113.80
Luxembourg	103.44	107.56	113.60	115.92
Netherlands	105.74	109.01	111.29	112.62
Portugal	103.51	110.94	110.26	109.06
Spain	100.82	112.56	112.88	111.43

Source: Calculated from data downloaded from Eurostat.

the position in 1999 and may reflect a misalignment of currencies at the time of the locking together of the national currencies with, for example, the German DMark entering at an overvalued rate followed by subsequent depreciation (in real terms) and the Irish punt entering at an undervalued rate followed by subsequent appreciation. Then the differential inflation rates are in effect an adjustment process bringing the real effective exchange rate closer to purchasing power parity. But we see these movements in the reer as a reflection of differences in inflationary pressures and trends between countries. It can, of course, be expected that the setting and changes in these exchange rates have significant effects on demand for their exports and subsequent effects on output and employment.

The evolution of the current account positions of EMU member countries is given in Table 2.6. The euro area as a whole is close to balance with regard to its current account position as indicated in Table 2.6. A number of countries report surpluses over the years 2002–08, which average over 5 per cent of GDP (Finland, Germany, Luxembourg and the Netherlands); while others report deficits of over 5 per cent of GDP (Greece, Portugal and Spain). These figures are obviously averages over a seven-year period and as such can be taken as reflecting an underlying issue rather than merely being random movements over a short period of time. The particular significance of any current account position arises from the question as to whether it is sustainable and what the consequences are for any required adjustment to the current account position as discussed above.

Table 2.6 Current account positions (percentage of GDP)

	1992–98	1999–2001	2002–2008	2009	2010	2011	2012
Austria	–1.89	–2.53	1.90	2.7	3.0	1.9	1.8
Belgium	5.29	4.17	2.86	–1.4	1.9	–1.4	–1.3
Finland	2.07	7.63	5.20	1.8	1.3	–1.3	–1.0
France	1.14	2.27	–0.34	–1.3	–1.6	–2.0	–2.1
Germany	–0.94	–1.03	5.06	5.9	5.9	5.7	6.4
Greece	–3.00	–6.90	–9.56	–11.24	–10.1	–9.9	–5.5
Ireland	2.26	–0.23	–2.76	–2.3	1.1	1.1	4.0
Italy	1.37	0.03	–1.81	–1.9	–3.5	–3.2	–0.9
Luxembourg	10.75	10.10	10.16	6.7	7.7	7.1	5.8
Netherlands	4.56	2.70	6.23	5.2	7.7	9.7	8.4
Portugal	–2.76	–9.53	–8.97	–10.9	–10.0	–6.5	–2.9
Spain	–1.09	–3.60	–6.86	–4.8	–4.5	–3.5	–2.0
Euro Area*	0.43	–0.07	0.47	–0.4	–0.4	–0.7	–0.6

Note: * Weighted average.
Figures for 2012 are forecast from OECD, *Economic Outlook*, November 2012.
Source: OECD, *Economic Outlook*, 79, 81 and 92.

The nature and significance of the current account and balance of payments positions of a country are rather different when the country has its own currency, the exchange rate of which can (at least potentially under a fixed exchange rate system) be varied and when it shares a currency with others and hence its exchange rate with fellow members cannot be changed. Under a fixed exchange rate, a balance of payments deficit can only be sustained so long as there can be depletion of the country's foreign exchange reserves. Measures such as control over capital flows can be brought in to try to preserve the exchange rate by removing the balance of payments deficit. In the context of a currency union, the exchange rate variation is no longer possible, nor in general are capital controls and the like. The balance of payments deficit of an individual country can only continue so long as money can drain out of the country concerned.

The relative economic performance of the euro area with the USA, Japan and the UK is indicated by figures in Table 2.7. In terms of growth, the period when the euro area matched the USA and the UK was 1999–2001. Since 2002, the euro area average growth rate has been below that of the USA and the UK every year, and broadly in line with the Japanese growth rate, although for the year 2012 it is expected to be well below Japan's. The figures on inflation reflect the worldwide low inflationary environment since the early 1990s. The euro area inflation record has been rather

Table 2.7 Relative economic performance (all figures in percentages)

	1992–1998	1999–2001	2002–08	2009	2010	2011	2012
GDP growth							
euro area	1.86	2.93	1.71	-4.2	1.8	1.7	-0.4
Japan	1.29	1.00	1.36	-6.3	4.1	-0.3	1.6
USA	3.53	2.97	2.16	-3.5	3	1.7	2.2
UK	2.70	3.07	2.33	-4.4	1.8	0.9	-0.1
Inflation							
euro area	2.28	1.87	2.34	0.3	1.6	2.6	2.4
Japan	0.76	-0.53	-0.01	-1.3	-0.7	-0.3	0.0
USA	2.59	2.80	2.84	-0.3	1.6	3.2	2.1
UK	1.90	1.10	2.03	2.2	3.3	4.5	2.6
Unemployment							
euro area	9.94	8.30	8.53	9.6	10.1	10.7	11.1
Japan	3.13	4.60	4.54	5.1	5.1	4.5	4.4
USA	5.84	4.33	5.34	9.3	9.6	8.5	8.1
UK	8.54	5.53	5.13	7.6	7.8	8.3	8.0

Figures for 2012 are forecast from OECD, *Economic Outlook* November 2012.

Source: OECD, *Economic Outlook*, 79, 81 and 92.

similar to that of the USA and the UK, noting the rather lower rate of inflation in Japan. Unemployment did improve in the euro area over the period from 2002 until the financial crisis though remaining significantly above that in the other countries featured in the table. The falls in unemployment during 2006 and 2007 would appear to have arisen from faster growth (and hence a result of higher demand) rather than from any labour market 'reforms'. Unemployment though increased again in 2009 as growth comes to a halt, and clearly unemployment remains a serious problem in many parts of the European Union, and elsewhere.

The budget deficits of member countries have been of significance largely because of the requirements of the SGP for the government budget of each member country to be in balance or small surplus over the course of the business cycle and for the budget deficit to not exceed 3 per cent of GDP in any year. The figures in Table 2.8 provide the background for more detailed discussion on budget deficits in the next chapter. It can be seen that there were a number of occasions on which the 3 per cent limit was indeed exceeded. The differences between countries in their average budget position should also be noted. It could well be expected that not only will the different positions in the business cycle lead countries to have different budget deficits, but also that, more significantly, differences in their savings and investment behaviour

Table 2.8 Budgetary positions of EMU member states (Budget surplus (+), deficit (–) as per cent of GDP)

	2002	2003	2004	2005	2006	2007	2008	2009	2010	2011	2012
Austria	–0.9	–1.6	–4.5	–1.8	–1.7	–1	–1	–4.1	–4.5	–2.5	–3.1
Belgium	–0.2	–0.2	–0.4	–2.6	0.3	–0.1	–1.1	–5.6	–3.9	–3.9	–2.8
Finland	4.1	2.4	2.2	2.7	4.1	5.3	4.3	–2.7	–2.8	–0.9	–1.4
France	–3.2	–4.1	–3.6	–3	–2.4	–2.7	–3.3	–7.6	–7.1	–5.2	–4.5
Germany	–3.6	–4	–3.8	–3.3	–1.7	0.2	–0.1	–3.1	–4.2	–0.8	–0.2
Greece	–4.8	–5.7	–7.4	–5.6	–6	–6.8	–9.9	–15.6	–10.8	–9.5	–6.9
Ireland	–0.3	0.4	1.4	1.7	2.9	0.1	–7.4	–13.9	–30.9	–13.3	–8.1
Italy	–3	–3.5	–3.6	–4.5	–3.4	–1.6	–2.7	–5.4	–4.3	–3.8	–3
Luxembourg	2.1	0.5	–1.1	0	1.4	3.7	3.2	–0.8	–0.3	–2	–1.7
Netherlands	–2.1	–3.2	–1.8	–0.3	0.5	0.2	0.5	–5.6	–5	–4.4	–3.8
Portugal	–2.9	–3	–3.4	–6.5	–4.6	–3.2	–3.7	–10.2	–9.8	–4.4	–5.2
Spain	–0.5	–0.2	–0.4	1.3	2.4	1.9	–4.5	–11.2	–9.7	–9.4	–8.1
Euro Area	–2.6	–3.1	–3.0	–2.6	–1.4	–0.7	–2.1	–6.3	–6.2	–4.1	–3.3

Figures for 2012 are forecast from OECD, *Economic Outlook*, November 2012.

Source: OECD, *Economic Outlook*, 88,92.

Table 2.9 Government debt as percentage of GDP

	1998	2002	2007	2012
Austria	64.8	66.2	60.3	75.6
Belgium	117.1	103.4	84.0	99.0
Finland	48.1	41.5	35.2	53.4
France	589.4	59.0	64.2	91.2
Germany	60.4	60.6	65.1	81.8
Greece	94.5	101.7	107.3	176.7
Ireland	53.6	32.0	25.0	117.3
Italy	118.0	105.2	103.1	127.8
Luxembourg	7.4	6.3	6.7	22.3
Netherlands	68.2	50.5	45.3	72.1
Portugal	56.4	56.6	68.3	115.5
Spain	67.4	52.6	36.3	86.1
Euro area	75.4	68.0	66.3	93.6

Note: The table uses the Maastricht definition of general government gross public debt (which tends to be a little lower than the general government gross financial liabilities). Figures for 2012 are forecasts from OECD, *Economic Outlook*, November 2012.

Source: OECD, *Economic Outlook*, various issues.

and in their trade position will lead to different budget deficits. This suggests to us that the appropriate budget stance (however appropriate is perceived) differs from country to country, and hence the SGP suffers from seeking to impose a 'one size fits all' fiscal stance.

Table 2.9 provides data on the government debt position in the euro area. It is evident that overall the euro area did not meet the 60 per cent debt limit, and that a number of countries, notably the larger ones, also exceeded that limit on many occasions. The figures for 1998 provide an indication of the degree to which countries did not meet the 60 per cent debt ratio target.

The path of the key interest rate set by the European Central Bank (the 'repo' rate) is described in Table 2.10, with some comparisons with the rate set by the US Federal Reserve (Federal funds rate) and the Bank of England. The sharp reduction in interest rates in the United States in the face of recession was clearly not followed by the ECB nor by the Bank of England. The latter two central banks began to reduce their respective interest rates well after the emergence of the 'great recession' in August 2007. It is clear from Table 2.9 that the Bank of England and the ECB rates only began to be reduced by 2009, well after the US rates started being reduced. However, by the summer of 2012 the euro area 'repo rate' is down to 0.75 per cent, while the US and UK short-term rates are the same as in 2011.

The euro exchange rate has moved substantially during its existence. Having started life at an exchange rate with the dollar of 1.1789, it initially tended to fall in value, reaching a low point against the dollar of 0.825 in October 2000. It remained below parity with the dollar until late 2002, and since then has been above parity. The highest rate against the dollar was at just below 1.60 in June 2008. Against the yen, the euro

Table 2.10 Short-term interest rates (percentage): euro area, the USA and the UK

year	Euro Area	USA	UK
1999	3.0	5.4	5.4
2000	4.4	6.5	6.1
2001	4.3	3.7	5.0
2002	3.3	1.8	4.0
2003	2.3	1.2	3.7
2004	2.1	1.6	4.6
2005	2.2	3.5	4.7
2006	3.1	5.2	4.8
2007	4.3	5.3	6.0
2008	4.6	3.2	5.5
2009	1.2	0.9	1.2
2010	0.8	0.5	0.7
2011	1.4	0.4	0.9
2012	0.6	0.4	0.9

Figures for 2012 are forecast from OECD *Economic Outlook* November 2012.

Source: OECD, *Economic Outlook*, 92 November 2012.

Table 2.11 Euro exchange rate

	euro: dollar	euro: yen
1999	1.0658	121.32
2000	0.9236	99.47
2001	0.8956	108.68
2002	0.9456	118.06
2003	1.1312	130.97
2004	1.2439	134.44
2005	1.2441	136.85
2006	1.2556	146.02
2007	1.3705	161.25
2008	1.4708	152.45
2009	1.3948	130.34
2010	1.3257	116.24
2011	1.392	110.96
2012	1.285	102.50

Source: Calculated from data on ECB website (accessed April 2013).

began at 133.7, falling to 89.3 by October 2000 (reaching its lowest level against the dollar and yen on the same day), and then tending to rise to reach a peak value of 169.24 in July 2008. The general pattern has been one of initial decline in value of the euro, with a gradual rise to a peak in mid-2008, which turned out to be just before the main blast of the financial crisis. The scale of the volatility is large with the peak value being near twice the lowest value, whether in terms of dollar or yen. The years of the financial crisis have seen the euro tending to fall in value, notably against the yen.

The exchange rate is, of course, a relative price and the weakness or strength of the euro can also be read as strength or weakness of the dollar, and it is perhaps perceptions of the relative strength or weakness of the US economy, which has played a substantial part in the variations of the exchange rate. Further, although the euro area and US economies can be considered to be relatively closed, nevertheless exchange rate movements have an effect. In terms of degree of closed or openness, US trade in exports is circa 15 per cent of GDP and imports over 20 per cent, and EU trade with non-EU countries of the order of 10 per cent of GDP.

The estimates of the effects of the euro on trade have varied enormously (from zero to 70 per cent), but a recent paper concludes 'For countries in the EZ ['eurozone'], the effect [of single currency on trade] appears more elusive: In particular, we could not find statistically significant effects on trade among EZ members following the introduction of the euro, though previous work has found positive, yet generally small, effects' (Santos Silva and Tenreyro, 2010a). No wonder the same authors' subsequent title said it all: 'Has the Euro Increased Trade? Short Answer: No' (Santos Silva and Tenreyro, 2010b).

2.3 Recent crisis experience

The global financial crisis of the late 2000s started to become evident in the second half of 2007 with the full force being felt in September/ October 2008 marked by the collapse in the USA of Lehman Brothers. The recessionary effects of the financial crisis became evident towards the end of 2008. Much of the financial crisis was initially located in the USA with the first signs emerging in 2007. But even in 2007 there were signs within some European countries that not all was well with the financial system, for example the liquidity problems and then collapse of Northern Rock in the UK in August/September 2007 and problems at a major French bank. It can be argued that the economic crisis in many European countries was closely linked with contagion – ranging from impacts on trade as the US economy went into recession through to the holding of 'toxic assets' on the balance sheets of many European financial institutions. It cannot be overlooked that there were many problems within the financial system of many European countries and collapses of many financial institutions, which could not be attributed to problems 'imported' from the USA. The British, Irish and (though delayed) Spanish cases stand out in that respect (one may also refer to Netherlands). The financial crises and the associated recession (now double-dip recession) highlighted a range of problems and difficulties for the Economic and Monetary Union, and also for the other members of the European Union and the ways in which EMU and the EU operated. In this regard we would highlight the following:

1. Financial institutions and banks are largely seen as the responsibility of the relevant national authorities. The regulation of financial institutions is undertaken by the national authorities (in general the national central bank), albeit within a common framework of regulation. Perhaps more significantly, 'bailout' of banks lies with the national authority which has generated difficulties ranging from the limits on State Aid imposed by the Treaty of Lisbon through to the impact on budget deficits (which are meant to be constrained by the SGP). Proposals for a banking union have been something of a response to this.

2. The scale of the recession threw most national governments' budgets into sharp deficit (see Table 2.7) and way beyond anything envisaged in the SGP with its intended upper limit on deficits of 3 per cent of GDP. Whilst in the early days, the automatic stabilisers of fiscal policy were allowed to operate, and in general attempts were not made to conform to the 3 per cent upper limit, that has been replaced by an enhanced drive for balanced budgets (as under the 'fiscal compact' discussed below).
3. The growing public debt and the need to fund a much larger budget deficit also put the relationship between national governments and the ECB into sharp relief. Whereas in the national setting, there is usually a close relationship between the central government and the central bank which is the issuing agency for the currency. The central bank acts as lender of last resort in two senses – the lender to the national government with the central bank always able to provide money for the budget deficit, and as accepting of government paper from banks and lending to those banks. Within the single currency, the national central bank no longer provided those functions, and the ECB was barred from direct funding of budget deficits.
4. Prior to the financial crisis, as discussed above, there were sharp current account imbalances, but those countries running deficits were able to finance them without difficulty within the single currency area. Indeed, the single currency area had not only lead to a single central bank interest rate but also for many a lower interest rate than prior to the formation of the euro zone – whether judged in nominal or real terms. Thus for many borrowing was not only easier but also cheaper. The borrowing and hence capital inflow enabled the current account deficit to continue. The economic crisis lead to even lower interest rates, but much credit dried up, leaving those countries with current account deficits in considerable difficulties. The collapse of investment along the surge in savings meant that the government was in deficit, and that the government in effect had to borrow from abroad.

2.4 Optimal Currency Area considerations

The use of a single currency across a number of countries brings the benefits of lower transactions costs between countries as the costs of currency exchange disappear, and as price calculations become simpler when only one currency is involved. There may be some spin-off benefits from the reduction of transactions costs as trade in effect becomes a little less expensive and expands, and economic gains accrue from that increased trade. The literature usually described as the Optimal Currency Area (OCA) literature asks questions on the downside of a single currency. It begins by noting that in a regime of national currencies, the exchange rate of a currency can be changed: the way in which changes in the exchange rate occur depends on the nature of the exchange rate regime (for example, fixed exchange rate, floating rate). There is then at least the possibility that a country whose economic fortunes have turned down to devalue their currency, thereby stimulating the demand for their production. The adoption of a single currency clearly removes that possibility in that the nominal exchange rates between members of the currency union cannot be changed. The nominal value of the single currency clearly can vary against other currencies, and such variations in value may well have differing effects on the members of the currency union; for example, a member country with greater trade links with countries outside the currency union would be more affected than a country with less trade links. But what matters for trade is the real exchange rate (that is, taking into account differences in the price levels), and a change in the nominal exchange rate is the easiest way of changing the real exchange rate. It becomes more difficult to change the real exchange rate under a single currency – in effect by one country's prices changing relative to another country's prices.

Although much of the academic literature on currency and monetary unions has been dominated by the OCA literature (starting from Mundell, 1961), it may be doubted whether that literature and the associated considerations had much impact on the formation of the EMU in that the criteria for the formation of a single currency appear not to have been applied when decisions were made on the formation of the single currency and on who would be a member. The political imperative for most, though not all, national governments and the EU itself was the formation of the EMU as the next stage of European economic integration.

The OCA literature can be interpreted as saying that two (or more) economic regions can share a common currency (with the implied fixed exchange rate between the two regions) if there is some combination of real convergence such that economic fluctuations (whether arising from random shocks or from systematic cyclical forces) are highly correlated and economic and policy responses, which cope with differences between the regions in economic shocks and fluctuations. In the OCA literature emphasis was placed on the roles of factor mobility, price flexibility and fiscal policy as mechanisms by which the economy of a region could adjust to asymmetric shocks.

The evaluation of factor mobility and price flexibility is made difficult by the absence of any precise criteria in the OCA literature – what is the necessary degree of potential factor mobility? One approach has been to compare the degree of mobility, particularly labour mobility, within the EU with that in the USA on the basis of being economically and geographically of similar sizes, albeit that the income differentials in the EU are larger, which could be expected to promote greater mobility. The general finding has been that factor mobility is rather lower in the EU for which there are ready explanations in terms of differences of language, culture and qualification regimes (Fertig and Schmidt, 2002). In the OCA literature the emphasis is on the response to asymmetric shocks when the response through exchange rate change is removed under currency union. The mobility of labour observed within the EU since 2004 would seem more related to large differences in income per capita and in unemployment rates than to responses to differential shocks. In the absence of substantial fiscal transfers, it would appear plausible to argue that the existing member countries of the EMU do not form an 'optimal currency area', and even more so the new member countries along with the existing member countries do not form an OCA.

Another possible route through which an economic area experiencing an economic downturn may be assisted is through fiscal transfers. The level of demand in the economic area in question would to some degree be sheltered from the full effects of the downturn through fiscal transfers. In a nation state there is some automatic element in these fiscal transfers – tax revenues to the central government are reduced as a consequence of the lower level of income, and some social security benefits (notably unemployment benefits) are increased. There would often be deliberate responses by the central government in the form of increased assistance of various forms to the economic area. Within a currency area without a central government (as in the case of EMU) there would not be these fiscal transfers.

The OCA literature had much influence in academic debates but appears to have little impact on the design of the Economic and Monetary Union (EMU). Many authors (see, for example, Eichengreen, 1997) who were attached to the OCA approach tended to conclude that the euro area was not an optimal currency area – or at least by comparison with the USA, the euro area had lower factor (notably labour) mobility, and lacked fiscal transfers. Insofar as regard was paid to the OCA criteria, the argument was put that there would be endogeneity in the fulfilment of the criteria, that is whilst at the time of formation of the euro the criteria would not be satisfied, the experience of the single currency and the enhancing trading between countries would lead in the direction of their fulfilment (see, for example, Baldwin and Wyplosz, 2009).

The OCA approach suffered from being developed within an essentially competitive demand/supply framework: that is a 'shock' in one country could potentially be addressed through a combination of price and quantity adjustments: if demand in one country fell, then prices of goods and services produced in that country could fall, and resources shift from that country. The exchange rate was similarly viewed as a price adjustment mechanism to shocks, with, of course, that adjustment mechanism being removed in the single currency case. The OCA approach then overstated the benefits of an adjustable exchange rate. The OCA approach overlooks the forces of cumulative causation and the degree to which imbalances between countries (or regions) can be reinforcing rather than self-correcting.

The OCA approach is based on an approach which starts with some equilibrium, then there is some 'shock', followed by an adjustment process which focuses on price and quantity adjustment to restore equilibrium. It pays little attention to situations of initial imbalance when the single currency is formed, and then how those imbalances could be resolved in the context of a fixed exchange rate system. This was in effect the position with the formation of the euro, with large differences in unemployment rates and current account positions. There were also substantial differences in income per capita and trend growth rates.

The OCA literature suggests three conditions for an 'optimal currency area' (Mundell, 1961):[7] factor mobility and openness of markets; relative price flexibility; and fiscal transfers within the monetary union. It would be desirable for a single currency to be used in an economic area within which there is openness of goods markets and mobility of factors of production (labour, capital); this is so since the mobility of factors is seen as one way in which adjustment is made to differences in economic performance. Further, member economies should share similar inflationary tendencies since a common currency imposes a common inflation rate. The Single European Act of 1986 and the implementation of the single European market by the end of 1992 were steps in seeking to ensure the mobility of goods and services and of capital within the European Union. But it is well known that effective labour mobility with the EU remains low, especially by comparison with the

USA, despite the large differences in real wages and unemployment rates across the EU. Price flexibility (in terms of relative prices across countries) remains low. The differences in labour market institutions, notably over wage determination mean that there are different inflationary tendencies and different responses to economic shocks. The convergence criteria ensured a convergence of inflation rates, which is not the same as the convergence of inflationary mechanisms and tendencies. Indeed, similar rates of inflation across the euro area countries in 1998 (the relevant year for the application of the convergence criteria) were accompanied by widely differing rates of unemployment from around 4 per cent in the case of Austria and the Netherlands to 17 per cent in the case of Spain (and the difference in unemployment between regions was much more marked from 3 per cent in the Oberösterreich region of Austria to 32 per cent in the Andulucia region of Spain and nearly 37 per cent in Reunion, France (these figures refer to 1997). The calculated output gap, as a sign of stage of the business cycle, varied (according to the OECD measure) from over +2 per cent in Ireland to –2 per cent in Italy.

The EU budget is small (set at a maximum of 1.24 per cent of EU GDP), required to be always in balance and dominated by the Common Agricultural Policy (CAP). There is clearly little role for fiscal transfers from relatively rich countries to relatively poor countries, nor is there any possibility of the EU budget operating as a stabiliser. About half of the transfers which do occur will be set by the requirements of the CAP, although much of the remainder (in the form of regional policy) do involve transfers from rich to poor areas. There is currently no mechanism for the operation of an EU level fiscal policy, which could have stabilising effects (as an automatic stabiliser) over time as well as significant redistributive element across economic regions.

There is, of course, the possibility that OCA contains an endogenous element in the sense of the question 'Is EMU more justifiable *ex post* than *ex ante*?' (Frankel and Rose, 1997, 1998). The answer given by Frankel and Rose (1997) was positive in their *ex ante* analysis; they argued that the EMU would be more justifiable in the *ex post* sense. However, more recently, Vieira and Vieira (2012) in an *ex post* analysis of the EMU's first decade in existence (including the initial group of eleven countries as members of the EMU plus Greece) conclude that the hypothesis does not hold for some countries. Utilising the OCA index, first proposed by Bayoumi and Eichengreen (1997), and comparing individual countries' compliance with selected OCA conditions before and after the adoption of the euro, they conclude that

> 'The distance separating peripheral and core economies before the introduction of the euro remains practically unchanged after 10 years of adopting the common currency' (p. 78). Vieira and Vieira (op. cit.) go further and suggest that 'the OCA index could have been a better indicator of countries' readiness to join the single currency than were the Maastricht criteria, as the latter were not able to identify the ill-prepared countries. The recent troubles of some euro area embers make this clear. (p. 90)

The optimists would tend to believe that the continuing effects of the single European market and the introduction of the euro will lead to further integration between the national economies. This integration could then be reflected in some convergence between national business cycles and (perhaps) some reduction in the extent of asymmetric shocks that impact on some countries but not on others. There could, in the fullness of time, be increased mobility of labour. But there seem little prospects of EU-wide measures, such as a common social security policy, which would enhance the mobility of labour. There would also seem little prospect of significant fiscal transfers, even up to the level of public expenditure and taxation at the EU level of 7.5 per cent as recommended the MacDougall Report (1977).

An OCA obviously introduces alongside a single currency a union-wide monetary policy. In much of the OCA literature the role of the common monetary policy is rather underplayed, but attention must be paid to the nature of the common monetary policy and who operates it, especially in an era where monetary policy has displaced fiscal policy as the main macroeconomic instrument. In the euro area context, this common monetary policy is operated by the ECB in pursuit of price stability in an environment where there is no union-level fiscal policy of any significance.

Fiscal policy can be differentiated, whether as a side effect of the design of the tax system (the obvious example being a progressive income tax system, which has a degree of redistribution from rich areas to poor areas) or through the allocation of public expenditure. Fiscal policy has the capabilities of being differentiated and of transferring resources though those capabilities need not be exercised. But monetary policy cannot be differentiated -- a common central bank discount rate must apply across all countries (or in the days of monetary targets, there is a single monetary aggregate to which the targeting applies). Monetary policy is likely to have differential effects on regions and countries. The mark-up of bank lending and mark-down of bank borrowing rates over the central bank discount rate may vary across countries (and also within countries). The responsiveness of aggregate demand in different regions is likely to vary, for example depending on the extent of fixed rate or variable rate borrowing. The difficulties of the 'one policy fits all' nature of monetary policy are well known and come into play whenever there are differences between economic areas in terms of economic performance, stage of the business cycle and inflationary pressures. These differences are exacerbated at the euro area level as economies are brought together under the single umbrella and with economies with different financial institutions and arrangements. It should also be noted that there is a sense in which the EU has adopted a one-instrument approach to policy, namely the use of monetary policy. Fiscal policy is restricted to an overall balanced budget position, albeit with variations of the national budget deficit positions over the business cycle.

The difficulties with the use of one policy instrument is well illustrated by the dilemma for the ECB during the past years – the inflationary position (of over 2 per cent) points to raising interest rates whereas the experience of economic slowdown point to further reductions in interest rates, though the objectives given to the ECB suggest that the former would have to dominate.

This discussion indicates to us that OCA considerations appear to have played little role in the formation of the euro area. Further, if the OCA literature is correct, then the euro area would appear not to be an Optimal Currency Area. Some of the departures of the euro area from an OCA arise from policy decisions (notably the absence of an EU fiscal policy) whereas others (notably lack of labour mobility) are more deeply embedded and some attempts have been made to address them (for example, development of the transferability of qualifications between countries). But to say that the euro area is not optimal is not the same as saying that the euro area is not better than the continuation of national currencies. However, we would argue that it is still the case that the criteria proposed by the OCA literature still have some relevance in judging whether the introduction of the euro is an improvement. Feldstein (1997) stated that 'what is clear to me is that the decision (on economic and monetary union) will not depend on the *economic* advantages and disadvantages of a single currency' (p. 23). This is a remark with which we would concur and in particular say that the OCA literature has been ignored.

Clearly, the ideas of the OCA had relatively little influence on the formation of the euro. Baldwin and Wyplosz (2009), for example, argue that 'The negotiators who prepared the Maastricht Treaty did not pay attention to the OCA theory' (p. 345). The same source also poses the question of whether Europe is an optimum currency area with the answer that 'most European countries do well on openness and diversification, two of the three classic economic OCA criteria, and fail on the third one, labour mobility. Europe also fails on fiscal transfers, with an unclear verdict on the remaining two political criteria' (p. 340). It is clear that EMU is not fiscally integrated. Taxpayers in one country do not pick up, for example, any of the costs of a bank bailout of another country. It is also true that while citizens of the EMU have the legal right to move freely in any of the member countries in search for employment, in practice citizens are much less geographically mobile than in countries like the US, for example. A currency union that works coincides with a nation that has a central government and a common language; EMU has neither.

The OCA literature clearly points out that a monetary union means that the exchange rate between constituent members cannot be changed in nominal terms. Hence, the possibility of using changes in the exchange rate as a means of adjusting to economic 'shocks' or indeed to continuing difficulties is ruled out. There can, though, be changes in the real exchange rate through a change in the relative prices of constituent members. The OCA literature points to the possibility of 'price flexibility' as a device through which a country could adjust to an 'economic shock'. But the expectation would be that a negative shock would be compensated by a fall in relative prices (of a country). In the euro area it appears that there have been substantial changes in the real exchange rate of countries, as relative prices of countries have changed reflecting differential inflation between countries. But it is rather unlikely that these changes in relative prices have been responses to differential shocks and that those changes are an adjustment process. If anything the changes in relative competitiveness have worsened rather than lessened the disparities in current account positions.

The emphasis of the OCA approach was on the ability (or otherwise) of an economy to adjust to shocks, where the adjustments were viewed in terms of market ones of price and factor mobility. What was little considered in the OCA, or other literature, was the consequence for an economy, which joined the currency union with an economy, which was 'unbalanced'. By the latter we mean an economy (or parts thereof), which had high levels of unemployment or one that had a large current account deficit. It is then not a matter of asking how an economy could adjust to a shock (particularly a negative one) to restore full employment but rather whether there is any prospect of an economy in a currency union escaping from high levels of unemployment. In order to reach a lower level of unemployment, the demand for the output of that economy has to be increased faster than output increases in other EMU countries. This would generally require that the productive capacity on which workers could be employed would also have to be created. Whilst there may be spontaneous increases in investment, there are clear limits on the policy instruments available to promote such investment. Further, those countries have to find additional markets for their exports without the benefits of devaluation.

In a similar vein, an economy that enters into a currency area with a current account imbalance lacks the ability to correct that imbalance. When that economy is able to borrow to meet any deficit, and similarly is willing to lend when there is a surplus, then the position would be sustainable, though its debts would mount, which serves to undermine that sustainability. But such an economy has to rely on borrowing from overseas and being able to continue to do so. In our interpretation it is difficulties arising from such borrowing, which underlies many of the problems of the EMU at present.

The development of a substantial EU budget, which operates to make fiscal transfers between the relatively rich and the relatively poor countries and to act as some form of stabiliser, that is a country experiencing a downturn receiving a greater inflow of funds, is a major policy way in which concerns of the OCA literature could be addressed. But the current account imbalances would remain, which would seem to require mechanisms by which a country with a current account deficit can in effect devalue in real terms, and hence a country with a surplus revalue. This is not possible, of course, within the EMU area, while the experience of the past decade in the EU area does not suggest that such adjustments would readily occur; indeed it appears that on the whole prices have adjusted in a manner opposite to that.

The OCA literature had considerable influence on academic debates but appears to have little impact on the design of the EMU. Many authors who were attached to the OCA approach tended to conclude that the euro area was not an optimal currency area – or at least by comparison with the USA, the euro area had lower factor (notably labour) mobility, and lacked fiscal transfers. Insofar as regard was paid to the OCA criteria, the argument was put that there would be endogeneity in the fulfilment of the criteria, that is whilst at the time of formation of the euro the criteria would not be satisfied, the experience of the single currency and the enhancing trading between countries would leads in the direction of their fulfilment.

The OCA approach suffered from being developed within an essentially competitive demand/supply framework: that is a 'shock' in one country could potentially be addressed through a combination of price and quantity adjustments: if demand in one country fell, then prices of goods and services produced in that country could fall, and resources shift from that country. The exchange rate was similarly viewed as a price adjustment mechanism to shocks, with, of course, that adjustment mechanism being removed in the single currency case. The OCA approach then overstated the benefits of an adjustable exchange rate. The OCA approach overlooks the forces of cumulative causation and the degree to which imbalances between countries (or regions) can be reinforcing rather than self-correcting.

The OCA approach is based on an approach which starts with some equilibrium, where a 'shock' is followed by an adjustment process which focuses on price and quantity adjustment to restore equilibrium. It pays little attention to situations of initial imbalance when the single currency is formed, and then how those imbalances could be resolved in the context of a fixed exchange rate system. This was in effect the position with the formation of the euro, with large differences in unemployment rates and current account positions. There were also substantial differences in income per capita and trend growth rates.

2.5 Concluding remarks

The euro has been running for over 10 years (and 13 if the period as a virtual currency is included). Its introduction was technically accepted and the switchover was perceived to have met few problems, though there was some perceptions that prices rose when the euro was introduced (a perception which does not show up in the statistics). Although there have been occasional rumblings against it, there had not been any concerted effort for a country to withdraw from the euro and revert to a national currency until the early 2010s. Most new member countries (or at least the political leaders) often appear eager to join though Sweden rejected the euro in a 2003 referendum. Denmark and the UK maintain opt-outs and appear unlikely to wish to join in the foreseeable future. Opposition often emerges in countries such as the Czech Republic and Poland. The euro area has expanded with the number now having reached 17.

The economic performance of the euro area countries, as briefly surveyed in sections 2.3 and 2.4 above, has been rather lacklustre – economic growth has been sluggish, inflation has remained low though often breaking the 2 per cent target (as for example again in summer 2012 when 2.7 per cent was reached), and unemployment has remained high. There are continuing disparities in economic performance. In reviewing the economic performance we have suggested a number of strains within the euro area. The disparities of unemployment and standards of living are highly significant as measures of economic well-being, and the framework of the euro area has little to address those disparities. But for the future operation and indeed survival of the euro area the differences in inflation, in budget deficits and in current account positions may be much more significant. If the differences in inflation rates continue, then those countries with relatively high inflation will see continuing decline in their competitiveness and ability to export. Under a common monetary policy, as discussed in chapter 3, there is a lack of policy instrument to address these differences in inflation. The differences in the budget deficit positions are suggestive of different requirements; namely, which economies have and point to the problems that the 'one-size fits all' approach of the Stability and Growth Pact presents: this is an issue we also return to in chapter 3. The differences in the current account position would suggest that there is substantial borrowing by some countries to fund their deficit and substantial lending by others. We have pointed to the absence of an adjustment process akin to changing the exchange rate in the context of a currency union; along with the current dangers of the current appreciation of the euro exchange rate. The alternative adjustment process would likely involve deflation in deficit countries to reduce their import bill.

Further decisions have been reached recently. The EU summit meeting, held on 28/29 June 2012, took a number of decisions, including: banking licence for the European Stability Mechanism (ESM); when the ESM is introduced in 2013 it would have access to the ECB funding and thus greatly increase its firepower; banking supervision by the ECB. Germany objects to the latter proposal on two grounds: the ECB should not be responsible for all 6,000 euro area banks (including small banks such as Germany's regional savings banks); and there should be a clean separation between ECB monetary policy and bank supervision. Furthermore, and at the same EU summit meeting of 28/29 June 2012, a 'growth pact' was proposed, which would involve issuing project bonds to finance infrastructure. Two long-term solutions are proposed: one is a move towards a banking union and a single euro area bank deposit guarantee scheme; and another is the introduction of euro bonds and euro bills. Germany has resisted the latter two long-term solutions, arguing that it would only contemplate such action only under a full-blown fiscal union. Such suggestion is pertinent not merely in terms of the introduction of the two solutions proposed but also for the long-term survival of the euro area, as we argue later in the book.

On 12 December 2012 the EU finance ministers reached a technical agreement to create a new single supervisor at the ECB. The ECB will supervise banks with assets worth more than €30 billion or 20 per cent of their country's GDP (it amounts to around 200 out of 6,000 euro area banks; the latter includes all but one German savings bank). National supervisors will run the day-to-day supervision of other banks, although the ECB has the right to supervise in an emergency and at the request of the ESM. The creation of the new supervisory body is to be set up by March 2013, although plans to use the ESM, the euro area bailout fund, to recapitalise banks directly, could not be in place before 2014. The plan has had political approval from the majority of the EU/EMU countries at their summit meetings of 13/14 December 2012. It now needs to be approved by the EU and individual country parliaments. The UK, Sweden and the Czech Republic refused to join the single supervisory agreement. It is the case, though, that they are members of the European Banking Authority that coordinates supervisors.

3
The Economic and Monetary Union Model: Theoretical Underpinnings of Macroeconomic Policy

3.1 Introduction

The Economic and Monetary Union (EMU) has a clear set of monetary and fiscal policies associated with the Stability and Growth Pact (SGP). We argue here that those policies have to be understood by reference to a particular macroeconomic analysis. Specifically, it is argued that the macroeconomic policy framework for fiscal and monetary policy with EMU is embedded in what is now known as the 'New Consensus Macroeconomics'.[1] Any specific macroeconomic analysis puts forward a view of how the economy operates, what are the issues which policy can and should address, and the effectiveness (or otherwise) of particular policies (for development of this argument at a general level see Arestis and Sawyer, 2010a), and the New Consensus Macroeconomics is no exception.

These macroeconomic policies govern the monetary policy of EMU as undertaken by the European Central Bank (ECB). They also govern the budgetary policies of EMU which amounts to the set of fiscal policy constraints for each of the nation states adopting the euro as there is no EMU budget as a whole and the budget for the EU as a whole is small (around 1 per cent of GDP) and has to be balanced. The national budgetary positions are intended to be governed by the Stability and Growth (SGP) Pact and the 'fiscal compact' as discussed in chapters 5 and 8 below.

In section 3.2 we set out the theoretical underpinnings of the 'New Consensus Macroeconomics' (hereafter NCM) framework. This is followed, in section 3.3, by a detailed discussion of the ECB macroeconomic model. Section 3.4 discusses the question of whether the ECB model is embedded in the NCM theoretical framework. We offer concluding remarks to this chapter in section 3.5.

3.2 Theoretical underpinnings

It is rather unlikely that economic policy pursued by any government or institution is fully consistent with some theoretical paradigm. Policy-making is a messy business, involving compromises and contradictions. It is, though, that the policy framework of EMU can be understood by reference to a set of theoretical positions, some articulated by its officials (see, for example, European Central Bank, 2008, p. 22 on the importance of the independence of a central bank and p. 34 on the neutrality of money). Specifically, the policy framework and approach of EMU should be viewed as embedded in the NCM paradigm. The approach can be viewed as 'new consensus' through its emphasis on the supply-side determined equilibrium level of unemployment (the 'natural rate' or the non-accelerating inflation rate of unemployment, the NAIRU), its neglect of aggregate or effective demand (essentially in the long run), and of the use of active fiscal policy, and the elevation of monetary policy at the expense of fiscal policy.

The key elements of the NCM with regard to the economic policies of EMU are:

(i) A market economy is viewed as essentially stable, and that macroeconomic policy (particularly discretionary fiscal policy) may well destabilise the market economy. Discretionary fiscal policy can, it is argued, be de-stabilising in that through decision and implementation lags, a fiscal stimulus (say) could come through when the economy is once again booming leading to an over-shooting. A particularly important assumption is that markets, and particularly the financial markets, make well-informed judgements on economic events and the future of the economy. This extends to economic policies and any attempt by government to pursue 'unsound' policies will be fully understood by the markets that will respond accordingly, and the responses of markets is intensified in the context of open and globalised financial markets. The idea that people (and after all markets are populated by people alone and not by mystical market forces) have good and accurate information on the future (the 'rational expectations' assumption) is a critical component of this view. It is also a key ingredient in this view that the financial system is seen as functioning smoothly and efficiently. The role of the financial system is the linking together of those who wish to save and those who wish to borrow to invest, and the financial system is viewed as undertaking that role efficiently. The global financial crisis of the late 2000s, has perhaps called some of that view into question!

(ii) Monetary policy is taken as the main instrument of macroeconomic policy, with the view that it is a flexible instrument for achieving medium-term stabilisation objectives, where those objectives focus on inflation, and that stabilisation of inflation is sufficient to ensure financial stability. Monetary policy can be adjusted quickly in response to macroeconomic developments with decisions on interest rates (even if the decision is to leave interest rates on hold) being taken on a frequent basis, for example monthly. Indeed, monetary policy is viewed as the main determinant of inflation, so much so that in the long run the inflation rate is the only macroeconomic variable that monetary policy can affect (see, for example, ECB, 2008, p.34). Indeed there is the 'the fundamental economic principle that, over the longer term, inflation is a monetary phenomenon' (ECB, 2008, p.37).

Fiscal policy is viewed as an impotent macroeconomic instrument (in any case it may often be subject to the slow and uncertain legislative processes and there are lags of implementation and effect). It is recognised that the budget position will vary over the course of the business cycle in a counter-cyclical manner (that is the deficit rising in downturn as tax receipts fall and some parts of public expenditure rise, and conversely the surplus rising in upturn as tax receipts rise with higher incomes). This helps to dampen the scale of economic fluctuations by increasing taxes in the upturn and fiscal policy then acts as a partial 'automatic' stabiliser. But these fluctuations in the budget position should take place around a budget position, which averages close to balance over the cycle. Fiscal policies 'based on clear mandates and rules reflect a macroeconomic policy design that is generally preferable to the ad-hoc discretionary co-ordination of day-to-day policy action in the face of shocks' (ECB, 2003c, p. 37). Indeed, in the ECB (2008) view, 'Stability-oriented fiscal policies are a pre-condition for sustainable economic growth and the smooth functioning of Monetary Union, as well as for avoiding unnecessary differentials across countries' (p. 75).

Even under conditions of financial crisis and recession when nearly all governments around the world have resorted to fiscal policy to rescue them from recession, the now ex-president of the ECB (Trichet, 2008) claimed that 'Regarding fiscal policies, the Governing Council considers it crucial that discipline and a medium-term perspective are maintained, taking fully into account the consequences of any shorter-term action on fiscal sustainability. It is of the utmost importance that the public's confidence in the soundness of fiscal policies is preserved, with the rules-based EU fiscal framework being fully applied and its integrity being fully preserved. The provisions of the Treaty of Nice and the Stability and Growth Pact require a medium-term perspective and allow for the necessary flexibility. Automatic fiscal stabilisers are relatively large in the euro area and provide a powerful source of fiscal support to a weakening economy. Where room for manoeuvre exists, additional budgetary measures could be effective if they are timely, targeted and temporary' (it is to be noted that this kind of statement has been repeated by the Presidents of the ECB ever since January 1999). In response to a question from the audience, Trichet (2008) is very clear: 'On ... fiscal discipline, as I have said on behalf of the Governing Council, we consider the Stability and Growth Pact to be absolutely essential. We are a single currency area which has no federal government and no federal budget. And we are told by observers from time to time that we have put the cart before the horse because we have a single currency, but no federal government. We respond by saying that, yes, we have an institutional framework that is not a federal government, but we have the Stability and Growth Pact, and the cohesion of the euro area is very much based on the Monetary Union, on the one hand, and on the Economic Union with the Stability and Growth Pact, on the other. This is very important and I will not elaborate more on this because it is the fundamental message that we give. We are telling all countries that they have to respect the orientations of the Stability and Growth Pact and, as I said on behalf of the Governing Council, that wherever there is room for manoeuvre, it can be used. Let us not forget on top of that that the various members of the European Union in general, but those of the euro area in particular, have already taken decisions with respect to the recapitalisation of their banks and the guarantees that they are giving to banks, as well as the rescue operations that have already been mobilised in some cases, as proof of their efforts. This is very important and we should not forget it. Nor should we forget that, when automatic stabilisation can be utilised and when there is room for automatic stabilisers to operate in full, we in Europe – in comparison with other industrialised economies – have a level of public spending as a proportion of GDP and a level of social safety net that is generally superior to what is observed in the other OECD countries. So, in terms of their volume, that makes automatic stabilisers more important in Europe – not only in the euro area – than is the case on the other side of the Atlantic, for instance,' Also that 'the Maastricht Treaty is the Maastricht Treaty, and the criteria are the criteria, and they will be applied. And, to my knowledge, absolutely nobody – irrespective of whether in the Commission or the Council, and certainly not in the ECB – has asked or is envisaging to change the rules and to change the criteria for entry into the euro area. On the timely, targeted, temporary fiscal measures, these are also the qualifications that I use myself, as are – to my knowledge – used by the Commission and by the Council. So, we are all using the same qualifications'.[2]

Monetary policy has, thus, been upgraded in importance in the attention paid to it and its assumed effectiveness, and fiscal policy has been downgraded to a budget balanced over the cycle format. Further, monetary policy becomes identified with the setting of interest rates, rather than any other interventions such as credit controls or reserve requirements.

(iii) Monetary policy can be used to meet the objective of low rates of inflation (which are desirable in this view, since low, and stable, rates of inflation are conducive to healthy growth rates). However, monetary policy should not be operated by politicians but by experts (whether bankers, economists or others) in the form of an 'independent' central bank, and this is the precise set-up of the ECB. Indeed, those operating monetary policy should be more 'conservative' where that term is used to mean greater weight on low inflation and less weight on the level of unemployment than politicians (or the general public) would (Rogoff, 1985). Politicians would be tempted, it is argued, to use monetary policy for short-term gain (lower unemployment) at the expense of longer-term loss (higher inflation), whereas central bankers by inclination and by mandate are not subject to such temptation when low inflation is set as overriding objective of monetary policy.

An 'independent' central bank would also have, it is argued, greater credibility in the financial markets and be seen to have a stronger commitment to low inflation than politicians do. This is reiterated by the ECB when they write that 'Economic theory and historical examples from previous decades represent strong evidence that central bank independence is a precondition for achieving and maintaining price stability. Against this background, the multi-dimensional independence of the ECB is stipulated in the Treaty, which legitimises its independence' (ECB, 2008, p. 22). Independence of a central bank is defined 'as *institutional independence*, implying a set of legal provisions that guarantee that the central bank carries out its tasks and duties without political, and more generally, external interference' (Issing, 2006, p. 67; italics included in the original).

The distinction between goal independence and instrument independence is made. It is recognised that in a democratic society goal-setting cannot be left to unelected officials, so that central banks should not be goal independent. However, full independence should be given in the setting of monetary policy to achieve the goal(s) set by the elected representatives. A number of quid pro quo requirements for central bank Independence are important: credibility of the central bank, accountability and transparency in the conduct of monetary policy. The independent central bank should explain and justify its decision to the public and its elected representatives with a high degree of transparency and credibility so that the actions of the central bank can be closely monitored and judged to be performed according to expectations. The ECB is, however, both goal and instrument independent, which makes it unique in this sense around the world: it is the most 'independent' central bank in the world when judged in terms of immunity to political and democratic control (though in terms of commitment to a neo-liberal ideology the least independent).

(iv) It is the credibility of monetary policy, which is viewed as paramount in the successful conduct of monetary policy, where here success would be generally seen in terms of the achievement of low inflation. It is argued that a policy which lacks credibility because of time inconsistency is neither optimal nor feasible (Kydland and Prescott, 1977). The only credible policy is the one that leaves the authority no freedom as to how to react to developments in the future, and that even if aggregate demand policies matter in the short run in this model, a policy of non-intervention is preferable. It is precisely because of the time-inconsistency and credibility problems that monetary policy should be assigned to a 'credible' and independent central bank. Such a central bank should be given as its sole objective that of price stability, interpreted in terms of an inflation target. An independent central bank is viewed as credible in that it is given the objective of price stability, its performance is to be judged by its achievement or otherwise of price stability, and the perception that a central bank would not fall for the temptation of an expansionary policy which may be politically popular as central bankers are seen as more committed to price stability than to low unemployment (and central bankers do not face re-election).

(v) The priority objective for macroeconomic policy should be that of low inflation. This is to be preferred to the focus on money supply targeting since it is generally recognised that achieving money supply targets is difficult or impossible. This is often formalised in terms of setting an inflation target (though 'inflation targeting' is formally speaking not a term adopted by EMU). Inflation targeting is neither a rule nor discretion (in practice only degrees of discretion prevail): it is rather a framework for monetary policy whereby public announcement of official inflation targets, or target ranges, is undertaken along with explicit acknowledgement that low and stable inflation is monetary policy's primary long-term objective. This improves communication between the public and policy-makers and provides discipline, accountability, transparency and flexibility in monetary policy. Inflation targeting has been described as 'constrained' or 'enlightened' discretion, in that inflation targets serve as a nominal anchor for monetary policy. As such, monetary policy imposes discipline on the central bank and the government within a flexible policy framework. For example, even if monetary policy is used to address short-run stabilisation objectives, the long-run inflation objective must not be compromised, thereby imposing consistency and rationality in policy choices (in doing so, monetary policy focuses public's expectations and provides a reference point to judge short-run policies). Although the ECB allegedly does not pursue an inflation targeting policy (Duisenberg, 2003a; Issing, 2003; see, also, our discussion below in this section), it does, nonetheless, pursue a monetary policy strategy with 'the clear commitment to the maintenance of price stability over the medium term' which 'implies a stable nominal anchor to the economy in all circumstances' (ECB, 2001b, p. 49). ECB (2008) has argued that 'Furthermore, price stability is the best – and, ultimately, the only – contribution that a credible monetary policy can make to economic growth, job creation and social cohesion. This reflects the fact that a policy-maker who controls only one instrument cannot meet, and be held accountable for the fulfilment of, more than one objective. The pursuit of additional objectives would risk overburdening monetary policy, and would ultimately result in higher inflation and higher unemployment. Over the longer term, monetary policy can only influence the price level in the economy; it cannot exert a lasting impact on economic activity. This general principle is referred to as the "long-run neutrality of money"' (p. 34).

The policy focus is then on inflation. There are caveats to the effect that monetary policy should also support other objectives but these are generally viewed as rather secondary. But further as indicated in some quotes given above it is argued that at least in the medium to long-term monetary policy (or indeed any macroeconomic policy) cannot influence the level of economic activity. At best, an expansionary monetary policy can stimulate economic activity in the short term, but then only at the expense of higher inflation at a later date. An upturn in economic activity, which is accompanied by inflation, does not present difficulties for this policy approach in that an increase in interest rates can serve to restrain output and employment and inflation. However, this inflation targeting approach can only address inflation which is demand-driven and cannot deal with inflation which is of a more cost push variety or of a global origin, or with inflation which is accompanied by a downturn in economic activity. Inflation targeting with interest rate as the policy instrument asserts that there are firm links running from interest rate to demand to inflation: for further discussion on that see below.

(vi) The level of economic activity is taken to fluctuate around a supply-side equilibrium, and in some sense remain close to that supply-side equilibrium in a stable environment. The supply-side equilibrium here corresponds to a level of economic activity at which inflation would be constant: this is often formalised in terms of a non-accelerating inflation rate of unemployment (NAIRU), and unemployment below (above) the NAIRU would lead to higher (lower) rates of inflation. The use of the word unemployment in the term NAIRU rather than some other word indicating or related to the level of economic activity is symbolic in that the general focus of attention is on the labour market. In general terms, a wide range of supply-side factors could influence the level of the NAIRU, but it is usually the rules under which the labour market operates which come into for policy attention. The ECB has argued, for example that 'the outlook for the euro area economy could be significantly improved if governments strengthen their efforts to implement structural reforms in labour and product markets. Such reforms are important to ultimately raise the euro area's production potential, improve the flexibility of the economy and make the euro area more resilient to external shocks' (ECB, 2003b, p. 6). In a similar vein, a more recent expression of this general view is: 'These are encouraging developments, which show that past labour market reforms, immigration and wage moderation have helped to overcome some of the constraints on growth stemming from rigid and over-regulated labour markets. It also confirms that monetary policy geared towards price stability is fully consistent with job creation and low unemployment. However, despite this progress, most euro area countries are still far from having exhausted the potential for further increases in participation rates and employment. Structural impediments emerging from rigid legal and regulatory environments, high taxes on labour and distortions associated with regulations such as minimum wages still prevent or discourage many people from actively participating in the labour market and thus keep employment rates low and unemployment high' (ECB, 2008, p. 69). Even under the circumstances of the financial crisis and the real thread of recession and deflation, Trichet (2008) argues that: 'Turning to structural policies, the ongoing period of weak economic activity and high uncertainty about the economic outlook imply the need to strengthen the resilience and flexibility of the euro area economy. Product market reforms should foster competition and speed up effective restructuring. Labour market reforms should help to facilitate appropriate wage-setting, as well as labour mobility across sectors and regions. The current situation should therefore be seen as a catalyst to foster the implementation of necessary domestic reforms in line with the principle of an open market economy with free competition.'

The source of domestic inflation (relative to the expected rate of inflation) is seen to arise from unemployment falling below the NAIRU, and inflation is postulated to accelerate if unemployment is held below the NAIRU. However, in the long run in this analysis there is no trade-off between inflation and unemployment, and the economy has to operate (on average) at the NAIRU if accelerating inflation is to be avoided. In the long run, inflation is viewed as a monetary phenomenon in that the pace of inflation is controlled by the rate of interest. Monetary policy is, thus, in the hands of central bankers. Control of the money supply is not an issue, essentially because of the instability of the demand for money that makes the impact of changes in the money supply a highly uncertain channel of influence. It should also be noted that control of the stock of money by the central bank becomes very problematic in a world of credit money created by the banking system, which is a world of endogenous money supply rather than exogenous money, and the world in which we live.

(vii) The essence of Say's Law holds, namely that the level of effective demand does not play an independent role in the (long-run) determination of the level of economic activity, and adjusts to underpin the supply-side-determined level of economic activity (which itself corresponds to the NAIRU). It was a fundamental aspect of Keynes (1936) to argue that Say's Law did not hold and that deficient aggregate demand (that is deficient with respect to productive potential) could and does exist and in the long term as well as the short term. There have been many attempts to revive Say's Law and the one currently in vogue is in effect to call on the operation of monetary policy in the setting of the (real) rate of interest equal to the so-called 'natural' rate of interest. It is asserted that there is a rate of interest (the 'natural rate of interest') at which the level of demand and the level of supply will be equated, savings and investment intentions brought into balance, and with actual output equal to potential output (zero output gap), and unemployment at the NAIRU level. The central bank sets the interest rate, and provided that it can be isolated and then target the 'natural rate of interest' (which corresponds to RR* in the equations below), then the economy would be able to operate with a zero output gap as well as a constant rate of inflation. But it does require the central bank to act appropriately. Keynes (1936) explicitly rejected the idea of a unique natural rate of interest, and in effect argued that there was a natural rate of interest corresponding to each level of effective demand, which would bring savings and investment into balance. 'In my *Treatise on Money* I defined what purported to be a unique rate of interest, which I called the natural rate of interest – namely, the rate of interest which, in the terminology of my *Treatise*, preserved equality between the rate of saving (as there defined) and the rate of investment... I had, however, overlooked the fact that in any given society there is, on this definition, a *different* natural rate of interest for each hypothetical level of employment. And, similarly, for every rate of interest there is a level of employment for which the rate is the 'natural' rate, in the sense that the system will be in equilibrium with that rate of interest and that level of employment. Thus it was a mistake to speak of the natural rate of interest or to suggest that the above definition would yield a unique value for the rate of interest irrespective of the level of employment. I had not then understood that, in certain conditions, the system could be in equilibrium with less than full employment' (Keynes, 1936, pp. 242–3). Keynes went on to argue that 'If there is any such rate of interest, which is unique and significant, it must be the rate which we might term the *neutral* rate of interest, namely, the natural rate in the above sense which is consistent with full employment, given the other parameters of the system; though this rate might be better described, perhaps, as the *optimum* rate... The above gives us, once again, the answer to the question as to what tacit assumption is required to make sense of the classical theory of the rate of interest. This theory assumes either that the actual rate of interest is always equal to the neutral rate of interest in the sense in which we have just defined the latter, or alternatively that the actual rate of interest is always equal to the rate of interest which will maintain employment at some specified constant level. If the traditional theory is thus interpreted, there is little or nothing in its practical conclusions to which we need take exception. The classical theory assumes that the banking authority or natural forces cause the market-rate of interest to satisfy one or other of the above conditions' (Keynes, 1936, pp. 243–4).

Most of these general ideas can be seen as formalised (explicitly or implicitly) in the 'New Consensus Macroeconomics' analysis summarised in terms of three equations, an example of which is given below. These three equations are relevant in the case of a closed economy (Arestis, 2007, for example, studies the case of the open economy; there are no significant differences from the point of view of the current analysis).

The equations are:

(1) $Y^g_t = a_0 + a_1 Y^g_{t-1} + a_2 E(Y^g_{t+1}) - a_3 [R_t - E_t(p_{t+1})] + s_1$

(2) $p_t = b_1 Y^g_t + b_2 p_{t-1} + b_3 E_t(p_{t+1}) + s_2$

(*with* $b_2 + b_3 = 1$)

(3) $R_t = RR^* + E_t(p_{t+1}) + c_1 Y^g_{t-1} + c_2(p_{t-1} - p^T)$

where Y^g is the output gap, R is nominal rate of interest, p is inflation, and p^T is inflation target, RR^* is the 'equilibrium' real rate of interest (that is the rate of interest consistent with zero output gap which implies from equation (2) a constant rate of inflation), and s_i (with $i = 1, 2$) represents stochastic shocks.

In these equations, equation (1) represents aggregate demand in that output relative to potential output, that is the output gap, is set by the level of aggregate demand, which in this equation is seen as dependent on past demand (output gap), expected future demand, and the real rate of interest. The demand for consumption and for investment is taken as dependent on these variables.

This equation has a passing resemblance to the traditional IS curve in macroeconomic analysis in that it is based on the demand side and involves the level of output (here in the guise of the output gap) and the rate of interest. It is though rather different from the traditional IS curve. In the approach here (elaborated at great length in Woodford 2003; see Arestis and Sawyer, 2008, for a critique) the expenditure decisions are based on the intertemporal optimisation of a utility function subject to a life-time budget constraint. The significant aspects of this are that (i) there is assumed to be well-informed forward-looking optimisation (in the context of 'rational expectations') where individuals in effect know the future. Further since individuals are subject to a life-time budget constraint and since they gain utility from consumption they push their consumption to the limit; that is over their life time in effect wish to consume all their income. In other words there is a tendency for income to equal expenditure, which is a way of bringing back Say's Law. Finally there are no credit constraints in this model, that is individuals can borrow or lend as much as they wish in any particular period of time, though they are subject to the overall budget constraint over their life time. The intertemporal utility optimisation is based on the assumption that all debts are ultimately paid in full, thereby removing all credit risk and default. This follows from the assumption of what is known technically as the transversality condition, which means in effect that all economic agents with their rational expectations are perfectly credit worthy. All IOUs in the economy can, and would, be accepted in exchange. There is, thus, no need for a specific monetary asset. All fixed-interest financial assets are identical so that there is a single rate of interest in any period. Over time the single rate of interest may change as borrowing and savings propensities change. Under such circumstance no individual economic agent or firm is liquidity constrained at all. There is, thus, no need for financial intermediaries (commercial banks or other non-bank financial intermediaries) and even money (see, also, Goodhart, 2007, 2008; Buiter, 2008; Arestis, 2009). In basing equation (1) of the NCM model on the transversality condition, the supporters have turned the model into an essentially non-monetary model. So it is no surprise that private banking institutions or monetary variables are not essential in the NCM framework.[3] It is rather amazing how such a non-monetary approach has been taken on board by central banks around the world.

Equation (2) is a Phillips curve in which the rate of inflation depends in a one-for-one manner on expected inflation and on the output gap. This is an essential ingredient in this approach for a number of reasons. First, it is the mechanism which links demand (as reflected in the output gap) to the rate of inflation. The rate of interest is assumed to influence the output gap through equation (1), and then output gap influences inflation through equation (2). Second, a constant rate of inflation where actual and expected inflation are equal implies the output gap would need to be zero. The zero output gap, where actual and trend output are equal, is the supply-side equilibrium in this framework. Third, the Phillips' curve illustrates the argument indicated above, namely that if there is a temptation to stimulate economic activity (positive output gap) then rising inflation is the consequence. Fourth, the Phillips' curve incorporates an 'accelerationist' view on inflation—the penalty of output gap even slightly positive is that inflation will not only be higher but rising. The argument is simply that for a given state of expectations on inflation, a positive output gap will lead to inflation being higher than those expectations. The experience of higher inflation generates a change in expectations on inflation, and the continuation of a positive output gap would lead to inflation higher than the now higher level of expected inflation. Inflation would then continue to rise indefinitely into hyperinflation if the output gap remains positive: and even a small but positive output gap would have this effect, albeit the rise in inflation would be slower than if there were a larger positive output gap.

The operating rule of monetary policy provides equation (3) (often labelled Taylor's rule, after Taylor, 1993) in which the interest rate is assumed to be set by the central bank in response to economic conditions in terms of inflation (relative to target) and the output gap. It is further assumed that the interest rate set by the central bank is translated in a one-for-one manner into other interest rates such as those on loans and deposits.

Under this rule, the real rate of interest would be raised in the face of inflation since the nominal rate of interest rises by more than 1 per cent for a 1 per cent higher inflation. This rule is designed to use interest rates to combat inflation. It reflects a demand-pull view of inflation in the sense that output gap and inflation are assumed to move in the same direction so that inflationary conditions (positive output gap and inflation high) lead to rise in interest rate. A stagflation situation, where the output gap is negative and inflation high, presents this approach with a policy dilemma – high inflation suggests putting up interest rates, negative output gap reducing them to combat recession.

There are then three equations and three unknowns in this model: output gap, interest rate and inflation. At any point in time, with the expectations and history of the economy, these equations would be sufficient to indicate the state of those three variables. It can here be noted that this approach endogenises the interest rate. The latter statement, though, needs a little elaboration. The rate of interest is still under the control of the central bank, but the latter's decisions to change or otherwise the rate under its control is determined by the variables that appear in equation (3). The monetary variable that is purely endogenous is the money supply as explained below.

This model has a number of additional, and relevant, characteristics. There are both lagged adjustment and forward-looking elements; the model allows for sticky prices (the lagged price level in the Phillips-curve relationship) and full price flexibility in the long run. For the present discussion the inclusion of the term $E_t(p_{t+1})$ in equation (2) is particularly significant for in effect it is those expectations, which drive inflation. A policy which convinces people that inflation is going to fall in the future will more readily be able to deliver low inflation. The credibility of the central bank argument can be reflected in the idea that the establishment of an independent central bank with the sole objective of too low inflation serves to create expectations of low inflation. A central bank that credibly signals its intention to achieve and maintain low inflation will be 'rewarded' by lower expectations on the rate of inflation. The inclusion of the term $E_t(p_{t+1})$ in equation (2) indicates that it may be possible to reduce current inflation at a significantly lower cost in terms of output than otherwise. The operating rule implies that 'policy' becomes a systematic adjustment to economic developments rather than an exogenous process.

This framework contains the neutrality of money property, with inflation determined by monetary policy (that is the rate of interest), and equilibrium values of real variables are independent of the money supply. But this model does not contain any mention of the stock or supply of money. It would be a straightforward matter to add an equation for the demand for money (willingness to hold money) and postulate that the stock of money is equal (perhaps with lags) to this demand for money (which we would interpret more as a willingness to hold money). There are two points to be made here. First, this reflects an essentially endogenous money approach. The stock of money adjusts to the demand for money as the amount of money is existence has to be held by some body and the overall amount of money will only be willingly held if the demand for money is aligned with the stock of money. Second, the stock of money though acts rather like a residual in that the stock of money clearly does not enter into the rest of the model.[4] The stock of money may though contain some information in the following sense. Suppose there is an upswing in demand, and that demand has to be financed if it is to become effective, that is demand leading to expenditure, and loans are sought to finance the increased demand. If loans are granted by the banking system, then corresponding bank deposits (part of the stock of money) increase and the higher level of expenditure can occur. A rise in the stock of money could be a sign that more loans are being granted and more expenditure is occurring. The manner in which the ECB operates represents some departure from this view in that the 'two pillar' approach (as discussed below) pays some attention to the evolution of the stock of money as well as to the rate of inflation.

The three equations in the NCM model above obviously represent a highly simplified view of the macroeconomy, albeit one, which reflects the crucial ingredients of the NCM. The NCM can be viewed as a simple representation of the approach of authors such as Woodford (2003) who provide very detailed analysis at the individual firm and household level which, by dint of assumptions of representative agents, can be summed to lead to equations the simplified form of which appear as equations (1) to (3) above. Models along the lines proposed by Woodford (op. cit.) are often described as dynamic stochastic general equilibrium (DSGE) models: dynamic in the sense that agents are assumed to be forward looking in their decision making, stochastic in that random errors terms are included (as can be seen in equations 1 and 2 above), and general equilibrium as based on equilibrium outcomes, which allow for interactions between economic agents, albeit that the 'representative agent' approach is used. These ideas can also be seen to feed into the formal macroeconomic models, which the ECB and others use.[5] How much impact these models and the forecasts derived from them have on decision-making is an unknown quantity, and the ECB often stresses the range of information on which it draws. The ECB states that 'Mathematical models of the economy have played an important supporting role in the quantitative assessment of current economic and monetary conditions in the euro area' (ECB, 2008, p. 37). The point to make here is that in clearly basing their macroeconomic models on a DGSE approach they have abandoned other approaches, for example, those with a more Keynesian flavour. The DSGE-based macroeconomic models, as we argue in Arestis and Sawyer (2008b), build in by assumption that fiscal policy is impotent. Obviously the model adopted is not neutral with regard to key questions such as the impact of monetary policy and of fiscal policy. Thus the use of DGSE approach in their modelling is supportive of the idea that the ECB works within that framework of which the NCM is a simplified manifestation.

The three relationships that summarise the NCM contain all the essential elements of the theoretical framework of the EMU (see, also, ECB, 2003a). There are, however, two important differences worth highlighting here, pursued further in the section on Monetary Policy (chapter 4). The first is that allegedly the ECB does not pursue inflation targeting. Duisenberg (2003a), then president of the ECB, was adamant that the ECB approach does not entail an inflation target: 'I protest against the word 'target'. We do not have a target ... we won't have a target'. The second is that in the ECB view the demand for money in the euro area is a stable relationship in the long run – most central banks would suggest the opposite in the case of their economies. Issing (2002) observes that 'Part of this controversy is, I believe, of semantic nature. If having price stability as a primary monetary policy objective, being forward-looking, and using all relevant information to achieve it, is what is meant by inflation targeting, then the ECB may be considered an inflation targeter and any central bank in the world should be one. But in my view inflation targeting means something else, and here more substantive differences arise.' Solans (2000) asks 'Does the inflation targeting strategy comply with the requirement of being all-encompassing and flexible (i.e. comprehensive, detailed and adaptable to change and to non-predictable conditions)? My answer is "no", unless we "bend" the meaning of the label "flexible inflation targeting" to a point at which it can accommodate almost any practice.'[6]

The ECB has sought to put some distance between their approach and that of inflation targeting. For example, 'The ECB's two-pillar strategy can be seen as a good example of a more procedural notion of a monetary policy framework... This meant that the ECB's strategy has certainly proved to be not easily digestible to academics. The strategy explicitly shuns the notion of a dominant model or all-encompassing forecast often associated with inflation targeting as well as simple, mechanical rules of the Taylor type or as under traditional monetary targeting. The ECB's strategy puts a premium on the notion of robustness and the need for complementary perspectives and approaches to inform the policy process. This makes it certainly look more complicated and more difficult to communicate than at least the simpler representations of inflation targeting. At the same time, the strategy acknowledges the need for an effective structuring of information, as in the two-pillar framework. It also gives a role to simple guideposts, like the medium-term reference value for money and regular staff projection exercises as a way to condense a large (but not all-encompassing) amount of information. The strategy emphasises procedural notions, such as the stress on 'cross-checking' of information coming from the two pillars. From this perspective the two pillars of the ECB's strategy offer a way to bring together and compare different analytical perspectives and to use – and present – all the information relevant to decision-making in a systematic way. The two-pillar structure of analysis and communication is, admittedly, more complex than the unitary, more monolithic message conveyed by inflation targeting at least in the simplest earlier vintages. At the same time it arguably provides a more explicit and stable framework than an eclectic multi-indicator approach of "looking at everything". ... Overall, the idea of a single "best practice" or universal textbook recipe to monetary policy and communication across the globe seems ill-advised to me.'[7] It is the case that with the ECB's emphasis on the two-pillar strategy it simply cannot be considered as an inflation targeting approach as the latter has been described above in section 3.2.

3.3 The ECB macromodel

We suggest that the ECB macroeconomic model can be captured by the following set of relationships (Arestis and Sawyer, 2008c; Cristoffel et al., 2007).

(4) $Y = C + I + G + X - Q$

(5) $C = C\ (Y, NW)$

(6) $X = X\ (rer, Y_w)$

(7) $Q = Q\ (rer, Y)$

(8) $rer = [(er)\ (P_w)]/P$

(9) $NW = K + PD + NFA$

(10) $Yg = Y - Y^P$

(11) $Y^p = (1 - a)\ K + aL^s + T$

(12) $K = (1 - \delta)\ K_{t-1} + I$

(13) $I = [(R - p), Y]$

(14) $p = p\ (w, Y^g)$

(15) $w = w(U, p^e)$

(16) $U = \dfrac{(L^s - L)}{L^s}$

(17) $L = L\ (Y^g, K)$

(18) $M^D = M(R, PY)$

(19) $R = R[(R - p)^*, (p - p^d)\ Y^g]$

where the symbols are Y is income and Y_w is world income, C is consumption, I is investment, G is government expenditure, X is exports and Q imports, NW is net wealth which is composed of K capital, PD public debt, and NFA net foreign assets. Y^g is output gap, Y^p is potential output, w is the wage rate, U is unemployment, p is rate of inflation, p^e is expected inflation, L is labour, Ls is labour supply, T is productivity trend, R is nominal rate of interest so that (R – p) would be the real rate of interest), $(R - p)^*$ is the long-run equilibrium real rate of interest, p^d is inflation rate target, *rer* stands for the real exchange rate, and *er* for the nominal exchange rate, defined as in equation (5) and expressed as foreign currency units per domestic currency unit, P and P_w are domestic and world price levels respectively, M is money (M3 definition in the case of the ECB) long-run . It should also be noted that G, Y_w, P_w, p^d, L^s, T, PD and NFA are treated here as exogenous for convenience.

Equations 4–9 capture the demand side of the economy, with equation (8) defining the real exchange rate, and equation (9) net wealth. The latter is arrived at by iterating over individuals' period-by-period budget constraints, and then aggregating over the whole population. An individual's wealth is defined as all the resources that are available for expenditure at the start of a period. Financial assets include money, the domestic currency value of foreign bonds, corporate bonds, government bonds, and shares, plus the interest returns and dividends arising from holding these instruments over from the previous period. Non-financial assets include human wealth, transfer wealth, and the value of dwellings.

We may summarise the key features of the first four equations succinctly: in terms of the consumption relationship in particular it should be noted that consumption is explicitly derived from forward-looking optimising behaviour, and it is based on income, the rate of interest and wealth. Economic agents maximise lifetime utility subject to their expected lifetime resources. Furthermore, goods markets are monopolistically competitive, with firms being in a position to charge non-competitive sticky prices. The latter help to clear domestic production to satisfy aggregate demand; that is demand for consumption, investment, including changes in inventories, government spending and exports, all net of imports. In view of the assumption of sluggish price and wage adjustments, actual output is determined by aggregate demand in the short run, with the standard equations for its main components: consumption, exports and imports, with government expenditure treated as exogenous and investment determined in the supply-side block.

Equations (10) to (17) refer to the supply side, with equation (10) defining the output gap. The supply side of the model depends on an aggregate Cobb–Douglas production function, equation (11), whereby output depends on capital stock, effective labour supply and technical progress. Equation (8) is more consistent with the approach of the ECB, where such a relationship is utilised. With equation (12) defining capital stock, investment (equation 13) and employment (equation 17) are determined by profit maximisation and inverting the production function, respectively.

The variables investment and capital stock specifically, although all variables in general, are scaled against the level of output. Hence, the desired capital stock, relative to output, depends on the cost of capital, and actual capital stock adjusts to the desired level, taking into account costs of adjustment. A change in the rate of interest through its impact on the cost of capital would change desired capital stock; there would be a relative price effect but the underlying growth of output would be unaffected. Investment (in terms of the desired capital stock) depends on the rate of interest (via the cost of capital), with the demand for capital depending on the relative prices involved. But it is scaled against the level of output, which is treated as growing at an exogenous rate. The growth of output pulls along the growth of the capital stock as in the neo-classical growth model.

Equations (14) and (15) represent the Phillips curve, and equations (16) and (17) define unemployment and labour supply respectively; the latter is related to the output gap and capital. Equation (15) is the Phillips curve itself (vertical in the long run), and equation (14) should be read as price as a mark-up on unit labour cost. The labour market is not perfectly competitive. Firms and unions bargain over wage levels, which generate unemployment, given private sector and public sector labour demand, labour supply and wage curves.

Unions bargain on workers' behalf. In any given period, a proportion of (randomly chosen) unions engage with firms in a bargain over the nominal wages of the workers they represent. This fraction is constant, so that we have Calvo (1983) nominal wage setting, rather than contracts for fixed terms as in Taylor (1980). Unions aim to maximise the welfare of an average worker, so the value of the 'outside' earnings that could be received if employed by the government or unemployed has a role to play. The private sector wage is determined as the Nash equilibrium in which the firms' and unions' strategies are both optimal. The wages of government employees are set according to a simple rule linking government and private sector wages.

Equations (18) and (19) represent the monetary side of the model. Equation (18) is the demand for the M3 definition of the money stock. Money is treated as a recursive variable in that it has no feedback on the rest of the model. As we will elaborate in the section that follows, this equation is prominent in the ECB model.

Equation (19) is the monetary rule relationship, of the Taylor rule variety. The variable $(p - pd)$ is by far the more important variable in policy decisions than Yg. $(R - p)^*$ is very important but highly problematic (see, for example, Weber et al., 2008). Clearly this is the long-run equilibrium real rate of interest. It is, in other words, the real rate that is associated with output being at its potential level (see equation (3) above). The nominal rate of interest in the hands of the central bank should be anchored to $(R - p)^*$ and to the target inflation as set by the central bank. Anchoring the real equilibrium rate of interest, though, is hazardous. If the central bank targets the wrong $(R - p)^*$ then it may drive the economy on a wrong path. Econometric evidence on the extent to which central banks can obtain the information necessary for a good knowledge of $(R - p)^*$ is by no means encouraging (Weber et al., 2008). The financial imbalances associated with the policy of manipulating the rate of interest to achieve an inflation target are overlooked by the NCM. These imbalances, which tantamount to investment and saving imbalances, are ruled out of the theory in the long run. This is due of course to the equality between the market rate of interest and the real equilibrium rate of interest. But these imbalances do exist!

3.4 Consistency of the ECB model with NCM

It is clear from the analysis of the latter section that the ECB macroeconomic model is consistent with the NCM. But there are differences as we alluded to in section 3.2. We elaborate further on differences and consider the possible consistency between the two approaches in the rest of this section.

The main objective of the ECB is to maintain inflation 'below, but close to, 2 per cent', an approach thought to be 'sufficient to hedge against the risks of both very low inflation and deflation' (ECB, 2008, p. 35). Achievement of this target is expected to take place in the medium term in view of the impact of monetary policy, which is expected to materialise with significant and variable time lags. Consequently, short-term volatility in inflation rates is accepted to be inevitable.

Indeed, the main hypothesis adopted by the ECB is that in the long run inflation is strictly a monetary phenomenon. This hypothesis leads to the policy implication that only monetary instruments, and more precisely the rate of interest, can control inflation. A two-pillar approach to evaluating the prospects of achieving price stability in the ECB case is adopted. There is an economic analysis and a monetary analysis. The ECB economic analysis attempts to assess price developments and the risks to price stability over the short to medium term. This broad range of indicators includes: 'developments in overall output; aggregate demand and its components; fiscal policy; capital and labour market conditions; a broad range of price and cost indicators; developments in the exchange rate; the global economy and the balance of payments; financial markets; and the balance sheet positions of euro area sectors' (ECB, 2004, p. 55). It is, thus, a broad outlook of price developments and the risks to price stability over the short to medium term. These factors and the analysis that accompanies them 'help to assess the dynamics of real activity and the likely development of prices from the perspective of the interplay between supply and demand in the goods, services and factor markets at shorter horizons' (ECB, 2008, pp. 35–6).

The 'second pillar' is a commitment to analyse monetary developments for the information they contain about future price developments over the medium and long term. It focuses 'on a longer-term horizon, exploiting the long-run link between money and prices' (ECB, 2004, p. 55). This is a quantitative reference value for monetary growth, where a target of 4.5 per cent of M3 has been imposed. Being a reference level, there is no mechanistic commitment to correct deviations in the short term, although it is stated that deviations from the reference value would, under normal circumstances, 'signal risks to price stability'. Monetary analysis is utilised by the ECB as a 'cross-check' for consistency between the short-term perspective of economic analysis with the more long-term perspective that emanates from the monetary analysis itself, essentially concern with the M3 definition of the money supply and its reference value, as described above (see, also, Issing, 2003).

The rationale of the 'two-pillar' approach is based on the theoretical premise that there are different time perspectives in the conduct of monetary policy that require a different focus in each case. There is the short to medium term focus on price movements that requires economic analysis. There is also the focus on long-term price trends that requires monetary analysis. In this analysis, there is the strong belief by the ECB in the long-term link between money (M3 in this case) and inflation. This focus, of course, reflects the notion that inflation is a monetary phenomenon. Short-term volatility of inflation is allowed but not in the long run, reflecting the view that monetary policy affects prices with a long lag.

It is important to note that the ECB Governing Council decided in 2007 to further enhance the monetary analysis along the following lines: 'First, money demand models are being refined and extended in order to improve the understanding of the behaviour of monetary aggregates over time and across sectors. Second, the robustness of money-based inflation risk indicators is being improved so as to develop further their use as a guide to policy decisions aimed at the maintenance of price stability. Third, structural models that embody an active role for money and credit in the determination of inflation dynamics are being developed and refined in support of the assessment of monetary developments. Finally, it is important to deepen further the analytical framework to support the cross-checking of information and analysis stemming from the monetary and economic analyses' (ECB, 2008, p. 38).

It is clear from this discussion that although the ECB analysis is embedded within the NCM framework, there is still one important difference that relates to the treatment of monetary aggregates as elaborated above. This makes the policy implications of the ECB monetary policy analysis different from those of the NCM. In other words, ECB monetary policy is not strictly speaking of the inflation targeting type. Especially so in view of the 'two-pillar' approach, which is clearly very different from that of the NCM, which pays very little, if any at all, attention to monetary aggregates.

There are, finally, a few problems in the case of the ECB macroeconomic model worth elaborating upon. The ECB's M3 growth has been consistently above the 4.5 per cent reference value and yet little inflation has been produced over the period.

Over the period since early 1999 M3 has been above the 4.5 per cent reference value for most of the period. The only exception was in mid-2000 when for a short period the M3 growth was below the 4.5 per cent reference value. It would appear that over this period the ECB has been caught between the economic analysis that suggested low or unchanged interest rates and the monetary analysis that implies higher interest rates for most, if not for the entire period. In other words, while the euro area inflation rate has been hovering just above the 2 per cent mark, the euro area M3 has been growing at rates well above the reference value of 4.5 per cent. The two-pillar approach sends different and contradictory signals more frequently than might be acceptable. The credibility of the strategy is obviously at stake (see CEPS, 2005, p. 29, which reaches a similar conclusion). It is also true to say that the ECB's special emphasis on the importance of monetary aggregates has been subjected to further criticism. Woodford (2006) offers a rigorous critique of this approach from the NCM perspective, suggesting that there is total lack of a theoretical foundation of the ECB monetary analysis. There is also the argument that money is an unreliable indicator of inflation in view of frequent shifts in velocity (see, for example, Estrella and Mishkin, 1997; Begg et al., 2002; De Grauwe and Polan, 2005).[8]

It would also appear to be the case that the economic and monetary analyses are not always consistent in the sense that they may point in different directions with regard to the prospects for inflation and the appropriate monetary policy response (Arestis and Chortareas, 2006).

There has been great reluctance to reduce interest rates even in obvious circumstances such as the financial crisis at its most intense in late 2008. The ECB reluctance to change interest rates as frequently as the rather reluctant BoE, and most certainly as the Fed in the US, can be explained by the chosen 'two-pillar' strategy. It is interesting to look at the period since January 1999 in terms of the conduct of monetary policy by the ECB. We may distinguish six periods. The first is the period early 1999 to mid-2001. That was a period of increasing rate of interest, which peaked at 4.75 per cent in October 2000 and remained at that level until May 2001. The period mid-2001 to mid-2003 was one of interest rate reductions. The period mid-2003 to end-2005 was one during which the official ECB interest rate remained unchanged. The period end-2005 to mid-2007 is one of interest rate increases, and the period of mid-2007 to mid-2008 of an unchanged rate of interest at 4 per cent. In the period from late 2008 onwards the ECB, along with other major central banks, has reduced the rate of interest to a low level of 1 per cent, although there was a short period in the mid-2011 when the rate of interest was increased.

The sole emphasis on price stability cannot be justified. History is replete with examples of relevant episodes when price stability had been achieved only to witness macroeconomic instability subsequently. These examples (see Angeriz and Arestis, 2007, for example) clearly demonstrate that price stability was followed by unsatisfactory economic performance. The price stability of the 2000s (even though inflation was not completely within the 2 per cent target) and the 'great moderation' which was claimed for that period (Bernanke, 2004) contained within it the seeds of a financial crisis which became apparent from late 2007 onwards.

Finally in this section, we note that the proposition that 'Over the longer term, monetary policy can only influence the price level in the economy; it cannot exert a lasting impact on economic activity' (ECB, 2008, p. 34). In a separate study (Arestis and Sawyer, 2004; see, also, 2008), we have argued that even the own macroeconometric model of the ECB does not seem to support this proposition. Empirical evidence drawn from these models suggests a relatively weak effect of interest rate changes on inflation. We also show in the same study, on the basis of the evidence adduced, that monetary policy can have long-run effects on real magnitudes. This particular result does not fit comfortably with the theoretical basis of current thinking on monetary policy by the ECB.

3.5 Concluding remarks

The central argument of this chapter has been that the policy framework of the EMU fits well with the analytical framework, which goes under the label of the 'new consensus macroeconomics'. This is true despite the differences we have highlighted in sections 2 and 4. The economy is envisaged as being essentially stable. Monetary policy is tasked with the control of inflation, and fiscal policy is downgraded to at most the role of automatic stabiliser in the context of an overall balanced budget. This forms our platform for the discussion of the macroeconomic policies of EMU in the next chapter.

4

Monetary Policy in the Economic and Monetary Union

4.1 Introduction

Our main focus of attention in this and the next chapter is on the EMU macroeconomic policy frameworks. We discuss monetary policy as implemented by the ECB in this chapter, and this is followed in chapter 5 by a discussion of the fiscal policy aspects of the Economic and Monetary Union (EMU). In this chapter we set out the specific elements of the monetary policy of the EMU, and consider the strengths and weaknesses of this policy as applied within the EMU.

We examine in this chapter the institutional framework of monetary policy along with the strengths and weaknesses of the theoretical and empirical aspects of this policy. We begin by discussing monetary policy itself in section 4.2, and this is followed in section 4.3 by a discussion of inflation problems. In section 4.4 we discuss problems with economic activity; this is followed in section 4.5 by a discussion of the potential future of monetary policy developments. Finally in section 4.6 we offer a number of concluding remarks.

4.2 Monetary policy

With the formation of the EMU, monetary policy has been removed from national authorities and from political authorities and placed with the ECB – that is, the ECB is not only supranational but also 'independent' of political (or other) authorities. The ECB and the national central banks are linked into the European System of Central Banks (ESCB) with a division of responsibility between them. The ECB has the responsibility for setting interest rates in pursuit of the inflation objective and the national central banks responsibility for regulatory matters.

The ECB is set up to be independent of the European Union (EU) Council and Parliament and also of its member governments. There is, thus, a complete separation between the monetary authorities, in the form of the ECB, and the fiscal authorities, in the shape of the national governments comprising the EMU. It follows that there can be little coordination of monetary and fiscal policy. Indeed, any attempt at coordination would be extremely difficult to implement. For apart from the separation of the monetary and fiscal authorities, there is also the constitutional requirement that national governments (and hence the fiscal authorities) should not exert any influence on the ECB (and hence the monetary authorities). Any strict interpretation of that edict would rule out any attempt at coordination of monetary and fiscal policies. Nor is it desirable to co-ordinate fiscal and monetary policy in the view of the ECB:

> there cannot be any scope for an active coordination of fiscal and monetary policies. Such active coordination is bound to be ineffective, given the inability of both fiscal and monetary policy-makers to fine tune economic developments. Commitments to ex-ante coordination between fiscal and monetary policies may blur the responsibilities of monetary and fiscal authorities and ultimately reduce their incentives to pursue their objectives. The economic outcome of such coordination is likely to be worse than the conduct of policies within the existing institutional set-up as only the latter ensures genuine accountability. (Duisenberg, 2003c, p. 5)

The ECB is the only effective federal economic institution, and it has the one policy instrument of the 'repo' rate to pursue the main objective of low inflation. The ECB is clear on this issue. In, for example, ECB (2003a) it is stated that

> In the field of monetary-fiscal policy coordination, the emphasis has shifted away from the joint design of short-term policy responses to shocks towards the establishment of a non-discretionary, rule-based regime capable of providing monetary and fiscal policy-makers with a time-consistent guide for action and thus a reliable anchor for private expectations...Therefore there will generally be no need for further coordination of day-to-day policy moves. (p. 38)

The perception of the ECB with regard to the way in which monetary policy operates is indicated in Figure 4.1. This represents the general

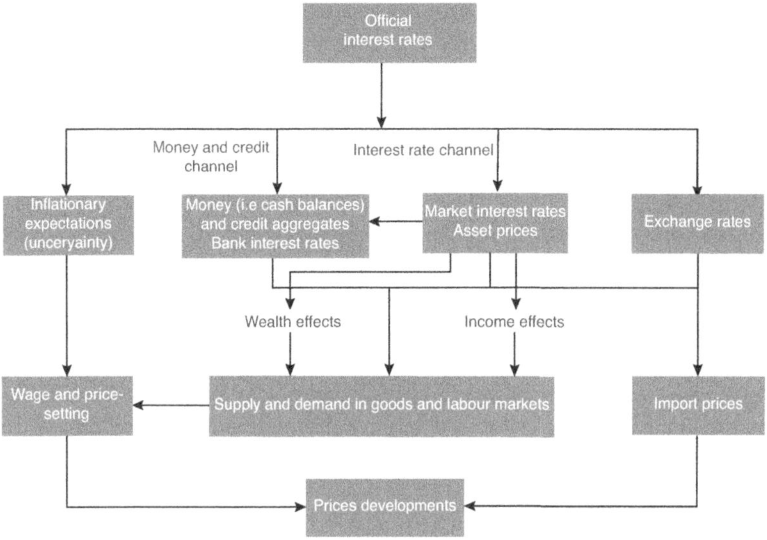

Figure 4.1 Schematic presentation of the monetary transmission mechanism
Source: ECB (2008, p. 60).

idea that decisions on the official (policy) interest rates are to be used to influence inflation (labelled price developments in the figure). The links from the official interest rates to the rate of inflation go through a number of stages. In the first stage, the official interest rate is seen to affect a wide range of other interest rates, including those charged by banks for loans and paid on deposits. Those interest rates are likely to affect the demand for loans and the willingness of the public to hold bank deposits, all of which is reflected in the volume of money. The market interest rates influence the way discounting is undertaken and thereby asset prices. There is expected to be an impact of interest rate changes on the relative attractiveness of domestic assets, which has effects on the exchange rate. Changes in interest rates can also have effects on the way people regard the future and specifically inflationary expectations. In the second stage, these developments have effects on the level of demand as depicted in the middle of the figure, and in turn (via some form of Phillips curve relationship, as for example equation 2 in the NCM model, as in chapter 3) are envisaged to have an effect on wage- and price-setting behaviour. The exchange rate movements can also be expected to influence the price of imported goods. The overall view is that an increase in the official interest rates would raise other market interest rates and boost the exchange rate. These effects would tend to lower demand, and that would be anticipated to bring down the rate of inflation; the appreciation of the exchange rate and the lowering of import prices as a result would be an added impact on lowering inflation.

Any currency necessarily has a corresponding central bank (or equivalent), which can issue the currency and set one or more key policy interest rates; the latter set the terms under which the central bank interacts with the banking system. The ways in which the central bank set interest rates and relates to the fiscal authorities are crucial to the success or otherwise of a currency. Furthermore, monetary policy faces an inevitable 'one size fits all' problem, that is a single interest rate (and more generally monetary policy) has to be set to apply to all members of the currency union; and the level of interest rate that may be appropriate for one region of the currency area may not be appropriate for other regions.

The Treaty and the Statute of the ESCB (Statute of the ESCB), attached to the Treaty establishing the European Union (EU) as a protocol, endowed the ECB with the responsibility for the single monetary policy within the euro area 'that is independent from political influence' (ECB, 2004c, p. 12). This monetary policy comprises of two main elements: a definition of price stability, and a two-pillar system of evaluating the prospects of achieving this stability over the medium term. We begin with a brief discussion of the price stability definition and this is followed by a discussion of the two-pillar monetary strategy.

The ESCB Treaty, Article 105 (1), states that 'the primary objective of the ESCB shall be to maintain price stability' and that 'without prejudice to the objective of price stability, the ESCB shall support the general economic policies in the Community with a view to contributing to the achievement of the objectives of the Community as laid down in Article 2'. The objectives of the Community mentioned in Article 2 of the Treaty are: 'a high level of employment ... sustainable and non-inflationary growth, a high degree of competitiveness and convergence of economic performance'. A clear hierarchy of the objectives of the euro area is thereby established, ensuring that price stability is by far the most important objective for ECB's monetary policy. Price stability in this definition was assigned a quantitative value, initially in the form of a 0–2 per cent target for the annual increase in the Harmonized Index of Consumer Prices (HICP) for the euro area (preferably hovering in the lower range of 0–2 per cent).[1] The ECB, however, after a comprehensive review of its monetary policy since inception, announced at a press conference on 8 May, 2003, its intention to maintain inflation 'close to but below 2 per cent' over the medium term, although the language of the ECB Monthly Bulletin since then, indicates the phrase 'inflation close to 2 per cent from below' to be more appropriate.[2] Issing (2003) insists on the 'clarification' aspect as being 'totally different from what is normally seen as inflation targeting'. Furthermore, the 'close to but below 2%' inflation 'is not a change, it is a clarification of what we have done so far, what we have achieved – namely inflation expectations remaining in a narrow range of between roughly 1.7% and 1.9% – and what we intend to do in our forward-looking monetary policy.'[3]

The official doctrine of the ECB, uniquely among leading central banks, is based on a 'two-pillar' monetary strategy. The 'first pillar', essentially an *economic analysis*, is an assessment of 'the short to medium-term determinants of price developments, with a focus on real activity and financial conditions in the economy' (ECB, 2004c, p. 55). It is, thus, a broad outlook of price developments and the risks to price stability over the short to medium term. This broad range of indicators includes: 'developments in overall output; aggregate demand and its components; fiscal policy; capital and labor market conditions; a broad range of price and cost indicators; developments in the exchange rate; the global economy and the balance of payments; financial markets; and the balance sheet positions of euro area sectors' (ECB, 2004c, pp. 55 and 57). The 'second pillar' is a commitment to analyse monetary developments for the information they contain about future price developments over the medium and long term. It focuses 'on a longer-term horizon, exploiting the long-run link between money and prices' (ECB, 2004c, p. 55). This is a quantitative reference value, not for a money supply target, but for monetary growth, where a 'reference value of 4.5 per cent of M3' has been imposed. Being a reference value, there is no mechanistic commitment to correct deviations in the short term, although it is stated that deviations from the reference value would, under normal circumstances, 'signal risks to price stability'. Monetary analysis is utilised by the ECB as a 'cross-check' for consistency between the short-term perspective of economic analysis with the more long-term perspective that emanates from the monetary analysis itself, essentially concerned with the M3 definition of the money supply and its reference value, as described above (see, also, Issing, 2003).

It is important to note, though, that monetary trends are no longer as 'prominent' as they used to be prior to the changes announced on the 8 May 2003 conference, to which we referred above. They are only used as a 'cross-check', and the monetary pillar has now become the second pillar, having been the first pillar before May 2003. In fact, the ECB has particularly stressed this argument in the past. ECB officials have argued that what the cross-checking implies is that the presentation of ECB policy decisions would first deal with 'the economic analysis, which identifies short to medium-term risks to price stability, and then turns to the monetary analysis, which assesses medium to long-term trends in inflation. It will conclude by cross-checking the analyses conducted under these two pillars' (ECB, 2003d, p. 5). Between the inception of the ECB and the time of the 'clarification', that is, May 2003, the presentation of the two analyses had been the other way round – monetary analysis was followed by economic analysis, as stated above. It is also important to note that ECB does not believe in a short-term close link between price and monetary developments, so that 'monetary policy does not therefore react mechanically to deviations of M3 growth from the reference value' (ECB, 2004c, pp. 62–3). This is due to special factors, which 'may not be very informative about the outlook of price stability' (ECB, op. cit., p. 65). Thus the ECB monetary analysis attempts 'to focus on underlying monetary trends by including a detailed assessment of special factors and other shocks influencing money demand' (ECB, op. cit., p. 65).

The rationale of the 'two-pillar' approach is based on the theoretical premise that there are different time perspectives in the conduct of monetary policy that require a different focus in each case. There is the short- to medium-term focus on price movements that requires economic analysis. In this analysis a 'broad range of economic/financial developments are analyzed, to assess economic shocks, dynamics and perspectives and the resulting risks to price stability over the short to medium term' (Issing, 2003). There is also the focus on long-term price trends that requires monetary analysis. In this analysis, 'The ECB singles out money from within the set of selected key indicators that it monitors and studies closely' (ECB, 2004c, p. 62). The rationale for this concern is the strong belief by the ECB in the long-term link between money (M3 in this case) and inflation. This focus, of course, reflects the notion that inflation is a monetary phenomenon. Short-term volatility of inflation is allowed but not in the long run, reflecting the view that monetary policy affects prices with a long lag. It may be noted in passing, though, that over the years since 1999, money growth has been in the main above the bank's 'reference value' of 4.5 per cent with inflation hovering around 2 per cent, and inflation expectations even just under 2 per cent. Issing (2003) leaves no ambiguity of the ECB belief in this relationship, when he argues that there is 'No evidence that long-run link between money and prices has broken down in the euro area; many studies show good leading indicator properties'; and that 'Excess money/credit may provide additional information for identifying financial imbalances and/or asset price bubbles, which ultimately may impact on price developments'. It is the case, though, that other studies have shown that instability in the demand for money in the euro area. For example, Arestis et al. (2003) demonstrate that over the period of their investigation, which is prior to 2003, the euro area demand-for-money relationship was highly unstable.

It is interesting to look at the period between January 1999 and mid-2007 in terms of the conduct of monetary policy by the ECB. We may distinguish three periods. The first is the period 1999 to mid-2001. There was a decrease in the rate of interest in April 1999, only for it to return to the same level by the end of the that year. A period of increasing interest rates followed that peaked at 4.75 per cent in October 2000 and remained at that level until May 2001. The period was characterized by concerns over price stability, emanating essentially from strong economic growth, increasing import prices, declining euro exchange rate and high growth in the money supply (M3).

It is also interesting to compare the period mid-2001 to mid-2007, when the official ECB rate was reduced, with the period mid-2003 to mid-2005, when the same rate remained unchanged. Rapid monetary growth is evident in both periods. In the first period this was explained (see the *Monthly Bulletin* of the ECB over the relevant period) by a shift from the uncertain stock markets to cash; it was felt that there was no risk to inflation, since credit growth was not increasing rapidly; the ECB decreased the interest rate over that period. Over the period mid-2003 to mid-2007, though, fast monetary growth was associated with an equally fast growth in lending. The slack in the real economy has not convinced the ECB to decrease interest rates; the fear was that monetary developments can be inflationary at that time. In some way the ECB was caught between the economic analysis that suggests lower interest rates and the monetary analysis that implies higher interest rates. At the time the two-pillar approach was sending different and contradictory signals. The credibility of the strategy was obviously at stake (see CEPS, 2005, p. 29, which reaches a similar conclusion).

In terms of the period since August 2007, the reaction of the ECB has been relatively modest. Initially, the upsurge in inflation enabled the ECB to keep interest rates relatively high for a long time. This was especially the case in July 2008, when it was obvious that an economic downturn was well on its way. Subsequently, the ECB was slow to push down interest rates. In the event when the banking crisis began to infect the real economy very seriously, interest rates were cut by a total of 225 basis points up to January 2009 and eventually to 1 per cent in May 2009. The reduction in interest rates by 225 basis points was done in four steps within a historically short period of time. But it was not as bold as that of other central banks. The interest rate was increased to 1.25 per cent subsequently only to be reduced to 1 per cent in November 2011. Nor has the ECB pursued 'Quantitative Easing' (QE) as, for example, the Federal Reserve System or the Bank of England. Although it has resisted QE, the ECB has, nonetheless, pioneered other types of policies. Under the acronym 'Enhanced Credit Support' (ECS) the ECB's has been a policy of providing unlimited liquidity to banks at its rate and under covered bonds.[4] Covered bonds are safe securities since in the event of default investors have redress to the issuer's balance sheet; they are, thus, of low risk of default. As discussed below, the ECB broadened the collateral it accepts in June 2009, when under the ECS scheme it extended the maturity of the collateral to up to 12 months. The reason for such a policy as opposed to QE is that in addition to the low risk, in Europe conventional loans comprise the bulk of credit, so that using covered bonds, which are issued by banks, could potentially affect bank lending. The banking system plays a much bigger role in providing finance in Europe than in, for example, the USA and the UK.

In the words of the ECB (2009) *Monthly Bulletin*,

> The euro money market has also been affected, at times severely, by the financial market tensions. Turnover declined substantially and spreads between interest rates on secured and unsecured lending rose to unprecedented levels. As a result, banks with liquidity needs could no longer be sure of obtaining funds in the interbank market, while other banks kept large liquidity buffers in their current accounts with the central bank and used the Eurosystem's deposit facility.... a breakdown of the money market would endanger financial stability, as solvent institutions could become insolvent due to liquidity shortages. (p. 75)

In fact,

> The euro money market was strongly affected by the tensions originating in the US sub-prime mortgage market on 9 August 2007, when rumours about large exposures of some European banks affected their ability to obtain liquidity in the US dollar market and subsequently

> led to a spike in euro money market interest rates. Activity in money markets decreased sharply, especially in the market for loans with maturities of over one week where activity almost came to a complete halt. At the same time, spreads between interest rates on unsecured and secured lending in those markets increased significantly. (p. 76)

It is, thus, the case that the financial market turmoil that commenced in August 2007 worldwide has been the greatest challenge to the resilience of the EMU monetary framework.

The normal ECB operational framework relies on three main aspects:

> (1) refinancing of the banking sector through open market operations; (2) standing facilities; and (3) reserve requirements. In the period up to October 2008, the ECB used this framework for its liquidity management, which aims to steer short-term money market interest rates to a level close to the minimum bid rate that signals the euro area's monetary policy stance. This minimum bid rate was applied to the main refinancing operations (MROs), which were conducted in the form of variable rate tenders with a minimum bid rate. With these operations, the ECB steered the marginal cost of refinancing for banks. To do so, the ECB essentially chose an appropriate level of aggregate liquidity provision to the banking sector, which needs central bank liquidity to fulfil its reserve requirements and to accommodate changes in autonomous factors. The ECB relied on the money market to distribute this liquidity among banks at market interest rates and to achieve a smooth fulfilment of the aggregate reserve requirements during the course of each reserve maintenance period. After August 2007 this approach was adapted to take into account the higher and more variable demand for liquidity from the banking sector, but was not significantly changed. (ECB, 2009, p. 75)

Changes, nonetheless, have taken place; this was necessary in view of 'the intensification of the financial market turmoil, and particularly in the months around the end of 2008' when

> the malfunctioning of the money market meant that the formation of short-term interest rates depended not only on the net aggregate liquidity situation, but also on the distribution of liquidity among individual banks and thus on the gross injections of liquidity from the central bank. In this environment, the Eurosystem had to also

> assume the role of an intermediary in the flow of liquid funds from one bank to another, by changing its operational framework in ways that facilitated its intermediation role. (ECB, 2009, p. 76)

The changes that did take place can be summarised succinctly.

The first type is 'liquidity management' measures. Perhaps this is the most important initiative in that the ECB has satisfied the liquidity demand of the banking sector. Prior to August 2007, the ECB had only met the liquidity needs of the banking sector by fulfilling the minimum reserve requirements. The second type is 'supplementary long-term refinancing' operations. By the end of October 2008, these operations emerged with maturities of three months initially and later also six months. The third type is measures in cooperation with other central banks. In December 2007, the ECB, in collaboration with the Federal Reserve System and other major central banks, initiated 'US dollar liquidity-providing operations, against collateral eligible for Eurosystem credit operations, in connection with the Federal Reserve System's US dollar Term Auction Facility (TAF)' (ECB, 2009, p. 79). All these measures, that is, the three types just discussed, implied that the aggregate liquidity provided to the banking sector was no longer determined by the ECB; it was, instead, demand determined. The fourth type is the one that was introduced in June 2009. The ECB decided, as from 23 June 2009, to carry out refinancing operations with a maturity of 12 months, applying a fixed rate tender with full allotment. It also proposed purchasing euro-denominated covered bonds issued in the euro area, and to grant the European Investment Bank the status of eligible counterparty in the ECB's refinancing operations.

The fifth element is the EU-wide bank regulation body, the European Systemic Risk Board (ESRB), which was established on the 16 December 2010 and has been operating since then. It is expected that the ESRB may provide an important test for the future of the EMU as well. The ESRB comprises all ECB governing council, other EMU central bankers, and representatives from the EU Commission; ESRB would be managed by the ECB.[5] The expectation is that the ESRB would track the stability of the European financial institutions and coordinate the supervision of risk by national bank regulators. Its task is for macroprudential oversight of the financial system in order to contribute to the prevention or mitigation of systemic risks to financial stability in the EU. It is expected to contribute to the smooth functioning of the internal EU market and thereby ensure a sustainable contribution of the financial sector to economic growth. The ESRB is an independent body of the European

Union and it is part of the European System of Financial Supervision (ESFS), the purpose of which is to ensure the supervision of the EU's financial system. The ESRB is designed to issue early warning signals on risk to EU's system of financial supervision. It cooperates with other international organisations, such as the International Monetary Fund (IMF), especially during crises. However, it does not have enforcement powers.

The sixth dimension, which also emerged in June 2009 and in the EU, was the proposal for a Pan-European Regime to regulate the financial markets and institutions, which is to be enshrined in European law. It comprises the ESRB, which will monitor financial stability, and of European agencies, which will police the banking, securities and insurance sectors. Neither the board nor the agencies would have powers to dictate fiscal action in case of financial emergency. Nor can they order governments to bail out or recapitalise banks.

The purpose of the changes just summarised, in combination with the easing of the ECB's key interest rates, was, in the words of ECB (2009), 'to promote the decline in money market term rates, to encourage banks to maintain and expand their lending to customers, to help to improve market liquidity in important segments of the private debt security market, and to ease funding conditions for banks and enterprises' (p. 86). As a result, and in unison with the major industrialised countries, the European authorities flooded the financial markets with liquidity. The ECB in the EMU pursued a similar approach; it also reluctantly reduced the repo interest rate to 1 per cent (May 2009), and then to 0.75 per cent (July 2012). Banks could be certain to obtain all desired liquidity at the ECB's weekly tenders, provided that they had sufficient assets eligible as collateral in the euro-area system of liquidity-providing operations. We may note in this context the enormous exposure of a number of EMU banks to Central and Eastern European (CEE) countries. Bank of International Settlements (BIS) data show that 90 per cent of loans to CEE come from EMU banks (Austria, for example, is exposed to CEE by about 80 per cent of its GDP; the Netherlands by 66 per cent of GDP). Clearly, this exposure provides risks to the current state of the EMU. Even so the ECB has acted more cautiously than other central banks, and certainly a great deal more so than the US Federal Reserve System.

This approach to monetary policy has been accompanied, however, by an unwelcome side effect. It was accompanied by a steady appreciation of the euro exchange rate, which was raised by around 8 per cent on a trade-weighted basis between August 2007 and 2009 according to OECD (2009); it has, however, fluctuated ever since in view of the euro crisis in particular. Indeed, this may explain the uneven but apparent economic recovery in the EMU. Italy and Finland, for example, where exports are more price-sensitive than elsewhere in the EMU, are recovering at a great deal slower pace than Germany and France. Furthermore, countries, such as Ireland and Spain, which are striving to enhance their competitiveness, may find the euro exchange rate gains as detrimental – even Germany's improved competitiveness is bound to suffer. These developments raise the old question of whether the EMU of 17 separate countries can function as a proper economy. Fiscal policy and much of the responsibility for bank and financial market regulation are still within the grip of governments and central banks of the individual EMU countries – save for the ECB which controls the rate of interest.

The ECB intervened on 21 December 2011, when €489.2 billion was injected into the euro-area banking system in the form of bank borrowing. This was undertaken through the Long Term Refinancing Operation (LTRO), one of the ECB mechanisms. There were more than 523 banks involved, encouraged by the policy makers of the region, who borrowed the €489.2 billion in three-year loans, equivalent to 5 per cent of the euro-area GDP; actually a much bigger take-up than had been expected. It is the largest amount provided in a single ECB operation so far. However, this amount is not as big as it might appear since the ECB switched funds from shorter-term facilities; in fact, the amount of fresh liquidity was only about €190 billion. The euro and equities also surged as a result. It was expected that the excess liquidity just mentioned would be used to finance purchases of peripheral euro area higher-yielding government debt, thereby helping to ease their debt crisis. Such optimism, however, never materialised!

The ECB continued to support Italian bonds so that Italy is not cut off from the financial markets. In the first three months of 2012, Italy had €300 billion of maturing debt. Unless this debt was rolled over in financial markets, no troika could cover these sums of money. The method applied could be more effective if the ECB were to announce a ceiling on bond yields or a floor on bond prices. In the case of Switzerland, for example, the mere announcement of such a scheme by the Swiss central bank had the desired effect without any real purchases. Further, the ECB was happy to salvage the financial system with the mere promise that governments would do their best to control budget deficits and public debts. Thus, the ECB provided three-year financing to 500 banks in the EU with loans that nearly hit €0.5 trillion. The ECB extended this package by another €530 billion with 800 banks involved (it costs them only 1 per cent per annum on a three-year loan deal) – banks had actually hoped for €1 trillion in the new round. Italian and Spanish banks dominated the take-up, which accounted for almost half of the funds on offer – half of the 800 banks were German. This kind of money may have prevented the meltdown of the EU financial system. However, it has done nothing to lift the economy out of recession. The reason is simply that banks do not trust each other and therefore prefer to park all this liquidity with the ECB. Interestingly enough, funds of €452bn after the first round (see *Financial Times*, 27 December 2011), and €777bn after the second round, were deposited with the ECB following the two operations referred to in the text. Furthermore, the ECB's financing operation has failed to boost bank lending to the real economy. Data released by the ECB showed that, despite injecting €1 trillion in long-term liquidity to the euro area banks, loans to non-financial firms fell by €3 billion during February. Corporate lending grew by just 0.4 per cent over the period since its introduction, lower than the growth that was recorded in November and December 2011 before its introduction.

The initial enthusiasm of the markets soon waned – Italian and Spanish government bond yields rose and equities as well as the euro retreated (as soon as the ECB intervened as suggested above). This is not surprising, though, for such measures only help to address the liquidity shortage in the euro area banking sector, but does not provide new loans to the private sector since banks shed assets in an attempt to abide by the new capital rules that commenced in June 2012. There is also the more serious problem that the weak economic performance of most euro area countries would not allow the necessary demand for credit by both business and consumers to materialise. The relevant experience of the period since August 2007 is very telling on this score; it suggests that banks are expected to hoard the cash, especially so in view of the looming refinancing needs in the first quarter of 2012 and also the gloomy expectations for the year 2012 and beyond. In fact, banks in the euro area had deposited €452 billion with the ECB by Tuesday 27 December 2011 (*Financial Times*, 29 December 2011), the week after the LTRO operation. Still it is expected that those countries where the economic difficulties emerged from their troubled banking sector, such as Spain and Ireland, would get some help out of this operation. Interestingly enough, on Wednesday 28 December 2011, €9 billion of six-month Italian bonds were sold at 3.25 per cent, down from the euro area record of 6.5 per cent reached in November 2011 – only for the yield to return to its original level on the same day once it became known of the €452 billion bank -deposits with the ECB. On 29 December 2011 the overall demand for the ten-year Italian bonds was low with the sale only raising €7 billion rather than the targeted €8.5 billion. As a result the interest demanded by investors on these bonds after the auction was above the critical level of 7 per cent, which is viewed as unsustainable by the markets. But here again the ECB is not prepared to act as a 'lender of last resort', and therefore does not intervene in government bond markets. This would be an illegal act according to the President of the ECB (see, for example, *The Economist*, 17 December 2011).

At the meeting of the finance ministers on 28/29 June 2012 a number of further decisions were taken. Perhaps the most important decision is that the European Stability Mechanism (ESM) is accelerated into entry as soon as it is ratified by 90 per cent of the member states with capital commitments to it. The objective was originally for the ESM to come into operation sooner than what had been planned for January 2013. However, it is now not expected to come into operation before 2014. The increase of its funding in addition to the €500 billion already planned for the ESM is another development. It is widely recognised that the amounts just referred to would not be sufficient to cover the borrowing needs of Italy and Spain, if required, over the near future. A banking union is planned but the details of its establishment are in the process of being developed. Three main components are contemplated: a unified supervisory framework to deter financial market fragmentation; a bank regulation authority to deal with problems of the weak financial institutions and facilitate orderly restructuring; and a deposit guarantee scheme to help depositors and reduce the risk of abrupt deposit movements across the EMU.

Another development worth mentioning is the pledge of €200 billion to the IMF by the EMU country-members to deal with the crisis. This amount is clearly not enough but the hope is that other countries outside the euro area would follow.

4.3 Inflation

It is clear that the only policy instrument which seeks to address inflation is that of monetary policy and that the prime objective of monetary policy is low inflation (with a target of below but near to 2 per cent). It is evident (by reference to our discussion in chapter 3) that the theoretical framework suggests that there are three sources of inflationary pressures, namely high level of demand (positive output gap), expectations of inflation and random supply-side shocks. The third of these can in effect be ignored within that framework since by assumption of their randomness they average out at zero. In that framework then monetary policy can be seen to address inflation in two ways. First, by varying the rate of interest the level of demand is influenced, which will in turn influence the rate of inflation. Second, it is hoped that by establishing a 'credible' and independent central bank with the objective of low inflation and the generated perception that the Monetary Policy Committee will be committed to the achievement of low inflation, relevant expectations will be generated that inflation is and will remain low.

The role of supply-side shocks reveals a significant weakness in this approach to the control of inflation in that there is little monetary policy (or indeed any demand approach to inflation) can do in the face of supply-side shocks, whether positive or negative. When there are substantial shocks to inflation from outside the economy, as evidenced by events in 2008, then the only policy which is available is to declare that these cost and price rises are a passing event and to reassert commitment to low inflation in the hope that the price rises not only prove to be temporary but also that they do not feed through into expectations about inflation, the so-called 'second round' effects.

Any interest rate policy faces a 'one size fits all' problem since the interest rate set by the central bank applies across the whole economy, even though there may be significant differences in the economic position of the different regions of the economy. These differences would include different positions in the business cycle, different inflation situations, and different responses of inflation to demand and other changes. In a relatively small country where there is a common set of institutional arrangements and where fluctuations in economic activity are closely coordinated, these differences may not generate a major problem. The difficulties were put in the following way by Eddie George, the then Governor of the Bank of England. 'Essentially the potential downside (of a single currency) can be summed up as the risk that the single monetary policy – the "one-size-fits-all" short term interest rate within the euro area, which is the inevitable consequence of a single currency – will not in the event prove to be appropriate to the domestic monetary policy needs of all the participating countries'. After noting that divergences within a national economy present problems for monetary policy, he argued that 'in the case of the Eurozone the risks are of divergent monetary policy needs between the different member countries – they apply at the national level. And if they materialised to any very significant extent, the resulting tensions could be serious, because alternative mechanisms – such as labour migration or fiscal redistribution through a central budget – which help to mitigate sectoral or regional disparities in the national context – are less developed at the Eurozone level' (George, 2000). There is, then, no way that a member country can offset undesirable effects of an interest rate set by the ECB, which is either too high or too low for the economic needs of that country. As George (op. cit.) suggests within a national economy there are measures which can address the different situations of regions within the country through fiscal transfers and expenditure plans of the central government. These fiscal transfers do not exist to any significant extent within either EMU or the EU.

In the euro area, it is evident from chapter 2 and Table 2.3 therein that there have been, and remain, relatively small but apparently persistent differences in the inflation record of the member countries. Indeed in some periods the differences in inflation between countries were such that some of those countries would not have met the Maastricht convergence criteria with regard to inflation. In September 2008, for example, and amongst the initial 12 members, the three countries with the lowest inflation were Netherlands, Germany and Portugal (Ireland also had the same rate as Portugal) and their inflation rates were 2.8 per cent, 3.0 per cent and 3.2 per cent respectively, hence averaging 3.0 per cent. The convergence criteria (as discussed in chapter 2) included national inflation rate not exceeding 1.5 per cent of the average rate of the three countries with lowest inflation. On that basis Spain (4.6 per cent), Finland and Greece (both 4.7 per cent) and Luxembourg (4.8 per cent) would not meet the criteria. As has already been mentioned, this type of situation poses particular difficulties for a single currency. It illustrates the 'one size fits all' problem in that a single interest rate set by the ECB cannot simultaneously address an inflation rate of 2.8 per cent in the Netherlands and 4.7 per cent in Greece. Further, the interest rate set will translate into a 1.9 per cent lower real rate in Greece as compared with the Netherlands. This would be so even though application of monetary policy rules, such as the Taylor rule (Taylor 1993), would indicate a higher real rate of interest in Greece than the Netherlands to address the higher inflation in the former as compared with the latter.

A severe problem, which is raised by the econometric evidence (largely generated by economists working with the ECB, see, for example, Fagan and Morgan, 2005), is that interest rate variations appear to have rather little effect on inflation, though the effects on output and particularly investment may be more substantial. We have surveyed elsewhere (Arestis and Sawyer, 2004a) the results of simulations undertaken by others of the effects of monetary policy using macroeconometric models. The survey is based on work undertaken for the ECB, the US Federal Reserve System, and for the Bank of England. The conclusion of that report is that the effects of interest rate changes on inflation tend to be rather small – typically a 1 percentage point change in interest rates may dampen inflation by 0.2 to 0.3 per cent after two years.

The figures given in chapter 2 (Table 2.3) indicate that the average rate of inflation in the euro area has generally exceeded the 2 per cent limit, albeit by a small margin, though a rather more substantial one in 2008 (later the figure reached 3.8 per cent). But it can be recalled that the interpretation of price stability is inflation between 0 and 2 per cent per annum, and the overrun looks a little more substantial if judged against the mid-point of that range of 1 per cent. The general theory, which lies behind the establishment of an independent central bank with a mission to use monetary policy to attain an inflation target, is that there should be some consequences for the central Bank if it failed in that mission. This may be the mild sanction of embarrassment as in the UK where the governor of the Bank of England is required to write a letter of explanation if inflation is outside the target range or as in New Zealand where an explanation has to be included in the Reserve Bank's quarterly *Monetary Policy Statements*.[6] There is no such sanction in the case of the ECB.

The problem with the ECB's methods of operation is partly the bank's secretiveness for it does not publish minutes of its meetings.[7] This is compensated to some extent by the ECB president's news conference once a month after the monetary policy meetings, by the president's testimony to the European Parliament on a regular basis, by the monthly publication of the ECB Bulletin, and by the ECB's GDP growth and inflation projections twice a year. The trouble is that the ECB has not learned to communicate its methods of operation, essentially because it does not publish minutes of the monetary policy committee's meetings.

4.4 Economic activity

The mandate of the ECB does include paying attention to the broad economic objectives of the EU though in its utterances the prime focus is always on inflation. Within the theoretical framework outlined in the previous chapter, there is essentially no conflict between the level of economic activity and inflation. In the short term, demand may need to be increased or decreased to influence inflation appropriately, but in the longer term the level of economic activity will move around the supply-side equilibrium. The perception of central bankers and others is generally to the effect that the most a central bank can do is to control inflation and it cannot have effects on levels of output and employment over the long term. This is also reflected in continuous call by the ECB to make markets, especially labour markets, more flexible; product markets more competitive and so on.

The set-up of the ECB may well foster a tendency for interest rates to be set higher rather than lower, and hence tend to be deflationary rather than reflationary. This is only a tendency, and reasons for it would include:

- i in the first years of its existence seeking to establish its reputation and credibility as being serious about the control of inflation;
- ii in a situation (like the one during much of 2008) where there is an element of stagflation – that is, higher inflation but lower economic activity – paying regard to inflation rather than to the level of economic activity. The underlying theoretical framework does not expect that to happen since via the Phillips curve higher inflation is associated with higher level of economic activity;
- iii adopting an overcautious approach to inflation and interpreting any signs of inflation to justify raising interest rates.

4.5 Potential monetary policy developments

In view of the problems discussed in this section the question arises as to whether or not changes in monetary policy are desirable. We discuss two such possible developments in this subsection. The end of inflation targeting and thus what might replace it and the end of ECB independence.

4.5.1 The end of inflation targeting?

Until recently, many would claim that inflation targeting had been able to provide a nominal anchor for the economy. After a number of other policies designed to provide nominal stability – notably control of the money supply, fixed exchange rates – had largely failed, inflation targeting appeared to have delivered. The experience of 2008 – and to some degree 2011 – with inflation rising well above the target levels, should raise considerable question marks against inflation targeting as it proved impotent in the face of cost-push inflation. For the present, inflation targeting (here seen to involve an independent central bank with the objective of achieving a stated target rate, or band, of inflation using the policy interest rate as the instrument) remains nominally in place, though whether decisions made by central banks recently could be said to be independent of central government or directed towards inflation is rather doubtful.

In previous writings we have cast doubt on inflation targeting along four lines (see, for example, Arestis and Sawyer, 2008b). First, the difference in inflation performance between inflation-targeting and non-inflation-targeting countries appears small in a general environment where inflation had been declining, and that inflation targeting was often introduced after inflation had been reduced. Roger Ferguson, then Vice Chairman of the Board of Governors of the Federal Reserve System, argues that

> Unfortunately, the empirical evidence for industrial countries available to date generally appears insufficient to assess the success of the inflation-targeting approach with confidence. For example, it is unclear whether the announcement of quantitative inflation targets lessens the short-run trade-off between employment and inflation and whether it helps anchor inflation expectations. In addition, some research, controlling for other factors, fails to isolate the benefits of an inflation target with respect to the level of inflation or its volatility over time, and output does not seem to fluctuate more stably around its potential for countries that have adopted numerical target. (Ferguson, 2005b, p. 297)

Second, variations in the rate of interest appear to have little effect on the rate of inflation (though rather more on the level of output). There seems to be weak empirical evidence on this proposition. And this evidence is obtained from typically econometric estimation results undertaken within central banks or by those closely associated with them. A 1 per cent hike in policy interest rate leads to a significant drop in output but reduction in inflation of the order of 0.1 to 0.2 per cent (Arestis and Sawyer, 2004a). Goodhart (2005b), drawing on his experience on the Monetary Policy Committee and the work done within the Bank of England, commented that "unless the shocks hitting the system were really quite small, the extent of policy-induced demand management, even if perfectly calibrated, could not be responsible for the achievement of the stability and successful growth that we have enjoyed)' (p. 169). A number of words of caution: the interest rate change is applied for a year, but this may be because the nature of the model is such that a departure from the equilibrium interest rate within the model would eventually cause the model to explode. And second, inflation in these models is tied down by expectations, and with the assumption of some form of forward-looking 'rational expectations' and that the inflation target is met. This does, however, point to the notion that the success or otherwise of monetary policy with respect to inflation comes not from variations in the policy rate of interest but through the generation of low inflationary expectations, and specifically that expectations are 'locked down' even in the face of changes in actual inflation.

Third, there is the attempt at ultra fine-tuning in the sense that monthly decisions (and hence potential change) on interest rates are made seeking to target inflation up to two years ahead. Fourth, the lack of strong theoretical link running from interest rate to economic activity to inflation. Sawyer (2009c) examines a number of the proposed links. The essence of the argument is that the interest rate and the level of economic activity are in *levels* whereas inflation is a *rate of change* (of prices). It is more usual in economics to relate levels with levels, and specifically the rate of interest with the level of prices (as initially postulated by Wicksell, 1898), and the level of demand (or level of economic activity) with the level of prices. For example, theories of price behaviour by firms focus on the determination of the price-cost margin, and that margin and costs themselves may vary with the level of demand (but not with the rate of change of demand).

A higher level of demand may then lead to higher prices, but that does not mean higher inflation, that is a persistent rise in prices. There are two situations where this could lead to inflation. First, in the period when higher prices materialise there is inflation, and if expectations of inflation jump in line with the experience of inflation, then the initially higher prices could set out inflation (in the sense of persistent rise in prices). Second, wages (or similar) also come into the picture and if higher output and employment means higher prices and higher wages, the intended increase in at least one of price/wage or wage/price cannot occur. In effect a wage–price spiral is set off.

It can therefore be disputed whether monetary policy is an effective means to control inflation – with the exception of the argument that having a central bank with an inflation mandate somehow convinces people that inflation will be low and so it might be.

4.5.2 Independence of a central bank

There has, of course, been a worldwide move over the past two decades towards the adoption of an 'independent' central bank generally with the objective of achieving (or maintaining) low inflation. The arguments for a central bank with operational independence (specifically from politicians) were based on two interconnected propositions. First, that the single instrument (interest rate)—single objective (inflation) was a viable one. This in turn rested on the Phillips curve-type approach in that interest rate could influence the rate of inflation and that there is an equilibrium rate of interest, which is simultaneously compatible with constant inflation and with supply-side equilibrium (expressed in the form of either the 'natural' rate of unemployment or a zero output gap). The achievement of a constant rate of inflation would secure the achievement of supply-side equilibrium (which was assumed to be uninfluenced by the path of aggregate demand and to have some desirable properties). The ability of the equilibrium rate of interest to secure the supply-side equilibrium was in effect sufficient to rule out any requirement for active fiscal policy.

Second, the short-run Phillips curve suggests that lower unemployment (higher output) comes with a higher rate of inflation, and that elected politicians at times will be tempted to boost demand with its benefits of lower unemployment and higher output at the cost of higher inflation. Central bankers are then viewed as uniquely able to influence the level of demand without falling to the temptation to raise demand at inappropriate times, to be more committed to low inflation and to avoid the problems of time inconsistency. The notion that the central bank has, or can acquire, credibility in terms of its commitment to the control of inflation, and that it is the central bank alone (the 'conservative' central bankers argument) that has this creditability with respect to the control of inflation.

Taylor (2008) claims to have been able to provide empirical evidence 'that government actions and interventions caused, prolonged, and worsened the financial crisis. They caused it by deviating from historical precedents and principles for setting interest rates, which had worked well for 20 years' (p. 18). This could suggest that the bankers were not 'conservative', at least as judged against Taylor's (1993) rule. In this context such a judgement may be warranted in that an operational rule akin to Taylor's rule would be needed to ensure the stability of the economy in terms of the NCM model.

The operational 'independence' of a central bank in any serious sense would preclude co-operation between the central bank and other public authorities. In a one instrument—one objective framework (bearing in mind the first point above, namely that constant inflation and the supply-side equilibrium are in effect two sides of the same coin) this could be acceptable. But once it is recognised that the interest rate tool is not adequate to achieve the objective so that more tools are required, and that there is more to life than low inflation, and that (at least intermediate) objectives such as the exchange rate and the level of and growth of output are on the agenda, then doubt must be cast on this isolation of the central bank. It can be argued that (as to some degree illustrated by the present crisis) there are 'get out' clauses, which enable coordination it times of crisis. But the argument would be that the institutional arrangements for coordination need to be in place, and further that the coordination is required at all times, not just in times of crisis.

4.5.3 ECB and policies on financial stability

Financial stability policies seem to have been taken on board by the EMU. A relevant proposal is the 'European Financial Stability Facility' (EFSF), formed on 1 July 2010 and endowed with a €250 billion fund, which was raised to €440 billion at a relevant meeting on 11 March 2011, and confirmed at another meeting of the European Commission on 25 March 2011. This is intended to be a temporary arrangement with an operational life of three years. It will then be replaced by the European Stability Mechanism (ESM) to help member indebted states when in acute cash flow difficulties; ESM will then become permanent. It was also decided at the meeting of 11 March 2011, confirmed on 25 March 2011, that the new permanent bailout mechanism should be able to lend up to €500 billion through increased guarantees from triple-A states and paid-in capital from those states with weaker balance sheets – in a subsequent meeting of the European finance ministers it was agreed to commit to €700 billion capital, of which €80 billion would actually be paid in; the rest would be 'callable' capital.[8] This facility aims to reassure financial markets and help out euro-area member states struggling to issue sovereign debt and faced with banking troubles. In terms of the funding arrangements of both the EFSF and ESM, however, the relevant decision was postponed until June 2011, which, however, did not change much. This was due essentially to the German negotiators who bowed at the last minute to domestic political pressures and persistently proposed a reduction of their contribution to the bailout mechanism. Under the deal reached on 25 March 2011, euro area and other governments will have to pay their share of capital over five years, instead of the four years initially agreed.[9] The rate of interest on new loans from this facility is expected to be lower by up to 1 per cent than previously.

The key element is the creation of a permanent liquidity facility under the aegis of the ESM. This would be available as a means of crisis resolution if there is a risk to the stability of the euro area as a whole. The crucial difference between the EFSF and ESM is that the credits of the latter would be more senior to those of private investors. This will reduce the risk to the budget of the creditor nations, since it is expected that by 2013 European banks should be in a better position to absorb losses. The ESM will not come into force before 2014.[10] These new measures reduce the cost of bailing out countries in trouble but increase it for those who have been, or potentially could be, in need of a bailout. They do not address the issue of high sovereign debt, which had appeared to have been the focus of the whole exercise. Still, the exercise has been turned into a political game, rather than what it should have been – a method to sort out the economic crisis. In this sense, it would not be surprising if the European leg of the 'great recession' is not contained any sooner.

It should be stressed that these arrangements had not been envisaged by the creators of the EMU. For one of the 'pillars' of the EMU and the euro was the 'no bailout, no exit and no default' clause. The sovereign debt crisis simply changed that principle significantly, at least in terms of the 'bailout' part of the clause. Still the agreed funds mentioned above should not be used to purchase government debt in the open market. Rather they should be used to buy the debt from struggling governments. But there is a condition attached. This is that the struggling governments should agree to implement significant austerity measures. Yet it all amounts to an increase in the level of debt in the countries concerned. This is justified on the premise that the new mechanism helps the countries involved in that the loan conditions are much better than the ones that they replace. Yet the debt of the countries involved piles up, thereby creating another serious danger, the possibility of default. This, however, entails a further danger in view of the high exposure of a number of European banks to the debts of weak countries. This may very well explain that despite the alleged seriousness of the European debt crisis, default has not been seriously considered yet. Indeed, it might not happen as long as support continues to be forthcoming. The weak country debt would continue to grow so long as support is forthcoming until the debt is all accumulated in, and held by, the official sector. Under these conditions the official sector will be the last holder of the assets that take the full loss. The taxpayer will carry the burden yet again, rather than the original bondholder. The ECB is trying very hard to avoid this problem. While helping the troubled countries, at the same time it attempts to sell debt to avoid excess liquidity in the market – the ECB does not undertake 'Quantitative Easing'. This is not always possible, though. It is not infrequent to find that since May 2010, when this operation started, the ECB has failed in its attempt to neutralise fully the effect on liquidity of purchasing government bonds.

4.5.4 Setting the policy interest rate

The attempt has been made to fine-tune the economy (or at least the rate of inflation) through the frequent change of the policy rate of interest (with monthly or thereabout decisions on the policy interest rate). In the previous section we cast doubt on the effectiveness of that policy with regard to inflation. The changes in the policy interest rate have implementation costs. But the most significant argument here is that the policy rate has effects on a range of variables, notably the exchange rate and asset prices. Indeed those variables are part of the channels through which changes in the policy rate of interest is supposed to influence the level of demand and thereby the rate of inflation. There are questions of the strength and reliability of those channels, but the point here is that there can be effects, and some of them may be adverse. For example, Goodhart (2005a) argues that a focus on domestic variables only in interest rate determination may provide 'a combination of internal price stability and exchange rate instability' (p. 301). In recent times, an important aspect of this can be the influence of low interest rates on asset prices, and whether the stimulus to asset price rises coming from low interest rates can be the spark setting off a price bubble. The argument of Wicksell (1898), and others, could be seen as one that suggests interest rate policy has an effect on asset price inflation – or at least on some subset of asset prices; asset prices develop a speculative element (meaning here purchase of assets to benefit from expected rise in their prices, rather than for income stream from asset holdings); it is obvious to say that asset price bubbles havedeveloped – including the dot.com and the pre-August 2007 house-price bubbles. Current arrangements are powerless to deal with those bubbles.

One of the curiosities of the present approach to monetary policy is that all of the attention is paid to 25 basis point variations in the interest rate on a monthly basis, and little attention is currently paid to what in the NCM is the key, namely the average/equilibrium/natural rate. There is virtually no discussion – there may be attempts to estimate the 'natural rate' but those are little more than the average of what has been actually observed. Yet a number of arguments point to the average rate being around the rate of growth – in Taylor's (1993) original formulation, the 'golden rule' of accumulation, the distributional argument (real rate = growth rate preserves the relative position of savings) and that (cf. Pasinetti, 1997) $b = d/g$ where b is debt/bonds, d is total deficit = primary deficit d' + interest payments $b.i$, and g is growth rate. Hence $b.g = d = d' + i.b$, and with $d' = 0$ the deficit equals interest payments.

The rule of 'rate of interest equal to the rate of growth' can be linked with other considerations. The 'golden rule of capital accumulation' in the framework of a neo-classical model with the marginal productivity of capital equal to the rate of interest generates such an outcome. Another is the 'fair rate of interest' (Pasinetti, 1981), which 'in real terms should be equal to the rate of increase in the productivity of the total amount of labor that is required, directly or indirectly, to produce consumption goods and to increase productive capacity' (Lavoie and Seccareccia, 1999, p. 544).

The setting of the interest rate has some clear and obvious implications for the operation of fiscal policy. The sustainability of a budget deficit depends on the level of interest rates (and specifically the post-tax rate of interest on government bonds, labelled r). If $r < g$, then any primary budget deficit of d (relative to GDP) would lead to an eventual debt ratio (to GDP) of $b = d/(g - r)$ (either both of g and r in real terms or both in nominal terms). If $r > g$ then a primary budget deficit would lead to growing debt ratio. In a similar vein, a continuing total budget deficit of d (including interest payments) leads to a debt to GDP ratio stabilising at d'/g where here g is in nominal terms. This implies that $b + rd = gd$, that is, $b = (g - r)d$ and hence if g is less than r the primary budget deficit is negative (that is, the primary budget is in surplus). The case where $g = r$ is of particular interest. Pasinetti (1997) remarks that this case 'represents the 'golden rule' of capital accumulation.... In this case, the public budget can be permanently in deficit and the public debt can thereby increase indefinitely, but national income increases at the same rate (g) so that the D/Y ratio remains constant. Another way of looking at this case is to say that the government budget has a deficit which is wholly due to interest payments' (p. 163).

The simplest way to implement such a policy would be to set the nominal policy interest rate at the beginning of the year, taking into account the expected rate of inflation for the coming year (with perhaps some adjustment based on difference between the actual and expected inflation in the preceding year). Outside of crisis (and perhaps even then) the nominal policy interest rate would be maintained for the year, with avoidance of the costs of further decision-making and implementation of interest rate changes. In some respects this could be seen as the equivalent to Friedman's constant growth of money supply rule to avoid problems of fine-tuning, but applied to the rate of interest!

There are some issues with such a policy approach to be resolved. The arguments for a constant real rate equal to the rate of growth relate to some market rate of interest, which is not equal to the policy rate, and which may bear a varying relationship with the policy rate. There can be international complications in so far as domestic interest rate relative to interest rates elsewhere can have implications for the exchange rate. This is neither to suggest some simple uncovered interest rate parity idea nor to suggest that the effects of interest rate differentials on exchange rate are firm and predictable.

In effect we wish to put forward two lines of argument here. First, to argue that the view against fine-tuning apply to the setting of interest rates, and that such fine-tuning should be foregone and rather the nominal rate of interest should be set to achieve a constant target real rate of interest. Second, there are a number of arguments to support the view that the target real rate of interest be the underlying rate of growth of the economy.

4.6 Concluding remarks

This chapter has elaborated on the nature of the monetary policy in the EMU. Our main focus has been on the weaknesses of this policy in terms of its design. We have highlighted the theoretical and empirical weaknesses in using interest rate policy to target inflation, and have also pointed to the failure, admittedly narrow, to achieve the inflation target and to the persisting inflation differentials between euro area countries.

We turn our attention in the chapter that follows to the fiscal policy aspects in the Economic and Monetary Union.

5
Fiscal Policy in the Economic and Monetary Union

5.1 Introduction

The history of monetary unions clearly suggests that their successful continuation may be closely tied to political union (see Arestis et al., 2003, for example). It can be further noted that there has to be a set of political authorities which determines the unit of account of money, and the forms of money which will be accepted as payment of tax and in settlement of debts. When the euro was created, powers over the issue of money which lie at the level of the nation with the central bank passed to a Federal institution in the form of the European Central Bank.

The Optimal Currency Area (OCA) literature, as discussed in chapter 2, suggests that there needs to be adjustment processes for constituent members of a currency union to respond to 'shocks' since the adjustment process of changing the exchange rate of the member's currency is now ruled out through membership of the currency union. Flexible prices and mobility of factors are mentioned frequently, but of particular significance here is the use of fiscal transfers. The argument is a simple one, namely that a downturn in a constituent economy can be slowed through a combination of automatic and discretionary fiscal transfers from the centre (and in effect from other constituent economies). Within a nation state, there are extensive fiscal transfers from relatively rich to relatively poor areas. A good example on this score is, of course, the United States of America.

Fiscal transfers within EMU (or more generally within the EU) could come from the development of a significant budget for the EU. The requirement for a significant EU budget was acknowledged in the MacDougall Report of 1977 (Commission, 1977, vol. I: 14), which estimated an amount of 7.5 per cent of EU GDP as necessary to manage a monetary union. Goodhart and Smith (1993) and Currie (1997) argue that a rather lower figure for the EU budget, provided that it was well targeted to aid stabilisation, would suffice; but their figures of around 2 per cent would still be double the current level of the EU budget. The Treaty of Lisbon, reinforced by the Treaty on Stability, Coordination and Governance, imposes the requirement that national governments balance their budget over the cycle and are subjected to the upper 3 per cent limit, even though many countries have broken this limit repeatedly. Following the Treaty on Stability, Coordination and Governance, the limits on budget deficits are now to be written into national law or constitution. It would be much more appropriate if a treaty were to set out the enduring objectives of the EMU economic policies, and for those to include full employment, equitable income distribution and the elimination of poverty, and the pursuit of sustainable development. The pursuit of the achievement of those values would come from, inter alia, macroeconomic policies, but macroeconomic policies inevitably change over time.

The Treaty of Lisbon often manages to combine statements, which are poorly defined but which are rather menacing. In the relevant article, it is stated that there shall be compliance with 'the following guiding principles: stable prices, sound public finances and monetary conditions' (article III-69). At one level this sounds eminently sensible for who could be in favour of unsound finance? But at another level it is an almost meaningless phrase for what constitutes 'sound finance': what does it imply for the balance between revenue and expenditure, or for the level of and rate of change of public debt? In the same article there is talk of 'the sustainability of the government financial position; this is apparent from having achieved a government budgetary position without a deficit that is excessive' (article III-92), which is close to a tautology but also it is not realised that any government deficit is sustainable in the sense that the debt to GDP ratio does not explode (see chapter 4 for the formula).

There is, however, a basic requirement for some coordination of fiscal policy across member countries. In part this arises from the recognition that fiscal policy has a significant impact on the well-being of economies. We thus continue in this chapter, after this introduction of section 5.1, with fiscal coordination within the EMU in section 5.2. We then turn our attention to fiscal policy within the SGP in section 5.3. Section 5.4 discusses relevant institutional considerations; section 5.5 deals with changes to the SGP ever since 1999 when the EMU was set up. Further developments are discussed in section 5.6. Section 5.7 summarises and concludes this chapter.

5.2 EMU fiscal policy coordination

There are (at least) two reasons for supporting fiscal policy coordination. First, the euro area as a whole requires mechanism for responding to adverse economic shocks, which impact on all economies, that is shocks that are widespread rather than being limited to a few countries. A coordinated fiscal policy is required to confront a 'coordinated' shock. Second, there are important spillovers between countries in the integrated economies of the EMU; expansion of demand in one country raises demand for the product of other countries, and in the EMU context where there is relatively little trade outside of the EU, most of the demand effects will be felt by other member countries. 'Coordination' of fiscal policy would mean that one country's fiscal policy would take into account the effects of fiscal policy in other countries.

The question then arises as to what type of 'coordination should be sought and the mechanisms of coordination to achieve the 'coordination'. There are (at least) two broad approaches to fiscal policy. The first, which is closely reflected in the present SGP, is to aim for some form of balanced budget, albeit allowing the budget position to vary over the business cycle. The second is to use the budget deficit in pursuit of economic objectives such as high levels of employment. The first approach is concerned with the budget being balanced over some time horizon and the objective of fiscal policy becomes the balance of the budget. There is some recognition that there may be some 'automatic stabilisers' in place, such that in an economic downturn the budget position tends to move into deficit and that helps to cushion the economic downturn. But there is no recognition that the general achievement of high levels of demand may require budget deficits (in the case where a high level of demand would generate a surplus of savings over investment).

The second approach views fiscal policy as one of the instruments of economic policy, which can be used to strive for specified economic objectives. A budget deficit or surplus (or indeed balance) is not then sought to meet some predetermined figure but rather is used in conjunction with other policies to maintain high levels of demand in the economy.

One of our major criticisms of the SGP is that some predetermined budget deficit limit is imposed, whether or not that budget deficit serves well the macroeconomic objectives. By focusing on limits on budget deficits, what should be the other objectives of macroeconomic policy, such as high levels of economic activity, are overlooked.

There is no reason to think that a budget balanced over the business cycle suits all countries (or indeed any). A budget deficit may often be required to attain high levels of economic activity, and that the size of such a budget deficit would be:

$$(G - T) = (sY^* - I(Y^*)) + (qY^* - X)$$

Where G is government expenditure, T tax revenues, Y^* is the high level of output, s the propensity to save, q the propensity to import, I investment and X exports.

On that basis the appropriate size of the budget deficit would depend on the level of economic activity, which is being targeted, and the propensities to save, invest, import and the ability to export. These are variables which are likely to differ across countries and there is little reason to think that the appropriate budget deficit would be the same across countries (or across time). A hint of that is given by the figures in Table 2.8 (chapter 2) where it can be readily seen that there are marked differences in the average budget deficit across the member countries.

The second approach to fiscal policy indicated above can be linked to a 'functional finance' approach (Lerner, 1943; Kalecki, 1944; see, also Arestis and Sawyer, 2004b) in which budget positions should be set to pursue macroeconomic objectives including the highest sustainable level of employment. Budget deficits should be incurred in so far as they are necessary to achieve these objectives, and not subject to arbitrary rules (such as balanced budget over the cycle).

Under the present arrangements, national fiscal policies could be said to be 'coordinated' by the SGP, though subordinated may be a better word than 'coordinated (except that in the outturn the rules of the SGP have frequently been broken). The rationale for the present form of coordination comes from the notion of spillover effects between national economies and the interests of one country in the effects of other countries' fiscal policy. In the approach taken here, the case for coordination of fiscal policies arises from the following considerations:

i when the euro area is impacted by shocks (for example, a general rise in price of oil), which effects all of the economies (albeit not to the same extent), a coordinated response to a generalised shock is appropriate;

ii there are likely to be substantial spillover effects between national economies given the extent of trade between them, and hence a fiscal stimulus in one country will raise demand in neighbouring countries. The setting of fiscal policy in one country then needs to take into account what is happening to fiscal policy in neighbouring countries;

iii monetary and fiscal policies both affect the level of aggregate demand, exchange rate and perhaps the rate of inflation, and that points towards coordination between monetary and fiscal policies.

The coordination of national fiscal policies faces many difficulties. A major one arises from the issues of what are the aims of fiscal policies and what are perceived to be the effects of fiscal policy. Under the present arrangements the aims of fiscal policy is a balanced budget and that the perceived effects of budget deficits are generally negative (that is, they lead to high interest rates and inflation). It is clearly difficult for two (or more) individuals (or countries) to coordinate their activities if the purpose and effects of coordination are matters of dispute amongst the parties concerned. Thus, we would argue, Coordination of national fiscal policies needs to be based on a shared set of objectives – and here we would advocate the inclusion of the objectives of high and sustainable levels of demand and economic activity. 'coordination' would also benefit greatly from shared views on the need for active fiscal policy and on the effects of fiscal policy. And this requires a sharp change from the prevailing 'conventional wisdom' embedded in the SGP.

Further reservations include the separation of the monetary authorities from the fiscal authorities. The decentralisation of the fiscal authorities inevitably makes any effective 'coordination' of fiscal and monetary policy difficult. Since the ECB is instructed to focus on inflation while the fiscal authorities will have a broader range of concerns, there will be considerable grounds for conflict. This suggests a need for the evolution of a body, which would be charged with the 'coordination' of EMU monetary and fiscal policies. In the absence of such a body, tensions will emerge in the real sector when monetary policy and fiscal policy pull in different directions. The SGP in effect resolves these issues by establishing the dominance of the monetary authorities (ECB) over the fiscal authorities (national governments).

The SGP has sought to impose a 'one size (of straightjacket) fits all' fiscal policy, namely that over the course of the cycle national government budgets should be in balance or slight surplus with a maximum deficit of 3 per cent of GDP.[1] It has *never* been shown (or even argued) that fiscal policy ought to be uniform across countries. The SGP imposes a fiscal policy, which may in the end fit nobody.

5.3 Fiscal policy within the Stability and Growth Pact

In this section we turn to the Stability and Growth Pact (SGP), which provides the macroeconomic policy framework for EMU. In setting out the SGP we seek to illustrate how this policy framework fits with the NCM theoretical framework discussed in chapter 2 and also to provide the basis for our more detailed critique of the SGP, which follows.

The SGP was developed in the mid-1990s during the passage to the establishment of the euro area, and could be seen to build on the thrust of the macroeconomic goals of the convergence criteria of the Maastricht Treaty. The SGP was enshrined in the Treaty of Amsterdam 1996, and has continued unchanged in terms of the wording in subsequent treaties, including the Treaty of Lisbon, although there were changes to the precise interpretation of the SGP in March 2005. The latest change took place in December 2011 as a result of the economic problems in Europe. A significant feature of all these changes (to which we return in section 5.5 below) is that macroeconomic policies are enshrined in law. In the context of EMU this has the effect that policies are difficult to change since changes in a EU Treaty requires the agreement of each of the (currently) 27 members of the EU, whether or not the country concerned is a member of EMU. Further, it can mean that a failure of a country to abide by the terms of the SGP can be challenged through the courts.

There is no fiscal policy that can be exercised at the EMU level. The budget of the EU is relatively small (around 1 per cent of EU GDP) and cannot be used for fiscal policy purposes since it must always be in balance. The fiscal policy of national governments is constrained by the rules of the SGP. In this regard, there are three core elements of the SGP: (a) to pursue the medium-term objectives of budgetary positions close to balance or in surplus; (b) the submission of annual stability and convergence programmes by the member states; and (c) the monitoring of the implementation of the stability and convergence programmes.

It is also necessary for national budgetary policies to 'support stability oriented monetary policies. Adherence to the objective of sound budgetary positions close to balance or in surplus will allow all Member States to deal with normal cyclical fluctuations while keeping the government deficit within the reference value of 3% of GDP.' Furthermore,

> Member States commit themselves to respect the medium-term budgetary objective of positions close to balance or in surplus set out in their stability of convergence programmes and to take the corrective budgetary action they deem necessary to meet the objectives of their stability or convergence programmes, whenever they have information indicating actual or expected significant divergence from those objectives. (Resolution of the European Council on the Stability and Growth Pact, Amsterdam, 17 June 1997)

The SGP imposes an upper limit of 3 per cent of GDP on budget deficits, with the view that budgets will be broadly in balance or small surplus over the business cycle. Automatic exemption was in place for falls of GDP of more than 2 per cent and discretionary exemptions for falls in output of between 0.75 per cent and 2 per cent, which would represent very major recessions. A system of non-interest-bearing deposits, which could turn into fines, was also in place but it has not been invoked despite of a number of budget deficits exceeding 3 per cent (in face of economic slowdown but not of declining output). It is then the intention that national budgets be broadly in balance but recognising that budget deficits and surpluses move with the business cycle and the expectation that deficits rise during recession and fall during booms. The argument is then that given the scale of fluctuations in the level of economic activity, an on-average budget balance can involve up to a 3 per cent deficit in a downturn; but that would be balanced by some surpluses on other occasions.

5.4 Institutional considerations

The official rationale for the SGP is twofold. The first is that a medium-term balanced budget rule secures the scope for automatic stabilisers without breaching the limits set by the SGP (see below for more details). Second, since a balanced budget explicitly sets the debt ratio on a declining trend, it reduces the interest burden and improves the overall position of the government budget. Underlying the approach to SGP, though, is the notion of sound public finances. The European Commission (2000) is emphatic on this issue:

> Achieving and sustaining sound positions in public finances is essential to raise output and employment in Europe. Low public debt and deficits help maintain low interest rates, facilitate the task of monetary authorities in keeping inflation under control and create a stable environment which fosters investment and growth ...

> The Maastricht Treaty clearly recognises the need for enhanced fiscal discipline in EMU to avoid overburdening the single monetary authority and prevent fiscal crises, which would have negative consequences for other countries. Moreover, the loss of exchange rate instrument implies the need to create room for fiscal policy to tackle adverse economic shocks and smooth the business cycle. The stability and growth pact is the concrete manifestation of the shared need for fiscal discipline. (p. 1)

It is further argued that these views spring from experience in that the emphases on both fiscal prudence and stability in the founding Treaty of the EMU spring from the firm conviction that

> the deterioration of public finances was an important cause behind the poor economic performance of many EU countries since the early 1970s. The subsequent decades taught Europe a salutary lesson of how economic prosperity cannot be sustained in an unstable economic policy environment. Inappropriate fiscal policies frequently overburdened monetary policy leading to high interest rates. On the supply-side, generous welfare systems contributed to structural rigidities in EU economies and fuelled inappropriate wage behaviour. The net effect was a negative impact on business expectations and on investment, thus contributing to a slower rise in actual and potential output. As a result, employment stagnated. (European Commission, 2000, p. 9)

The figures in Table 2.8 (chapter 2) indicate that over the period 2002–08 the budget deficit for the euro area as a whole varied between 0.7 per cent of GDP and 3.1 per cent of GDP, and averaged just over 2 per cent. Although this period of seven years may not be a complete business cycle, the figure is nevertheless suggestive that the overall intention of budgets in balance or with a small surplus was not attained. The same table also indicates that all the initial 12 euro area members, with the exception of Luxemburg, have on at least one occasion breached the 3 per cent of GDP upper limit on budget deficits. It is clear from this table that there are three groups of countries: one group includes those countries that had deficits that were near to the 3 per cent SGP ceiling in their budget throughout the period; another group which, although had a deficit it was a small percentage of GDP; and a third group that had surplus at the beginning of the period, which turned into deficit after a fashion. Finland was the only country with surplus over the entire period. The euro area as a whole, though had a deficit throughout this period, which was rather substantial. In terms of government debt, for the euro area as a whole, the government debt to GDP ratio has been consistently over the 60 per cent ceiling imposed by the Maastricht criteria. Two groups can be identified; the first comprises those countries with a ratio that exceeds the 60 per cent ceiling; and those countries, the majority of the member states, with a ratio of less than 60 per cent. We may also note that for the whole euro area, the government debt to GDP ratio has been consistently over the 60 per cent ceiling imposed by the Maastricht criteria.

Table 2.9 (chapter 2) has indicated the position over the debt to GDP ratios for the euro area countries for selected years. The figures for 1998 indicate the degree to which countries missed the convergence criteria figure of 60 per cent. The situation was not much different in 2007 and 2012. If anything by 2012 the debt to GDP ratio, although improved in some countries by 2007, it was worse by 2012 in all the countries reported in Table 2.9.

The imposition of an upper limit of 3 per cent of GDP on the size of the budget deficit and the declaration of the aim of a balanced budget over the cycle represented a significant tightening of the fiscal position as compared with the 3 per cent of GDP target for the budget deficit in the Maastricht Treaty convergence conditions. In those conditions, the 3 per cent was to be achieved at a particular point in time: under the SGP the 3 per cent limit is to be exceeded only under extreme conditions. Although no justification was ever given by the European Union for the choice of 3 per cent in the convergence conditions, others advanced two arguments. Buiter et al. (1993), for example, suggested that the choice of the 3 per cent figure for the deficit to GDP ratio arose from a combination of advocacy of the so-called "golden rule" (that current expenditure should be covered by current revenue) and that 'EC public investment averaged almost exactly 3% of EC GDP during 1974–91' (p. 63). Another argument suggests that the 3 per cent figure corresponded to the range of deficits run by a number of countries, notably Germany, and was achievable. For example, in the decade up to 1992 the German general government financial balance averaged 1.8 per cent deficit, and the euro area as a whole averaged 4.45 per cent deficit (calculated from OECD *Economic Outlook*, various issues). These possible justifications prompt two points to be made. The first is that typically governments have run budget deficits. The imposition of a balanced budget requirement represents a major departure from what governments have done in the past. The second is that governments invest, and it is generally accepted that governments can and should borrow to fund their investment programmes. The SGP imposes the requirement that governments generally fund their investment programmes from current tax revenue. A balanced budget (on average) means, of course, that current government expenditure will be much less than tax revenue since that tax revenue would also need to cover interest payments on debt and to pay for capital expenditure.

The general requirement that the budget be in balance or small surplus over the course of the business cycle is more deflationary than it sounds when allowance is made for inflation and the deficit is calculated in real terms. For example, with a 60 per cent debt to GDP ratio inflation of 2 per cent per annum would mean that the real value of the outstanding debt declined by 1.2 per cent of GDP, and hence in real terms a balanced budget in nominal terms equates to a 1.2 per cent of GDP surplus.

There is anyway an essential contradiction between the 60 per cent debt to GDP ratio and a balanced budget. It can readily be shown that a persistent overall budget deficit (that is, including interest payments on government debt) of d (relative to GDP) would lead to public debt stabilising at $b = d/g$ where g is the nominal rate of growth.[2] Taking as an example $g = 0.05$ (a 5 per cent growth rate built up from say 2½ per cent real growth and 2½ per cent inflation) then the debt ratio would be 20 times the deficit ratio. In that example a 60 per cent debt ratio would be consistent with a persistent 3 per cent deficit ratio – indeed that precise calculation was given as a justification for the 3 per cent deficit, 60 per cent debt target in the convergence criteria.

The general stance of the SGP with its requirement of an overall balanced budget and maximum deficit of 3 per cent of GDP is a deeply flawed one on four counts. First, no reasons are given for thinking that a balanced budget position is consistent with high levels of employment (or indeed with any particular level of employment). Second, there is the imposition of a common 'one size fits all' approach. Third, there is little reason to think that the 3 per cent limit can permit the automatic stabilisers to work, and striving to reach the 3 per cent limit in time of recession is likely to push economies further into recession. Fourth, the balanced budget requirement does not allow governments to even borrow to fund capital investment projects.

The first two of those flaws can be seen by reference to a well-known identity (though generally forgotten by advocates of the SGP) drawn from the national income accounts The equation of (Private Savings minus Investment) plus (Imports minus Exports) plus (Tax Revenue minus Government Expenditure) equals zero can be expressed in symbols:

$$(S - I) + (Q - X) + (T - G) = 0$$

Individuals and firms make decisions on savings, investment, imports and exports. For any particular level of employment (and income), there is no reason to think that those decisions will lead to:

$$(S - I) + (Q - X) = 0$$

But if they are not equal to zero, then $(G - T)$, the budget deficit, will not be equal to zero, since,

$$(G - T) = (S - I) + (Q - X)$$

The SGP in effect assumes that any level of output and employment is consistent with a balanced budget ($G - T = 0$), and hence compatible with a combination of net private savings and the trade position summing to zero. But no satisfactory justification has been given for this view. Two possible arguments could be advanced. First, it could be argued that budget deficits cannot be run for ever as the government debt to income ratio would rise continuously and that would be unsustainable. Hence governments eventually have to run balanced (on average) budgets. However, that depends on whether post-tax rate of interest (on government bonds) is greater or less than the growth rate, the debt to income ratio being unsustainable in the former case but not in the latter case. Further, it relates to the size of the primary deficit, which is the deficit that excludes interest payments. The relevant deficit here is the total including interest payments, and it was indicated earlier that an overall budget deficit of d leads to a sustainable debt ratio of d/g.

Second, some form of Say's Law could be invoked to the effect that intended savings and investment are equal at full employment (or modified for foreign trade, domestic savings plus trade deficit equals investment). Even if Say's Law held (which we would dispute), what is required here would be that the level of private demand could sustain the supply-side equilibrium – that is, the non-accelerating inflation rate of unemployment, and the NAIRU does not correspond to full employment. In particular, there is no reason to think that a balanced budget position is compatible with employment at the level given by the NAIRU.

If we expand the equation given above slightly to read:

$$(G - T) = (sY - I(Y)) + (qY - X)$$

where Y is income level, s propensity to save and q propensity to import. If a level of income Y^* is to be achieved, then the required budget deficit (or surplus) would be given by equation (1) above.

The deficit or surplus then required would clearly depend on the propensities to save, to invest, and to import and also on the state of exports. The appropriate budget position for a country then depends on those factors (plus the level of economic activity it seeks to achieve). There is clearly no reason to think that these propensities would lead to the same general deficit in each country. Indeed the figures in Table 2.8 are suggestive of quite different requirements: Finland's budget surplus averaged 3.6 per cent over the years 2002–08, France's budget deficit averaged over 3 per cent in that period.

The SGP clearly seeks to impose an upper limit on the budget deficit of 3 per cent of GDP with some limited exceptions for a severe recession. Countries will differ in terms of their overall budget deficit requirements (as argued above) and also in the degree to which their GDP varies in the course of a business cycle and in the extent to which the budget position varies with GDP. The latter could be expected to depend on the structure and progressivity of the tax regime as well as the degree to which social security and other transfer payments rise with falling GDP. Buti et al. (1997) found that the budget balance is negatively linked to GDP growth, but in a way which varies between countries with estimates of changes in the deficit to GDP ratio of up to 0.8 per cent and 0.9 per cent for the Netherlands and Spain respectively for a 1 per cent slowdown in growth. The notable feature is the differences amongst countries, and that the rules of the SGP make no allowance for that.

One other notable feature of the SGP is that no distinction is made between the current account and the capital account of the government budget, and that it is the size of the overall budget which is to be constrained. This stands in contrast with, for example, the 'golden rule' adopted by the UK government as part of its Code of Fiscal Stability (Treasury, 1998) whereby over the course of the business cycle the current budget position should be in balance but borrowing for capital investment is not so constrained (see Sawyer, 2007, for further discussion on all these matters). In a similar vein, many states within the United States of America are constitutionally constrained to aim to balance their budget with respect to current expenditure but are able to borrow for capital projects. In terms of the impact on aggregate demand, it is the overall budget deficit which is relevant for whatever purpose the borrowing is put. But the focus on the overall budget position rather than the current budget serves to impose a more deflationary approach. It also runs counter to the potent argument that capital expenditure by government stimulates future productive potential and private investment, and that it is reasonable to borrow to fund that capital expenditure, which yields future benefits to the economy from which some additional tax revenues will be forthcoming.

The operation of the SGP has managed to combine the losses from an insistence on reducing budget deficits in the face of economic slowdown with a loss of reputation through not doing so consistently or effectively. The case of Portugal illustrates the former where attempts to reduce the budget deficit (not always successfully) were associated with a rise in unemployment. The figures in Table 2.8 (chapter 2) clearly indicate that there have been a number of occasions on which the 3 per cent deficit limit has been breached.

5.5 Stability and Growth Pact changes

There have been some movement in the interpretation of the SGP with regard to fiscal policy, and the main changes are enumerated in Table 5.1.

In September, 2002, the European Commission admitted for the first time that the SGP fiscal rules relating to the single currency need to be changed. They would be more flexible in the future in view of the euro area economic weaknesses. The European Commission actually relaxed the deadline of 2004 by which Germany, Portugal and France should balance their budgets. These countries were given until 2006 to balance their budgets. In return the Commission demanded that the members reduce their deficit by 0.5 per cent a year starting in 2003. It was at the 2002 summer summit in Seville of the 15 European Union members that they all signed a commitment 'to achieve budgetary positions close to balance or in surplus as soon as possible in all Member States and at the latest by 2004' (Council of the European Union, 2002, p. 8). The European Commissioner for Economic and Monetary Affairs admitted at the time that it was of great concern to them that the original political commitment of national governments to uphold the SGP was substantially weakening.

Table 5.1 Summary of decisions relating to the Stability and Growth Pact

February 2002: European Commission recommends that early warning be given to Portugal for having missed its budget target for 2001 by a wide margin (projected deficit for 2001 was 2.2 per cent). Also to Germany whose projected deficit for 2001 was 2.6 per cent.
February 2002: ECOFIN Council decided not to endorse the European Commission's recommendation, thereby abrogating the 'early warning' signal. That was based on the commitment by Germany and Portugal to take action to avoid the occurrence of excessive deficits in the future.
October 2002: European Commission recommends that excessive deficit exists in Portugal; deficit in 2001 of 4.1 per cent and in the absence of a rectifying budget, the 2002 deficit could be above 3.5 per cent.
November 2002: ECOFIN Council decides that Portugal has excessive deficit; the 2001 deficit was revised to 4.1 per cent.
November 2002: European Commission recommends to give early warning to France; in fact, France refuses to start cutting deficit in 2003 (thereby breaking promises made under the SGP); European Commission projects deficit of 2.7 per cent (2002) and 2.9 (2003).
January 2003: European Commission recommends that excessive deficit exists in Germany (in October 2002 Germany admits that it will break SGP for the first time).
January 2003: ECOFIN Council decides that excessive deficit exists in Germany; deficit in 2002 expected to be 3.8 per cent. ECOFIN Council also decides to give an early warning to France.
May 2003: European Commission recommends that excessive deficit exists in France; in 2002 deficit is 3.1 per cent and forecasts for 2003 estimate it to be 3.7 per cent.
June 2003: ECOFIN Council decides that excessive deficit exists in France.
October 2003: France admits of breaking the SGP for third successive year in 2004. European Commission gives it until 2005 to comply. Germany confirms it will also break pact for third year.
November 2003: Germany tries to draw the SGP's remaining teeth by calling for countries that 'co-operate' to be exempted from possible sanctions.
November 2003: ECOFIN Council suspends disciplinary procedures against France and Germany. European Commission shows grave concern.

January 2004: European Council pledges to take ECOFIN to the European Court of Justice for allowing France and Germany to flout the SGP rules. The ECB in the words of its President 'respects the Commission's decision to seek legal clarity' (Trichet, 2004).

July 2004: European Court of Justice condemned ECOFIN for 'suspending' the SGP's recommendation on deficit reduction, but upheld the right of national governments to ignore these recommendations and all the disciplinary procedures that were so painstakingly attached to them in 1996.

September 2004: European Commission announces proposals for the reform (although the Commission prefers to call them 'an evolution') of the SGP (in response to the June, 2004, European Council call for proposals by the Commission that strengthen and clarify the implementation of the SGP).

March 2005: The European Commission proposal are adopted formally by the EU Finance ministers (ECOFIN), subsequently endorsed by the European Council. The agreement went through marathon meetings with a great deal of acrimony, which nearly put a hold to the reformed SGP. The main points of the agreement are: more budgetary consolidation in good times; more flexibility in reducing deficits in bad times; more focus on cutting the debt to GDP ratio; more room for manoeuvre for countries carrying out structural reforms; countries with sound finances allowed to run small deficits to invest. These changes aim 'to improve governance, strengthen the preventive arm, and improve the implementation of the corrective arm' (ECB, 2005b, p. 60) of the original SGP.

November 2008: The EU package, 'European Economic Recovery Plan' (EERP), is introduced. A fiscal stimulus that amounted to 1.5 per cent of EU27 GDP should be implemented in 2009, and applied through national policies under their total discretion. The EERP aggregate fiscal input would be consistent with the SGP deficit ceiling of 3 per cent of GDP for the euro area as a whole. The GDP escape clauses introduced in 2005 would apply.

December 2011: The European Leaders agreed in principle at their meeting in Brussels on the 8th/9th of December 2011 to adopt tougher sanctions on the euro-area countries that break the 'new' rules of the Stability and Growth (SGP; the so-called 'fiscal pact'), what is now called the 'fiscal compact' (FC). This is an inter-government treaty, not a change to the EU treaties, whereby tax and spending plans will be checked by the European officials before national governments intervene. There will be automatic actions against those countries that overspend.

June 2012: The EU summit of 28/29 June 2012 proposed a 'growth pact'. This would involve the issue of 'project bonds' to finance infrastructure. The 'growth pact' also includes raising the capital base of the European Investment Bank. The 'growth pact' is to be finalised in the future.

The Commission also said that they would pay more attention to structural deficits so that a country's fiscal deficit would be judged in relation to cyclical conditions. Those changes took place alongside Germany, Portugal and France, showing evidence of having breached the conditions of the SGP. Portugal became the first country to breach the 3 per cent rule, and it admitted in July 2002 to a budget deficit in excess of the 3 per cent of GDP upper limit for the financial year 2002. Germany and France followed soon afterwards. In the same year Italy's budget deficit was also criticised by the European Commission for having reached 'dangerous proportions'. The charge was made that the Italian government was massaging the figures. France, too, was criticised by the European Commissioner for Economic and Monetary Affairs, for the 2003 tax and spending plans of this country (European Commission, 2003a); and expressed concern that France may not be able to meet the new deadline of 2006. In fact in October 2002, France refused to adhere even to the 2006 deadline, arguing that its expenditure plans were affordable, and also claiming that 'other priorities' were in place.

In his testimony to the European Parliament in October 2002 the ECB president actually accused France, Germany and Italy of being responsible over the uncertainty surrounding the economic recovery in the euro area; he argued that 'Three of the larger countries have not used the time when there were good economic conditions...to consolidate their budgets. Now they bear the burden of it' (Duisenberg, 2002).

Germany was told in January 2003 by the European Commission to draw up urgent plans to bring its deficit below 3 per cent. In June 2003 Germany announced plans to bring forward €15.5 billion of tax cuts, and admitted that it may break the SGP in 2004 for a third successive year. In April 2003, when it became apparent that France had a public deficit of 3.1 per cent in 2002, with European Commission (2003a) provisional forecasts putting it to 3.7 per cent for 2003 and 3.6 per cent for 2004, and Germany (where the budget deficit was thought to rise to 3.6 per cent in 2003) and Portugal (with an expected 3.2 per cent deficit in 2003), all three might have been fined. The Commission was of the opinion that 'an excessive government deficit' already existed in France. It recommended that France should eliminate the deficit by the end of 2004, 'at the latest', and also by 2004 France should bring back to a declining path its government to GDP ratio. France was asked to have relevant measures in place to achieve those objectives by October 2003. France never adhered to that dictum by October 2003, claiming that the deficit was justified by economic circumstances, but pledging to bring the budget deficit below the 3 per cent by 2005, thereby showing co-operation.

According to the SGP rules, France should have been penalised, but instead was offered an extra year to comply. France even refused to abide by the European Commission's 'flexible' interpretation of the SGP, which was asking that country to cut its structural deficit by 1 per cent in 2004, instead of the 0.7 per cent planned by France, and 0.5 per cent in 2005; instead France vowed to fresh spending cuts in 2004. Germany by that time was also predicted to violate the 3 per cent fiscal rule for the third successive year in 2004. The European Commission expectation was that this country would be treated in the same way as France. Germany responded by proposing that countries that show 'co-operation' in reducing their deficits should be exempted from the SGP's sanctions mechanism, regardless of 'success'. Sanctions would only apply to those countries that refuse to co-operate. In the event, the European Finance Ministers (ECOFIN) at their meeting on 24 November, 2003, decided not to penalise France and Germany. A compromise solution required Germany and France to cut their deficit by 0.60 per cent and 0.77 per cent, respectively, of GDP in 2004 and by 0.50 per cent and 0.60 per cent, respectively, in 2005. This was under the proviso that those reductions would not be required if economic growth was not solid. The European Commission and the ECB governing council responded showing grave concerns. The Governing Council of the ECB in a press release (25 November, 2003), 'deeply regrets these developments and shares the views made public by the Commission on the ECOFIN Council conclusions' (the European Commission expressed their deep regret at the decision). It goes on to suggest that 'The conclusions adopted by the ECOFIN Council carry serious dangers. The failure to go along with the rules and procedures foreseen in the Stability and Growth Pact risks undermining the credibility of the institutional framework and the confidence in sound public finances of member States across the euro area'. Trichet (2004) was as concerned when he declared that

> as regards the Stability and Growth Pact, the Governing Council shares the concerns of the European Commission regarding the conclusions of the ECOFIN Council in November last year. The Commission is the guardian of the Treaty and the ECB respects the Commission's decision to seek legal clarity. Furthermore, we do not see a need to change the Treaty and, in our view, the Stability and Growth Pact in its current form is appropriate. We are in agreement

> with the Commission that the implementation of the Stability and Growth Pact could be further improved, in particular in terms of the analysis of structural imbalances and the strengthening of incentives for sound fiscal policies during good economic times. Clarity and enforceability of the fiscal framework should be enhanced.

It is worth commenting, however, on the September 2004 European Commission proposals for the reform (although the Commission prefers to call them 'an evolution') of the SGP (in response to the June 2004, European Council call for proposals by the Commission that strengthen and clarify the implementation of the SGP). The main elements of the proposals were: (i) placing more focus on government debt and sustainability in the surveillance of budgetary positions; (ii) allowing for more country-specific circumstances in defining the medium-term deficit objective of 'close to balance or in surplus'; (iii) considering economic circumstances and developments in the implementation of the Excessive Deficit Procedure. Two elements are emphasised under this item: catering for prolonged periods of sluggish growth through the 'exceptional circumstances clause'; and allowing for country-specific elements in the enforcement of the correction of excessive deficits (the adjustment path). Both the identification of an 'excessive deficit' and the recommendations and deadlines to correct it may benefit from taking better into account the budgetary impact of periods of exceptionally weak economic growth; (iv) ensuring earlier actions to correct inadequate budgetary developments. Budgetary surveillance should ensure the achievement of surpluses in good times to prepare for the ageing of the population, to create sufficient room for dealing with economic slowdowns and to ensure an adequate policy mix over the cycle (it is argued in this context that had member states undertaken more consolidation efforts during the good years of 1999 and 2000, some of the subsequent excessive deficits might have been avoided). In addition, a strong emphasis is placed on economic policy 'coordination' for the euro area as whole, especially on the interaction between European and national levels, before a draft budget is prepared for the following year. There is still the question of policy 'coordination' between fiscal and monetary policy and between fiscal and structural type of policies so much favoured by the ECB and the Commission. ECOFIN, at its meeting on 10 September accepted the proposals but sharp differences remain on the definition of 'exceptional circumstances' under which countries can run big deficits.

The reaction to the reforms is also of some interest. The ECB reaction was that 'improvements could be introduced in the implementation of the Stability and Growth Pact' but the 'Pact is an appropriate framework for dealing with countries' fiscal developments on a level playing field', and there is thus 'no need for changes to the text of the Maastricht treaty and of the SGP'. The president of the ECB repeated the position on a number of occasions in statements at the press conferences after the ECB governing body meetings at the time of the introduction of the changes in 2005. One such an example is Trichet (2005), where he states that

> on a number of points improvements to the implementation of the SGP could really be effective, especially as regards the 'preventive arm' of the Pact, where we could strengthen the compliance in 'good times'. As regards the 'corrective arm' we would insist that we do not see a need to change the wording of the Pact. In particular the 3 per cent threshold, which is in the treaty itself, is to be observed in nominal terms and not in cyclically adjusted.

What emerges from these statements is that the reform package dodges the key issue of the SGP debate: countries that join the single currency must abandon all efforts to stabilise their national macroeconomic conditions, as well as giving up a large part of their budgetary, and therefore political, independence. Only a country that is willing to sacrifice these two parts of its national autonomy can responsibly join a currency union.

It became apparent that the slowdown in economic growth brought about, largely through the operation of the 'automatic stabilisers' rather than discretionary fiscal policy, the scale of budget deficits, which could readily predicted from the size of the slowdown. Buti et al. (1997) found that a 1 per cent change in GDP produced on average a 0.5 per cent change in the average budget deficit in the EU countries. The economic slowdown in the euro area also showed clearly that the fiscal rules of the SGP are counterproductive during a slowdown and the budget rules cannot cope with the effects of recession. Moves to enforce the fiscal rules will inevitably add further deflationary pressures.

The SGP case assumes some significance over the period since 2005, but especially so since the beginning of the current crisis in August 2007. In this context, the EU package, 'European Economic Recovery Plan' (EERP), which was introduced in November 2008, indicates that a fiscal stimulus that amounted to 1.5 per cent of EU-27 GDP should be implemented in 2009,[3] and applied through national policies under their total discretion (the debt to GDP ratio is 64 per cent).[4] The plans are thereby uncoordinated. The EERP aggregate fiscal input would be consistent with the SGP deficit ceiling of 3 per cent of GDP for the euro area as a whole.

5.6 Developments since August 2007

In early August 2007, when the US subprime crisis began to spread outside mortgage and real-estate finance, central banks around the world turned their attention to enhancing the liquidity of their banking sectors. A unique element of the 'great recession' is the activist role played by central banks and Treasuries around the world. Monetary and fiscal policies were employed extensively and in an unparalleled way in the history of similar crises.

The Fed and the ECB were probably the first to commence it. The ECB began to lend to the EMU banks through the discount window or fine-tuning operations and the Fed through its repo operations. At the same time the Bank of England, Bank of Canada, and the Bank of Japan announced similar measures to address elevated pressures in the short-term funding markets. In December 2007, the Fed along with the Bank of England, Bank of Canada, the Bank of Japan, the ECB and the Swiss National Bank introduced the 'Term Auction Facility' (TAF). This is a scheme whereby the Fed, and the other central banks, auction term funds to depository institutions under collateralised agreements. Also under this scheme the Fed allows temporary dollar swaps to other central banks, so that the latter can pass on to counterparties in local operations.

The crisis worsened, especially in March 2008 and subsequently. The rescue in the USA of the investment bank, Bear Stearns, by JP Morgan with funds from the Fed was only the beginning. The rescue was justified on the argument that the Bear Stearns exposure was so extensive to third parties that a worse crisis would have developed without the bailout. It was followed by the Fed/Treasury bailout and partial nationalisation of Fannie Mae and Freddie Mac in July 2008 on the grounds that they were crucial to the functioning of the mortgage market.

In September 2008 the Fed and US Treasury allowed the investment bank Lehman Brothers to collapse in an attempt to prevent moral hazard by discouraging the belief that all insolvent institutions would be saved. Shortly afterwards, the insurance US giant American International Group (AIG) was bailed out and nationalised in an attempt to avoid the impact on insurance contracts on securities if it were allowed to fail. The Lehman Brothers incident turned the liquidity crisis into a confidence crisis, thereby causing panic in capital markets and a virtual freeze in global trade. There was a widespread collapse of confidence in the banking systems in the industrialised world, especially so in the interbank market, and with the money markets becoming dysfunctional. The transmission mechanism of monetary policy itself was thereby disrupted. That led to an unprecedented and synchronised downturn in business and consumer confidence around the world; a significant drop in aggregate demand thereby ensued. A fully-fledged global credit crunch and stock market crash emerged, as interbank lending was effectively frozen on the fear that no bank was safe anymore.

By early October 2008 the crisis had spread to Europe and to the emerging countries as the global interbank market stopped functioning.[5] The crisis prompted significant government and central bank interventions, both to restore confidence in the financial system and to contain the impact of the crisis on the real economy. Monetary and fiscal policy responses became very accommodative in many countries around the globe. At the same time, though, it became clear that macroeconomists and central bankers knew less than what they had thought they did. Central banks responded by flooding the financial markets with liquidity, while fiscal authorities attempted to deal with the decline in the solvency of the banking sector.

The European authorities also flooded the financial markets with liquidity. The ECB in the EMU pursued a slightly different approach under the banner of 'enhanced credit support' or 'liquidity-enhancing' policy.[6] The latter 'comprises non-standard measures that support financing conditions and credit flows above and beyond what could be achieved through reductions in key ECB interest rates alone' (ECB Monthly Bulletin, January, 2010, p. 68). The ECB also reluctantly reduced the repo interest rate to 1 per cent (May 2009). Banks could be certain to obtain all desired liquidity at the ECB's weekly tenders, provided that they had sufficient assets eligible as collateral in Eurosystem liquidity-providing operations. The focus has been on banks since they are the primary source of financing for the real economy in the euro area. The ECB decided that, as from 23 June 2009, it would carry out refinancing operations with a maturity of 12 months, applying a fixed rate tender with full allotment. Also, to purchase euro-denominated covered bonds issued in the euro area[7] and to grant the European Investment Bank the status of eligible counterparty in the ECB's refinancing operations. The ECB Governing Council decided, at its meeting in early December, to gradually phase out those non-standard measures, beginning in the first quarter of 2010. The reason in the view of the Governing Council is the improvement observed in the financial conditions. Money markets were performing better, so that: 'there would have been an increased risk of adverse side effects had all measures been extended in the current circumstances' (ECB Monthly Bulletin, January, 2010, p. 70). As a result of these decisions: the 12-month operations were terminated in December 2009, and the six-month operations were terminated in the first quarter of 2010. The number of three-month operations was also reduced in the first quarter of 2010; and they returned progressively to a variable tender.

In its March 2010 monthly meeting the ECB decided to restrict its unlimited liquidity facility only for short-term maturities. An EU-wide bank regulation body, the European Systemic Risk Council (ESRC), was proposed, comprising all ECB governing council and other central bankers, and managed by the ECB, while providing a critical role for the Bank of England. It was designed to issue early warning signals on risk to EU's system of financial supervision, which began to operate in 2011. Also in June 2009 and in the EU, a Pan-European Regime has been proposed to regulate the financial markets and institutions, which is to be enshrined in European law. It comprises of the European Systemic Risk Council, which will monitor financial stability, and of European Agencies, which will police the banking, securities and insurance sectors. Neither the Council nor the Agencies would have powers to dictate fiscal action in the case of financial emergency; nor can they order governments to bail out or recapitalise banks.[8]

Turning more precisely to the fiscal measures, these relate to the decisions of the G20. G20 Agreement (London, 2 April, 2009) included amongst other the following measures that are relevant to our discussion: IMF Resources: the centrepiece of the agreement, whereby a dramatic increase in the funding for the IMF is recommended – from the current \$250 billion to \$750 billion increase to enable IMF to lend to countries facing financial difficulties; the IMF to sell off gold reserves to establish a new \$50 billion fund to help developing countries; emerging countries, China for example, to be given a greater 'say' in the running of the IMF; bankers' pay: a crackdown on pay and bonuses for bankers; Global 'Quantitative Easing': the IMF will increase the amount each country has in Special Drawing Rights (SDRs) by \$250 billion; fiscal stimulus: no explicit commitment, other than to reiterate that \$5 trillion had already been pledged; and to quote from the G20 communiqué, 'deliver the scale of sustained fiscal effort necessary to restore growth'; clamp down tax heavens: countries that refuse to provide full information to foreign tax authorities to help catch potential tax evaders will face sanctions. The subsequent G20 Agreement (Pittsburgh, 25 September, 2009) decided to designate the G20 as the 'premier forum for our international cooperation', thereby establishing the new 'framework for strong, sustainable and balanced growth'. The latter objective is to be achieved: with national leaders agreeing priorities for the world economy in annual G20 summits; countries submit reports to show how their domestic policies match the G20 priorities; the IMF assesses whether national plans come together to support global objectives; the enforcement mechanism will be based on peer review with the thread of 'naming and shaming'. In fact, the G20 countries adopted fiscal measures subsequently, which saved the world from a 'second depression', which ended being a 'great recession'. But those initial promising efforts did not last for very long. Subsequent political developments emerged, which were very much along the lines of the 'New Consensus Macroeconomics' as discussed earlier in the book (see chapter 3 in particular), and have produced the poor performance of current economic activity throughout the world.

Further developments did emerge. At their meeting in Brussels on 8/9 December 2011 the European leaders agreed in principle to adopt tougher sanctions on the euro area countries that break the 'new' rules of the Stability and Growth Pact (now the so-called 'fiscal compact' (FC)). This is an intergovernmental treaty, not a change to the EU treaties (European Council, 2011a).

The Treaty on Stability Coordination and Governance (which incorporates the 'fiscal compact') was signed on the 1 March 2012 by all EU members, with the exception of the UK and the Czech Republic; further details also became available subsequently (European Union, 2012). It requires that tax and spending plans will be checked by the European officials before national governments intervene. There will be automatic actions against those countries that overspend. In effect the Fiscal Compact retains the principles of the previous 'fiscal pact' versions but with the added one that breaking the deficit rules may actually be punished in some way. The limits of the revised and old SGP are, in effect, to balance overall budget over the cycle and limit the national budget deficit in any year to a maximum of 3 per cent of GDP. In place of the previous threat of 0.2 per cent of GDP as a 'fine' (though never implemented even though there were 40 cases where the 3 per cent limit was breached), there is now a change, which is as follows: euro area states' budgets should be balanced or in surplus; this principle will be deemed respected if, as a rule, the annual structural deficit does not exceed 0.5 per cent of gross domestic product, unless the ratio of government debt to GDP is significantly below 60 per cent in which case the annual structural deficit should not exceed 1 per cent; and this is to be written into national constitutions. In the case when a euro area member state is in breach of the 3 per cent deficit ceiling, the old SGP ceiling, there will be automatic consequences, including possible sanctions, unless a qualified majority of euro area states is opposed. There is also the problem in this context, which is that it is really unbelievable to mandate in terms of the EMU countries' constitutions notions that are so vague in terms of their calculations, like 'structural deficits', 'output gaps; and 'potential GDP'. Its predecessor, the SGP did not work and there is absolutely no reason the 'fiscal compact' will work for it is not very different in any case.

The fiscal compact requires that tax and spending plans are checked by the European officials before the intervention of national governments. There are automatic actions against those countries that overspend. In effect, the new agreement tightens the rules of the old SGP, which had already been revised in 2005, but with no apparent improvement. In effect, the 'fiscal compact' retains the principles of the previous 'fiscal pact' versions but with the added one that breaking of the deficit rules may actually be punished in some way. The limits of the revised and old SGP are, in effect, to balance the overall budget over the cycle and limit the national budget deficit in any year to a maximum of 3 per cent of GDP. In place of the previous threat of 0.2 per cent of GDP as a 'fine' (albeit one that was never implemented even though there were 40 cases where the 3 per cent limit was breached), there is now a change, which is as follows: euro area states' budgets should be balanced or in surplus; this principle will be deemed respected if, as a rule, the annual structural deficit does not exceed 0.5 per cent of gross domestic product; and this is be written into national constitutions. In the case when a euro area member state is in breach of the 3per cent deficit ceiling, the old SGP ceiling, there will be automatic consequences, including possible sanctions, unless a qualified majority of euro area states is opposed.

It is readily apparent that the revised SGP did nothing to address the perceived problems of national governments with large budget deficits, which cannot be funded through the capital markets except insofar as it somehow changes the European Central Bank's attitudes to directly or indirectly funding those deficits. More seriously it does nothing to address the major problem of the Economic and Monetary Union, namely the large current account imbalances – ranging (figures for 2013) from a surplus of 6 per cent in the case of Germany to a deficit of

1.8 per cent in the case of France on a quarter-to-quarter basis. There is also the serious issue of whether existing European institutions can be used to implement what is in effect an intergovernmental treaty. The French and the Germans would like to see the European Commission and the European Court of Justice involved in enforcing and overseeing these new rules. In the words of the European Commission (2011),

> Member States in Excessive Deficit Procedure shall submit to the Commission and the Council for endorsement, an economic partnership programme detailing the necessary structural reforms to ensure an effectively durable correction of excessive deficits. The implementation of the programme, and the yearly budgetary plans consistent with it, will be monitored by the Commission and the Council. (p. 3)

Even so, the implication is that it is by far not a fiscal union arrangement.

Before writing a commitment into a national constitution, it would be worth examining whether a country can ever achieve a 'balanced structural budget'. Some countries may but others not, yet this is being imposed on all. Consider what a balanced structural budget means: at a level of output, which is deemed to be potential (or others such as corresponding to a high level of employment) government revenue and expenditure are in balance. In turn, this implies that private investment equals private savings plus capital inflow (equal to current account deficit); and that this equality holds at potential output and that the equality holds for the intention to invest and intention to save. It is not that the equality holds at some level of output but at a specified level of output. The NCM model assumes that savings intentions and investment intentions can be aligned at potential output (or full employment), but where is the evidence?

There is a clear lack of symmetry here – structural deficits cannot be more than 0.5 per cent but any level of structural surpluses is allowed. Those countries which have conditions (such as strong net exports, high rates of investment) conducive to budget surpluses can have such surpluses: those which have conditions requiring budget deficits to sustain demand (net imports, high levels of savings relative to investment), cannot deploy deficits.

This approach assumes that an upper limit of 3 per cent of GDP is consistent with a near balanced structural budget despite the swings in economic activity and associated swings in budget deficits as the automatic stabilisers take effect. As a rule of thumb a 1 per cent fall in GDP below trend leads to around a 0.7 per cent rise in the budget deficit – hence a more than 3 per cent drop in GDP before trend with a structural deficit of 0.5 per cent would lead to a country breaching the limit. Note that this is a drop in GDP below trend – and could come from an actual drop of more like 1 per cent (with a 2 per cent trend growth rate). The implication of automatic sanctions is that the sanction is applied whenever the budget deficit exceeds 3 per cent of GDP whatever the reason. A shortfall in demand, a financial crisis which brings recession, the need to respond to a national disaster are not apparently to be countenanced.

The aim of a balanced average ('structural') budget is actually a significant budget surplus when calculations are made (as they should) in real terms; that is, with allowance being made for the impact of inflation on the real value of government debt. But, more significantly, it would involve a very substantial excess of tax revenue over current government expenditure (excluding interest payments). Further, it makes no allowance for governments to be able to borrow to fund public investment. The profoundly undemocratic nature of this approach is clear: the unelected European Commission can 'request' that the elected national parliament and government to change its budget. Let us also note the problematic nature of assessment of budgets. The forecast of budget for the year ahead requires forecasts of economic variables such as growth, employment, inflation and so on for that year. The assessment of structural budget position requires estimates of potential output (which have often been subject to revisions many years after the event).

It is clear that the major objections to the 'fiscal compact', and the old SGP, is that it seeks to impose without any justification a balanced budget and that it poses restrictions in the use of fiscal policy in the face of economic crises. And, as we have argued recently, proper fiscal union is the only way forward (Arestis and Sawyer, 2012a).

It should be noted that at the EU summit of 28/29 June 2012, a 'growth pact' was proposed, which would involve the issue of 'project bonds' to finance infrastructure. €130 billion, equivalent to 1 per cent of the EU GDP, would be included in the 'growth pact'. But this amount comes from existing funds and does not represent a new economic stimulus package. The 'growth pact' would also include raising the capital base of the European Investment Bank by €10 billion in an attempt to raise its capital base (see Table 5.1, last item).

We may conclude this section by repeating what we have argued widely in this book that the major objections to the fiscal compact, and the old SGP, are that it seeks to impose without any justification a balanced budget and that it poses restrictions in the use of fiscal policy in the face of economic crises. And, as we argue in chapter 9 of this book, and also elsewhere recently, proper fiscal union is the only way forward (Arestis and Sawyer, 2011a; Arestis et al., 2013).

5.7 Summary and conclusions

Fiscal policy has been criticised for its striving for a balanced budget and the failure of the SGP to allow countries to tailor their fiscal policies to the needs of their own economies. This contribution is concerned with macroeconomic policies and the European constitution. In doing so it has attempted to throw light on a number of questions: the objectives of economic policy; the underlying 'model' of the policies, which are portrayed in the proposed EU constitution; the nature of the imposed neo-liberal agenda; the question of whether the constitution proposes a federal Europe or a collection of nation states; and the way democratic deficits might be corrected. The answers to these questions clearly suggest that changes should take place. A great deal more thinking and ingenuity are vital before a relevant and acceptable EU constitution might be acceptable.

6
Labour Markets, Employment Policies and the Single Currency

6.1 Introduction

The general focus of immediate attention, with respect to the euro single currency, is on macroeconomic issues, fiscal and monetary policy and current account imbalances. Such a focus has been prominent in this book. In this chapter we discuss some labour market and employment policy issues. We remarked in chapter 1 that labour market and employment policies are not the remit of the Economic and Monetary Union (EMU) but rather a combination of policies at the level of the European Union (EU) and policies coming under national 'competencies'. Insofar as there is coordination of policies, this largely comes under the 'open method of coordination' rather than being subordinated to EU-level decisions. However, within a currency union, some highly significant questions arise, and two related ones are the focus of attention in this chapter.

The first question concerns issues of whether coordination between national labour market and employment policies is a requirement for the successful operation of a currency union. Within a national currency union there tends to be common institutional and legal arrangements across the country, employment and labour market policies are centrally set and in that way there could be said to be coordination. But in an international currency union such as the EMU that does not necessarily apply. Within EMU there are some common policies (notably free movement of labour), and some degree of coordination of policies as just mentioned. There are many aspects of coordination, and we mention here just two of rather different dimensions. The first relates to coordination of wage policies and how far that would be a component of generating common inflation rates within the currency union, which we have argued above is necessary within a currency union but which has not been fully evident within EMU so far. The second relates to the degree to which there should be attempts to develop similar institutional and legal arrangements for the operations of the labour market across countries. The operation of macroeconomic policies at the EMU level is made more complex through the different institutional and legal arrangements.

The second question, which relates to some degree with the last point made, is the nature of employment and labour market policies at the EU and national levels, and specifically within EMU the direction of travel in terms of labour market and employment policies. There have been frequent calls from institutions such as the ECB for 'more flexible labour markets' and for 'structural reforms'. These calls have been reflected in the nature of the policies being imposed on member countries such as Greece as part of the financial rescue packages. In the Treaty on Stability, Coordination and Governance there is specific mention of the need for 'structural reforms', although there is little attempt to define within the Treaty what is meant by 'structural reforms'. However, it would be reasonable to regard those 'structural reforms' as in the direction of deregulation, liberalisation, the reduction of trade union rights, diminished social protection and minimum wages and so on (as further discussed below). The Treaty threatens to impose 'structural reforms' whether or not they are appropriate to the institutional, social and political arrangements of the country concerned. It has yet to be established that a neo-liberal agenda is the appropriate one for all countries (and whether it would be acceptable to the peoples of the countries). A general question to be raised here relates to the implicit view that there is a single 'best' model which is appropriate for all countries no matter what their previous policies, institutions and traditions. In this chapter we specifically address another question, namely whether there is any evidence to support the view that the type of 'structural reforms' which the EMU, ECB and the Treaty promotes would bring improved economic performance.

Within the Optimal Currency Area (OCA) perspective, the question with regard to the labour market is whether in the face of 'shocks' there will be relative wages and prices responses and the movement of labour. A negative 'shock' to an economy would be seen to involve a decrease in wages in the country concerned (relative to wages in other countries), decrease in relative prices, and the movement of labour from areas of low demand to areas of high demand. In other words, the question is whether the labour (and other) markets will respond in the ways envisaged in neoclassical competitive labour market theory.

However, underlying debates over the single currency, which invoke OCA arguments, are considerations drawn from the labour market in terms of wage flexibility and labour migration. These considerations relate (as seen in chapter 2) to the degree to which an economy (and specifically here the labour market) responds to 'shocks' through price and quantity adjustments. Further, a similar inflationary experience across member countries is viewed as required for the sustainability of the currency union (for otherwise prices in one member country would rise relative to those in other countries), and hence there are implications for the rate of increase of wages relative to labour productivity. Unit labour costs are, by definition, wages divided by output, and rate of increase of unit labour costs (in nominal terms) is equal to the rate of increase of wages minus the rate of increase of labour productivity. These latter two terms may not be independent of one another – for example, a fast rate of overall growth may foster relative fast increases in wages and in productivity.

This simple formula suggests that over any significant period of time, wage inflation can only differ between countries to the degree to which labour productivity growth differs, or otherwise there will be substantial changes in the pattern of competitiveness. And indeed in chapter 2 above we suggested that there had been these substantial shifts in competitiveness with consequent effects on current account imbalances. The rates of increase of wages and of productivity will be strongly influenced by the ways in which the labour market is structured and operates, though as will be seen below there are strongly conflicting views on the labour market structures which are conducive to wage increases in line with productivity and to growth of productivity. The operation of a 'one size fits all' policy (as is monetary policy in a single currency) relies on the policy instrument having similar impacts across the countries of the currency area. In the EMU case, the specific example is the operation of monetary policy designed to control inflation, and the transmission mechanism of monetary policy includes the effects which aggregate demand (assumed to be influenced by interest rate) has on inflation, and the structure and operation of the labour market can be a significant element in the effects (if any) of demand (for labour) on wage inflation.

There is something of a paradox at the heart of the currency union. When two (or more) countries come together in a customs union (or indeed any form of lowering trade barriers), then the gains from the customs union depend on the degrees of differences between the countries concerned. In a simple model of trade, the gains from trade come from specialisation by the countries involved in the areas of production in which they have a comparative advantage, and the extent of the benefits will depend on the degree to which the countries differ in their comparative advantages. If countries were very similar in the range of product which they produced and in the relative costs of production, then there would be little to gain from trade and specialisation. But in the context of a currency union, differences in the structure of economies make the currency union more problematic. One major issue on which we focus later in this chapter is then the significance of the clear differences between the EMU member countries with regard to labour market institutions and their operations, and more generally differences in policy perspectives in that regard. These differences may well be reflected in, for example, the inflationary processes, the general speed of inflation and the responsiveness (or otherwise) of wage inflation to changes in interest rates.

It would be trite to observe that countries have differing histories, in this context relating to employment relations, wage determination and so on. With regard to the Economic and Monetary Union with its membership grown to 17 (and even more the case of the European Union with its expansion to 28 members) a highly pertinent question is how differing modes of employment and wage determination interact in the context of a single market and currency.

The detailed specifics of labour market structures will necessarily differ across countries. The question here is whether those differing labour market structures are in effect such as to represent different 'models' of the labour market. If they do, the questions we would then ask are: (i) how can an overarching set of policies with regard to the labour market be imposed which respects the basic differences?; (ii) does this mean that the different labour markets behave in some quantitatively important different ways? In this context this would include in terms of wage and employment determination.

There are clearly major institutional and political differences between the labour markets, employment relations and wage determination processes of the member countries of EMU (and EU). An illustration of that comes from the classification into different types of labour market arrangements which have been attempted.

Van Veen (2006, Table 6.2, p.115), for example, identifies four types of labour market models, namely:

(i) 'Nordic or social democratic model', which has centralization of wage bargaining with 'relatively high level of employment protection and high levels of social security benefits' ;

(ii) 'Continental European or conservative corporatist model' with social security safety nets and institutions to dampen class conflict (and Austria, Germany and the Netherlands are given as examples);
(iii) 'Mediterranean model or traditional rudimentary model' with low labour market regulation and low social security benefits (with Greece, Portugal amongst those given as examples);
(iv) 'Anglo-Saxon model or liberalist-individualistic model' with decentralised wage bargaining and relatively low levels of employment protection (the UK is given as the example within the European Union).

The 'varieties of capitalism' literature provides a strong argument that there are major differences in institutional arrangements and policy approaches between market capitalist economies. Amable (2003), for example, provides a five-way classification, of which the first four are relevant for EMU: market-based Continental European capitalism, Social Democratic economics, Southern European capitalism and Asian capitalism.

In the context of a single currency and the associated single monetary policy, the differences illustrated can have macroeconomic implications. The theory of inflation targeting (as outlined in chapter 4) is that the policy interest rate is set so as to influence economic activity and thereby inflation. The ways in which wages are determined and the manner in which the level of demand may (or may not) influence the rate of wage inflation (and then the rate of price inflation, which will, of course, be influenced by many other factors including international inflation) are not clear. The effects of the policy interest rate (as set by the ECB) will likely vary between countries, exacerbating the 'one size fits all' problem of monetary policy which we have mentioned above. As we have seen in chapter 2 there were significant differences in the rates of inflation between EMU member countries, though that may not necessarily be ascribed to the differences in labour market institutions (albeit that the low growth of wages in Germany and the associated changes in competitiveness may well be ascribed to the German labour market institutions and the wage policies of the German government (Hein and Mundt, 2012)). We have mentioned the implications of these inflationary differences for the real interest rates (being lower in countries with higher inflation) and for the evolution of competitiveness and the current account imbalances.

6.2 Labour market institutions and unemployment

There are major differences in the ways in which economists (and others) have viewed the interactions between labour market institutions and the levels of employment and unemployment and wage determination, which are relevant for the operations of a currency union and policies to be adopted. We express those differences along the following lines:

Insofar as there is a rate of unemployment which is consistent with a constant rate of inflation, the forces determining such a rate of unemployment are viewed rather differently: the term non-accelerating inflation rate of unemployment (NAIRU) is generally used though we prefer a more neutral term such as inflation barrier. The first approach to be identified views the conditions in the labour market as setting the NAIRU. The 'natural rate of unemployment' can be seen as a forerunner of this view when Friedman (1968) envisaged the natural rate as 'the level that would be ground out by the Walrasian system of general equilibrium equations, provided there is embedded in them the actual structural characteristics of the labour and commodity markets, including market imperfections, stochastic variability in demands and supplies, the cost of gathering information about job vacancies and labor availabilities, the costs of mobility, and so on' (p. 8).

The 'New Consensus Macroeconomics' (NCM) portrayed a supply side in which inflation responds to demand and in which there is a supply-side equilibrium consistent with constant inflation and an equilibrium which is seen as generating desirable outcomes. Insofar as the supply-side equilibrium is one of significant unemployment of labour, the blame is laid at the feet of inflexible labour markets. The NCM which we elaborated on in chapter 2 as having a close correspondence with the policy framework of the EMU asserts that there is a supply-side equilibrium which is consistent with constant inflation. In the model presented in chapter 2 that equilibrium corresponds to a zero output gap where actual and trend output are equal to each other. In relationship to the supply-side equilibrium in spite of the way it is represented in the NCM the predominant approach has been to talk in terms of concepts such as the NAIRU in which the position of the supply-side equilibrium depends on the characteristics of the labour market. It is then asserted that a high rate of unemployment associated with a NAIRU is the consequence of overregulated labour markets: the regulations range from minimum wages, through trade union rights, limitations on firing and on the use of temporary workers.

In developments such as Layard et al. (1991), features of the labour market such as trade union density and industrial relations legislation, the level of unemployment benefits, minimum wages and so on serve to impact on the level of the NAIRU. Further, there is the postulate that higher trade union density, industrial relations legislation, which limits rights of employers to fire workers ('employment protection laws'), higher and/or more extensive minimum wages, higher unemployment benefits (relative to average wages) would all serve to raise the NAIRU.

The second approach places emphasis on the role of the amount of productive capacity of the economy as a limiting factor on the levels of employment and economic activity, and the interaction of price and wage determination in the inflationary process. The inflation barrier is not only a level of economic activity at which (it is postulated) inflation would be constant, but also wages and prices would be rising at a rate, which differs by the rate of increase of productivity and hence the distribution of income between wages and profits constant. When demand in the economy is high relative to the productive capacity, prices can be expected to rise as unit costs are high and profit margins rising, and in that manner the scale of productive capacity will impact on the 'inflation barriers'. Further, as investment is ongoing, the productive capacity is ever-changing, and the rate of investment (relative to depreciation and scrapping of existing capital stock) will influence whether productive capacity is expanding. The alternative view is that a 'poor' supply-side equilibrium results from a lack of productive potential. We have argued (Arestis and Sawyer, 2005), as a number of other authors have, that any inflation barrier should be viewed in terms of a lack of productive capacity (relative to that which would be required to sustain full employment of labour). Any inflation barrier may be described as a NAIRU but it is important to distinguish between the different perceptions of the underlying determinants. The crucial elements of the view here is that the level of aggregate demand is always important for the determination of the level of economic activity and hence employment, and that investment adds to productive capacity, which is continuously changing and thereby the positioning of the inflation barrier is changing. Periods of recession have long-term effects through the suppression of investment and thereby the size of the capital stock.

Both approaches can involve what is often termed hysteresis effects though those effects are rather stronger and more self-evident in the second approach. These hysteresis effects, whereby the level of demand and the experiences of unemployment and low economic activity impact on the NAIRU, 'inflation barrier' arise in two broad ways. The experience of unemployment, particularly long-term unemployment, can lead to loss of skills and detachment from the workforce. Low levels of demand are associated with low levels of investment, and subsequent lower (than otherwise) capital stock (Sawyer, 2002).

These two broad approaches point towards rather different policy perspectives. The first approach focuses on the labour market, with the policy agenda of labour market 'reforms' (meaning reducing the power and influence of organised labour, and lowering minimum wages and social security benefits). The second approach would place more emphasis on developing the productive capacity (and its distribution across all regions), and less on the labour market. But even when the labour market is viewed as significant, it would not assume that deregulated labour markets would necessarily be more conducive for a low level of unemployment for reasons which are akin to those discussed below.

(ii) At the risk of gross oversimplification, we can identify two broad views on what type of labour market arrangements are conducive to good economic performance (and what is deemed to constitute good performance differs also). One broad view would envisage that a competitive labour market, which approximates the conditions envisaged in a perfectly competitive vision of the economy, would be conducive for good economic performance. Wages would be set in a flexible manner by the interaction of demand and supply, bringing the labour market into equilibrium. Relative wages would adjust to ensure that there is a balance between demand and supply, and that labour is efficiently allocated between different sectors and between different skill levels and so on. Overall, there would be a balance between demand for and supply of labour, which in effect would mean full employment (in that all those who seek work at the going wage would be employed). This approach would emphasise the roles of flexibility of relative wages, the determination of wages without intervention of government (in say the form of minimum wage legislation) and without trade unions and collective bargaining, and the allocative function of relative wages with movement of labour from low-demand to high-demand sectors.

The other broad view would emphasise the positive role of secure employment and long-term contracts, supported by employment protection legislation. The encouragement for training and skill formation, the push for higher productivity rather than lower wages as the way to reduce unit labour costs and so on, would feature here. Further, trade union involvement, worker representation can have positive effects on issues such as work organisation, skill formation and so on. Higher wages encourage capital–labour substitution, raising labour productivity and induced technical change. Long-term contractual relationships encourage commitment and loyalty, and the development and retention of idiosyncratic knowledge. See, for example, Vergeer and Kleinknecht (2010) for arguments along these lines.

These differences of approach have relevance for debates within the EU and EMU and can be related to the idea of a Social Europe The term European Social Model (and similar phrases such as Social Europe) does not have a universally accepted meaning, and it could be said (whether as something, which actually exists or as an aspiration) to have the feature of standing in contrast with the American model (or perhaps the Anglo-Saxon one). However, 'although the [European Social Model] is far from being a well-developed analytical concept, in essence it is characterised by three main features: The universalistic character of welfare provision, a high degree of coordination between economic actors, the acknowledgement that workers need special protection and have a right to collective interest representation, and widespread public ownership, especially in public services' (Hermann, 2009, p. 88). An alternative expression is

> one of the central tenets of the ESM [European Social Model] involves the creation of social partnership between employer and employee representatives in order to develop positive sum solutions to issues pertaining to industrial relations. Social partnership between peak level actors is, additionally, intended to develop a wider legitimacy for the EU's decision-making process, and tailor directives to meet the requirements of those most closely affected by work-related relations. (Whyman et al., 2012, p. 222)

The ESM has strong overtones of what was seen as the German model.

> At the core of what was long described as the German variant of 'coordinated' or 'Rhenish' capitalism was a combination of economic dynamism and relatively little social inequality. Until about 20 years ago, institutions such as the industrial relations system, labour legislation and the welfare state helped the economy as a whole, as well as large swathes of society to benefit from the success of its export-oriented industry that was based on high value added and high-quality

manufacturing, and reliant on 'patient capital' and skilled employees. (Lehndorff, 2012, p. 79)

Following from the quote given above, Whyman et al. (2012) state that 'this model of inclusivity is contrasted against another stated aim advanced by the EU in the years since the production of the Lisbon Treaty, namely the promotion of a more flexible labour market' (p. 222). Lehndorff (2012) continues from the quote above by speaking of 'today's German model of capitalism – a hybrid consisting of a few preserved components of 'Rhenish capitalism', neoliberal-inspired reconstructions and demolitions of this classic model over the past 20 years, along with stubborn refusals to reform the conservative welfare State' (p. 97). The ESM (or since each country has its own 'model' perhaps social models) may lack a precise definition but the general contours of such a notion are there (as reflected in the quote from Hermann, 2009, above). The key question which is to be addressed is how the ideas associated with the term European Social Model relate to the Economics and Monetary Union and the policies being advocated there and to the more general policy approaches of the European Union. As suggested in the quote from Whyman et al. (2012) above, and becomes evident in the proposals on a 'fiscal compact', the policy drive is much more in the direction which may be described as neo-liberal, deregulation of labour markets and the advocacy of 'flexible labour markets'.

6.3 Labour market 'reforms'

The 'fiscal compact' incorporates not only the constraints on budget deficits but also a call for 'structural reforms'. Under Article 5 of Treaty on Stability, Coordination and Governance 'A Contracting Party that is subject to an excessive deficit procedure under the Treaties on which the European Union is founded shall put in place a budgetary and economic partnership programme including a detailed description of the structural reforms which must be put in place and implemented to ensure an effective and durable correction of its excessive deficit' (p. 14).

Mario Draghi, president of the ECB, stated that the most important structural reforms were

first is the product and services markets reform. And the second is the labour market reform which takes different shapes in different countries. In some of them one has to make labour markets more flexible and also fairer than they are today. In these countries there is a dual

> labour market: highly flexible for the young part of the population where labour contracts are three-month, six-month contracts that may be renewed for years. The same labour market is highly inflexible for the protected part of the population where salaries follow seniority rather than productivity.[1]

This echoes the sentiments which have been repeatedly expressed by the European Central Bank in the various issue of their *Monthly Bulletin*. The ECB has been at the forefront of calling for more 'flexible' labour markets and for changes in the pension arrangements. For example,

> The Governing Council [of the ECB]...urges all euro area governments to decisively and swiftly implement substantial and comprehensive structural reforms. This will help these countries to strengthen competitiveness, increase the flexibility of their economies and enhance their longer-term growth potential. In this respect, labour market reforms are key, with a focus on the removal of rigidities and the implementation of measures which enhance wage flexibility. In particular, there is a need for the elimination of automatic wage indexation clauses and a strengthening of firm-level agreements so that wages and working conditions can be tailored to firms' specific needs. These measures should be accompanied by structural reforms that increase competition in product markets, particularly in services – including the liberalisation of closed professions – and, where appropriate, the privatisation of services currently provided by the public sector, thereby facilitating productivity growth and supporting competitiveness. (ECB, 2011, p. 7)

It is almost self-evident that one would want to be 'flexible', for who would wish to be seen as 'inflexible'? But if other words were used, such as volatile wages, uncertain employment, then it would not be so self-evident. The more serious point to make here is that 'flexible' (or similar) can have a number of meanings in the context of labour markets. It can refer to the market being rather like that portrayed in neoclassical economics as akin to what may be described as a spot market – that is when there is any change in demand and supply conditions then wages adjust accordingly in the context where individuals are hired on a short-term basis with rapid adjusting wages. It can be taken to refer to low or no costs associated with hiring and firing. But flexible can also relate to what is termed functional flexibility – the ability of an individual to move from one task to another; at another level the facility for a worker to retrain when the job requirements change or when the demand for the skills which the worker possessed declines. Although there is range of meanings which can be associated with 'flexible labour markets', the intention of authors such as the ECB can reasonably be taken to mean the direction towards the greater movements in wages and employment.

6.4 European labour market and employment policies

The Economic and Monetary Union has, in general, said little about labour market and employment policies, although as noted below the ECB has often pontificated on the need for labour market reforms, and 'structural reforms' feature in the fiscal compact. Insofar as there are labour market and employment policies for EMU countries coming from a central federal level they are those of the EU and its employment strategy, but that of course is at the EU level rather than the EMU level. The EU does have a Directorate of Employment, Social Affairs and Inclusion, and its title is suggestive of a broader approach than that of the structural reform agenda of the 'fiscal compact'.[2] And as Grahl (2006) argues,

> Labour market policies have a specific place in the EU, in that they represent an intermediate zone between the economic sphere where the EU has extensive powers and the sphere of social policy where member states retain almost complete competence. It is also the case that the doctrines which inform these policies are an amalgam – although neoliberal conceptions have predominated since the 1980s, there are also commitments to social partnership, social dialogue and, more recently, to the "European Social Model" (ESM) which are certainly more than cosmetic and which have influenced both the form and its content of EU labour market policies. (p. 170)

The European Employment Strategy is viewed as providing a framework for EU countries with regard to employment policies, and through the 'open method of coordination') for the sharing of information, discussion and coordination of their employment policies.[3]

Within the Europe 2020 Strategy, the Employment Strategy is intended 'to create more and better jobs throughout the EU' (European Employment Strategy web page). In order to reach such an objective, the EES encourages measures to meet three headline targets by 2020:

- 75 % of people aged 20–64 in **work**;
- school dropout rates below 10%, and at least 40% of 30–34-year-olds completing third level education;
- at least 20 million fewer people in or at risk of **poverty** and social exclusion' (emphasis in original).

These constitute three of the five Europe 2020 targets, with the other two being 3 per cent of EU GDP invested in research and development, and greenhouse gas emissions 20 per cent (or 30 per cent if conditions are right) lower than 1990 with 20 per cent of energy from renewable and a 20 per cent increase in energy efficiency (these being group under climate change/energy).

These are laudable targets which raise rather fundamental questions, namely are the policies being actually pursued conducive to their attainment, and in the present context will the employment and labour market policies being advocated by the EC (and more particularly by EMU) contribute to their achievement. The guidelines of employment policies (European Union, 2010) highlights four, namely:

> Guideline 7: Increasing labour market participation of women and men, reducing structural unemployment and promoting job quality;
> Guideline 8: Developing a skilled workforce responding to labour market needs and promoting lifelong learning;
> Guideline 9: Improving the quality and performance of education and training systems at all levels and increasing participation in tertiary or equivalent education;
> Guideline 10: Promoting social inclusion and combating poverty.

It is under guideline 7 that there is most evidence of a neo-liberal thrust to the policy guidelines. It argues that

> Member States should integrate the flexicurity principles ... Member States should therefore introduce a combination of flexible and reliable contractual arrangements, active labour market policies, effective lifelong learning, policies to promote labour mobility, and adequate social security systems to secure labour market transitions accompanied by clear rights and responsibilities for the unemployed to

actively seek work. ... Policies to make work pay remain important. In order to increase competitiveness and raise participation levels, particularly for the low-skilled, and in line with economic policy guideline 2, Member States should encourage the right framework conditions for wage bargaining and labour cost development consistent with price stability and productivity trends. Member States should review tax and benefit systems, and public services capacity to provide the support needed, in order to increase labour force participation and stimulate labour demand.' But this is 'modified' by 'together with the social partners, adequate attention should also be paid to internal flexicurity at the work place. Member States should step up social dialogue and tackle labour market segmentation with measures addressing precarious employment, underemployment and undeclared work. ... Member States should combat in-work poverty and promote occupational health and safety. Adequate social security should also be ensured for those on fixed-term contracts and the self-employed. (European Union, 2010).

A central feature of the EU general approach to labour markets has become 'flexicurity', which is seen as

a new way of looking at flexibility and security on the labour market. It sets out from the awareness that globalisation and technological progress are rapidly changing the needs of workers and enterprises. Companies are under increasing pressure to adapt and develop their products and services more quickly. If they want to stay in the market, they have to continuously adapt their production methods and their workforce. This is placing greater demands on business to help their workers acquire new skills. It is also placing greater demands on workers with regards to their ability and readiness for change ... Flexicurity promotes a combination of flexible labour markets and a high level of employment and income security and it is thus seen to be the answer to the EU's dilemma of how to maintain and improve competitiveness whilst preserving the European social model.

Flexicurity can be defined, more precisely, as a policy strategy to enhance, at the same time and in a deliberate way, the flexibility of labour markets, work organisations and labour relations on the one hand, and security – employment security and income security – on the other (http://ec.europa.eu/social/main.jsp?catId=116&langId=en; see also 'Towards Common Principles of Flexicurity: More and Better Jobs Through Flexibility and Security', EC, 2007).

However, it is recognised that 'each Member State has a specific labour market situation and culture. The European Commission is therefore not aiming for a one-size- fits-all 'flexicurity recipe' for all Member States, but rather to establish 'pathways' to be developed towards achieving more flexicurity. Pathways are sets of measures that can, if introduced in conjunction with each other, improve a country's performance in terms of flexicurity.' A number of pathways are set out: (i) tackling contractual segmentation; (ii) developing flexicurity within the enterprise and offering transition security; (iii) tackling skills and opportunity gaps among the workforce; and (iv) improving opportunities for benefit recipients and informally employed workers (http://ec.europa.eu/social/main.jsp?catId=117&langId=en).

These remarks are only intended to illustrate some aspects of employment and labour market policies coming from the EC and EU. For the purposes of the discussion of the euro, we would make three sets of comments. The first is that the labour market policies of the EU are difficult to categorise in terms of, for example, being neo-liberal or not, and – as briefly indicated – contains many competing elements. It is also seen that these policies are subject to the 'open method of coordination' which relies more on peer pressure than legislation. It is, of course, the case that the EMU countries are only a subset of the EU, and as such these labour market policies apply to all countries rather than being tailored to the requirements of a single currency.

The second is that whilst the EU has set an employment rate target, the route to its achievement is intended to be labour market policies rather than attention to demand factors and the creation of productive capacity. It is perhaps not surprising that an employment strategy should emphasise labour market policies, rather than the creation of productive capacity. But within the European policy framework much less attention is paid to the level and distribution of investment. Further, and particularly relevant for the operation of the single currency, there are no policies which address the coordination of wage inflation and the evolution of unit labour costs.

The third is that the nature of the 'fiscal compact' represents a considerable departure as far as the EMU countries are concerned with regard to labour market policies in two important respects. First, the implementation of 'structural reforms' in a particular country can be dictated by EMU as whole. Second, the policies associated with the term 'structural reform' represent a big step in the direction of neo-liberal 'flexible labour markets' and away from the type of policies associated with the term European Social Model.

In the next section, we consider the evidence with regard to 'flexible labour markets' and levels of employment and unemployment. It is clear that underlying the drive for 'structural reforms' is an implicit view of what constitutes 'good' labour market policies and what constitute 'bad' ones, with the 'flexible labour market' falling into the 'good' category. The evidence in the next section challenges that view, and hence whether 'labour market reforms' can indeed bring higher rates of employment. In the subsequent section, we consider some of the differences in labour market institutions and perspectives on policies between the member states of EMU.

6.5 Do more 'flexible' labour markets lead to better economic performance?

This advocacy of labour market 'reforms' is consistent with the theoretical framework, which has been discussed in chapter 3, in which it can be seen that demand has no long-lasting effects on output, and in which the supply side of the economy is viewed to determine the level of economic activity. It is a stage further to argue that relevant changes in the labour market will lead to changes in the level of unemployment but a stage which is often followed. But the evidence that labour market 'flexibility' favourably impacts on the level of employment is weak. It must be noted here that labour market 'flexibility' is used here to mean lack of regulation and the promotion of wage and employment flexibility in the face of demand shocks (which may be more pejoratively be labelled as 'hire and fire' mentality). As noted above, there are other notions of flexibility (such as functional flexibility) which are valuable but do not come under the heading of 'flexibility' here.

The first point to note is that notions of labour market 'flexibility' do not fit well with the experiences of unemployment within the European Union. It would generally be seen that the direction of travel in terms of labour market regulation has been in the direction of deregulation. After the formation of the euro, as figures in chapter 2 indicate, unemployment did indeed generally fall, but those falls were quickly reversed with the onset of the financial crisis, and more 'flexible' labour markets have not prevented unemployment in 2012 standing at higher figures (in general, Germany being an exception) than in the late 1990s. Further, unemployment varies between and within countries. The inter-country comparisons do not readily support any idea that more 'flexible' labour markets are associated with lower unemployment: the rate of unemployment in the EU countries in 2004 ranged from 4.5 per cent in Ireland, 4.6 per cent in the Netherlands to 11.5 per cent in Spain: in 2012 it ranged from over 26 per cent in Greece and Spain to under 5 per cent in Austria, where the correlation between unemployment and labour market 'rigidity' is not self-evident. For example, Tridico (2012) concludes 'that countries which performed better during the economic crisis of 2007–2011 are countries which do not have a flexible labour market and have managed to keep stable employment levels. These countries combine a very good mix of economic policies and social institutions oriented to stabilize the level of consumption and the aggregate demand. Coordination mechanisms, higher level of financial regulation and monitoring are also important features of these economies. Clearly, this group of countries identifies better, in the EU, a coordinated market economy model' (p. 1).

The intra-country comparisons of unemployment between regions indicate substantial variations. There is a wide range of unemployment within a country (e.g. Spain where in 2004 it varied from 5.5 per cent in Comunidad Foral de Navarra to 17.1 per cent in Andalucia, and in 2011 from 12 per cent in Pais Vasco through to 30 per cent in Andalucia). These variations of unemployment cannot in general be explained by appeals to differences in the degree of 'flexibility' of labour market (or other differences in labour market institutions) since there are broad similarities across the regions. It is generally the case that employment laws, regulation and deregulation of labour markets, organisation of trade unions apply at the national level, and hence are effectively the same for each region. But there are large differences in regional unemployment.

The rate of unemployment also differs significantly amongst countries, and on average remained over 7½ per cent throughout the 2000s. By 2012 it had reached near 12 per cent across the euro area confounding those who claimed that 'Employment has risen by almost 15% since the launch of the single currency while unemployment has fallen to about 7% of the labour force, the lowest rate in more than fifteen years.... The bulk of these improvements reflect reforms of both labour markets and social security systems carried out under the Lisbon Strategy for Growth and Jobs and the coordination and surveillance framework of EMU, as well as the wage moderation that has characterised most euro area countries' (European Commission 2008, p. 6).

A study by Baker et al. (2002) provides empirical evidence on labour market regulations and unemployment for 20 OECD countries spanning the 40 years 1960–99. Different time periods are utilised and different combinations of variables. The most comprehensive measure of labour market institutions and policies utilised can only account for a minor part of the differences in the evolution of unemployment. The evidence in Baker et al. (2002) provides little or no support for the labour market rigidity, and in general for labour market institutions, explanations. An index of the extent of labour market deregulation in the 1990s is constructed, but this variable too, showed no meaningful relationship between labour market deregulation and shifts in the NAIRU. The same study poses the question of 'reverse causality' in the studies they discuss, to conclude that 'While clearly not universal, this evidence of reverse causation provides serious grounds for viewing test results showing a correlation between high unemployment and long benefit duration' (p. 28). Glyn et al. (2006) found the evidence linking 'various indicators of the implementation of labor market reforms and unemployment' to be unconvincing (p. 20). This was following up on Baker et al. (2004, 2005) studies, which have challenged the robustness of the findings that 'rigidity effects of labor market institutions explain the pattern of unemployment across developed countries' (Glyn et al., 2006, pp. 20–1). They conclude that

> proponents of labor market deregulation have not produced robust evidence of systematic positive effects of their proposed reforms on cross-country employment performance, though this result has evidently not dimmed the confidence with which such reforms are promoted.... Deregulationists often argue that demonstrating any negative effect of labor market institutions on the unemployment rate is sufficient to pare back or eliminate those institutions. In fact, since these institutions typically provide substantial economic and social benefits, the burden of proof should be set much higher. (pp. 20–1).

Palley (2001), by accounting for micro- and macroeconomic factors, and also for cross-country economic spillovers, concludes that unemployment in Europe emanates from 'self-inflicted dysfunctional macroeconomic policy' (p. 3).

Palley (2001) seeks to account for a range of microeconomic labour market institutional and macroeconomic variables in exploring unemployment for a range of European countries. He concludes that

> the evidence clearly shows that macroeconomic factors matter for unemployment, and these factors are robust to changes in the empirical specification of the model. However, when it comes to microeconomic factors the evidence is much more problematic. The level of

> wage bargaining coordination and the extent of union coverage matter consistently, but they need not raise unemployment if they are appropriately paired. The level of benefit duration and the level of union density are both consistently insignificant. The significance of other microeconomic variables (employment protection, replacement rate, tax burden) is unstable and not robust to changes in specification. (Palley, 2001, p. 5)

Baccaro and Rei (2006) summarise their empirical results as follows: they provide

> very little support for the view that one could reduce unemployment simply by getting rid of institutional rigidities. We find that an increase in interest rates raises unemployment and that countries that augment the level of independence of their central bank end up augmenting the unemployment rate as well. Changes in employment protection, benefit replacement rates and tax wedge do not seem to have a significant impact on unemployment. The one institutional variable we find to be positively associated with changes in unemployment is the union density variable. Other interesting results from our analysis concern the bargaining coordination variable, which turns out to be mostly an insignificant predictor when fixed effects are controlled for, in contrast with most literature that attributes to it a negative impact on unemployment. (p. 150)

An OECD (1999) study is more damning to the 'labour-market-flexibility' thesis. It covers the period late 1980s to late 1990s and utilises new and improved data on employment legislation in 27 OECD countries. It utilises multiple regression analysis and techniques, so that it is able 'to control for other factors that can influence unemployment' (p. 88). The study demonstrates that employment protection legislation (a measure of labour market flexibility) has small or no impact at all on total unemployment.[4] Consequently, dismantling employment protection would not solve the current unemployment malaise in the 27 countries considered in the study.

A recent OECD study (OECD, 2012) is more sympathetic to a structural reform agenda, but concludes that 'the benefits from reforms often take time to materialise', though 'concerns about possible negative short-term effects of structural reforms seem exaggerated'. However, 'cyclical conditions matter for the short-term effects of reforms. There is some evidence that in 'bad times', certain labour market reforms (of unemployment benefit systems and job protection in particular) can make the economic situation temporarily worse. In still depressed economies, such reforms would therefore be more quickly beneficial if carried out only once the labour market shows clear signs of recovery. In view of wide remaining spare capacity, constrained macroeconomic policies and impaired fiscal positions in most OECD countries, policy priority should be given to reforms that offer comparatively strong short-term gains, especially in terms of strengthening the jobs recovery' (OECD, 2012, p. 166) with the promotion of active labour market policies.

Many of the measures associated with labour flexibility (such as a more stringent approach to unemployment benefits, reduction of minimum wages) would tend to reduce the wage share in national income, tend to depress demand and to increase the budget deficit. The budget deficit could then only be expected to decline (following a more 'flexible' labour market) if an investment boom were stimulated. A similar argument is deployed by Tridico (2012) in relating labour market flexibility with the financial crisis.

> The flexibility agenda of the labour market and the end of wage increases...diminished workers' purchasing power. This was partly compensated with increased borrowing opportunities and the boom of credit consumption, all of which helped workers to maintain unstable consumption capacity. However, in the long term, unstable consumption patterns derived from precarious job creation, job instability and poor wages have weakened aggregate demand. Hence, labour market issues such as flexibility, uneven income distribution, poor wages and the financial crisis are two sides of the same coin. (p. 17)

Our conclusions echo those of Whyman et al. (2012) (based on literature which substantially overlaps with those we have cited above) when they write that 'there are a large number of studies which have found little or no significant impact arising from labour market deregulation' (p. 229).

The European Commission (2008) sums up by suggesting that

> the assessment of whether the single currency led to less or more progress with structural reforms depends largely on the data source used. OECD and Eurostat data do not replicate the negative impact of the single currency emerging from the BEPGs and Fraser indicators. Obviously, the small size of the control groups constitutes a severe

> handicap, and no sweeping conclusions can be drawn. Even so, from the findings can be safely inferred that there is no overwhelming evidence of the 'TINA' argument that giving up of the exchange rate and interest rate instruments in EMU would spontaneously produce incentives for structural reform so as to heighten the flexibility of markets in the pursuit of alternative adjustment mechanisms. There is no evidence that this has occurred, which is of concern given the sizable reform needs. (p. 92)

A later European Commission (2012b) study also suggests that

> All employment and social indicators point to a growing divergence between the Southern and peripheral European countries, that seem to be trapped in a vicious circle of recession, while most of the countries of Northern and Central Europe have so far shown greater resilience. Part of this is driven by how the economy has performed overall but much of the overall performance is the result of how labour markets and social systems reacted to the severe global downturn. The shockwaves from the crisis appear to be asymmetric but the different institutional setups saw very different resistance to the generally experienced major shock from the initial financial crisis: very often countries with relatively un-segmented labour markets and strong welfare systems have fared better than those with highly segmented labour markets and weak welfare provisions. The (in)ability to cope with the shock was frequently compounded by the initial public debt and deficit levels, as well as the property market situation, and subsequent developments followed by the reaction of financial market. (p. 17)

The same study goes on to argue that

> In the area of labour market policies, feasible fields for action include minimum wages, taxation and social spending and all involve rebalancing in one form or another. On wages, the action would involve raising or introducing minimum wages and greater social partners involvement through exchanging views on wage developments at European level. Taxation measures would see rebalancing within income tax shifting the burden from the lower paid to the higher wage earners and rebalancing taxation away from labour onto property and onto environmental 'bads'. Social spending would be rebalanced to improve efficiency in terms of reducing inequality. More

> generally, a social investment approach to social protection expenditure would be taken. (p. 49)

Vergeer and Kleinknecht (2010) address the issue of the effects of labour market deregulation on productivity across a panel of 19 OECD countries. They conclude that the 'Superior growth of labor input in flexible Anglo-Saxon economies is *not* due to superior GDP growth. Over a long period (1960–95), it has been due to a lower growth of labor productivity when compared to 'rigid' European economies' (p. 391). Only after 1995 did the picture change as the ICT boom enhanced US labour productivity growth. At the same time, several European countries experienced a worsening labour productivity performance as they gradually engaged in wage-cost saving flexibilisation of their labour markets. These authors note that

> the call for more flexible labor markets is one for lower wages. It is interesting to confront such claims to evidence from micro-data. For example, firm-level estimates in the Netherlands show that firms employing high shares of flexible personnel pay lower wages and flexible workers earn less per hour, compared to similar workers with tenured jobs. Estimates of sales equations, however, also show that firms with high shares of flexible labor do *not* conquer market shares from 'rigid' firms—in spite of paying lower wages. The explanation is that firms with plenty of flexible labor realize lower productivity gains (Kleinknecht et al. 2006). ... Clearly, downward wage flexibility is paying less than expected: lower wages are, to a significant degree, compensated by lower labor productivity gains. (p. 394)

In this section, we have summarised a range of evidence which runs against the idea that the route to higher employment and better economic performance is labour market deregulation and 'flexibility'. This should, at a minimum, raise serious questions on the desirability of a rush to 'structural reforms' within the 'fiscal compact'.

6.6 Concluding remarks

From the discussion above there are two important features of labour markets and their institutions which have major importance for the single currency and its operations. The first is the notion that labour markets and their institutions differ substantially and significantly across the member countries which raises issues for the operation of common macroeconomic policies. Further, these differences in labour market institutions could lead to marked differences in economic performance, notably with regard to wage inflation and productivity trends. This is not to imply there is some optimal set of labour market institutions which would be consistent with the best macroeconomic outcomes. But it is to point to possible differences in economic performance which can generate divergences (or at least non-convergence) within the Economic and Monetary Union. Between countries which have separate currencies some adjustment to those differences can be accommodated by changes in the (real) exchange rate. This is notably the case with differences in rates of inflation and in growth of productivity. Many of those differences may generate difficulties within a single currency area, as appears to have been the case with respect to differences in inflation rates between member countries (as discussed in chapter 3).

Labour market institutions evolve, and the creation of a single market alongside the free movement of labour and the creation of a single currency will undoubtedly exert pressures on labour market institutions. As a result of those pressures, alongside the construction of a European Employment Strategy (not to mention the pressures for 'structural reforms' within the 'fiscal compact'), some convergence of labour market institutions is likely to occur. But the processes of convergence and evolution are likely to be relatively slow, and major differences in labour market institutions will long remain. The policy challenge is then how to construct policies at the EMU level which will address the differences of institutions and the differences in macroeconomic performance. In this regard we would suggest that important elements would be policies which rectify differences in competitiveness which has emerged between countries, and to limit future differences in wage and price inflation.

The second feature is the degree to which the policy thrust of EMU and of the EU more generally (though it is more readily apparent in the policy pronouncements of EMU institutions, notably the ECB) is the neo-liberal direction of deregulation and labour market 'flexibility'. The complexities of the European Employment Strategy mean that this is not a uniform push in that direction, and there are numerous caveats which would need to be entered against that simplification. But the policy agenda of the ECB and now of the 'fiscal compact' are difficult to interpret other than in terms of this neo-liberal direction. This approach runs into the 'one size fits all' problems which monetary policy has faced. Countries differ in their histories and experiences, which precludes a simple read over of imposition of a set of uniform policies. It has also been argued here that the evidence does not support the view that labour market 'reforms' (in the direction of deregulation) are strongly associated with improved economic performance.

7
Macroeconomic Policies for Full Employment and Low Inflation

7.1 Introduction

What should the macroeconomic policies of the Economic and Monetary Union (EMU) look like? In trying to give an answer to this question we proceed in three stages. The first, which picks up from our discussion in chapters 4 and 5, is to consider what the objectives of economic policy should be, specifically in relation to macroeconomic policy. The second is to consider the instruments of economic policy and how they can be used to achieve the stated objectives. In this we look at the instruments of monetary policy and argue that monetary policy should be geared towards ensuring financial stability (rather than being narrowly focused on inflation) and that additional tools of monetary policy should be developed to move away from sole reliance on the central bank interest rate policy. In the case of fiscal policy we argue for such a policy that is geared towards achieving a high level of economy activity and low unemployment. For national governments this would entail setting the budget position in an appropriate manner without constraint from the Stability and Growth Pact and similar measures. At the federal level there is a need to develop a budget of some significance and one which can play a stabilising role. This can raise questions such as whether this would be a budget covering just the EMU countries or whether it should be extended to all EU countries. The third is to consider changes to the institutional arrangements. We start with the role of the ECB and its relationship with the ESCB and national central banks. In this regard we first argue for the democratisation of the ECB and its integration into the macroeconomic decision-making process. This would enable some coordination between monetary and fiscal policies, a very important dimension of such economic policy coordination. The ECB would no longer be independent and able to pursue its own agenda. The split of responsibilities between the ECB and national central banks with the latter being responsible of the national banking sectors and therefore being in charge of the national banking regulation needs to be examined in the context of the aftermath of the 2008 financial crisis and the internal market.

We proceed, after this introduction, with a discussion in section 7.2 of the economic policy implications of our theoretical framework as in chapter 3, followed in section 7.3 with monetary policy, in section 7.4 with fiscal policy and in section 7.5 with international relations and exchange rate policy. Section 7.6 turns briefly to considerations relevant to inflation before we summarise and conclude in section 7.7.

7.2 Economic policy implications

It is our firm starting point for the discussion of macroeconomic policies that the overall focus of the relevant policies should be on sustainable and equitable economic development and growth. A specific part of that general focus is the objective of the achievement of full employment of the labour force. Achieving such an objective requires the maintenance of both a high level of aggregate demand and the provision of sufficient productive capacity. The development and analysis of macroeconomic policies arise from interactions between those macroeconomic objectives and the theoretical framework outlined earlier in the book and more specifically in chapter 3.

7.2.1 Objectives of economic policy

We begin by briefly commenting on the objectives of economic policy. In our perspective, the objectives of economic policy should be: (i) full employment of the available labour supply, and thus sustainable growth; (ii) constant rate of inflation consistent with output growth rather than target rate of inflation; and this in view of the evidence that inflation and output move together up to an inflation rate of around 10–15 per cent, as discussed below in section 7.6; and (iii) financial stability.

The instruments of economic policy may be briefly summarised:

(i) fiscal policy is crucial. We consider the operation of fiscal policy in terms of movements in the fiscal stance in the short run and also in respect of the long-run setting. In the short term, variations in the fiscal stance can be used in conjunction with automatic stabilisers to offset fluctuations in economic activity arising from, inter alia, variations in private sector aggregate demand. In the longer term, the general fiscal stance should be set to underpin the desired level of output and employment;

(ii) interest rate policy should be set so that the real rate of interest is as low as possible in line with the trend rate of growth. In this sense, a real rate of interest in line with the perceived trend rate of growth could be targeted so that the nominal rate is set by the central bank equal to the target rate plus the expected rate of inflation. Further, the operations of the central bank should ultimately be directed towards financial stability and this objective of financial stability should be placed as the most significant one for the central bank, requiring the development of alternative policy instruments alongside the downgrading of interest rate policy and of any notion of inflation targeting;

(iii) exchange rate policy is also important. Changes in the exchange rate affect the domestic economy: primarily in terms of the level of demand and hence economic activity and, rather weakly, in terms of inflation. Intervention by the central bank in the foreign exchange market with the specific aim to stabilise the exchange rate may be important in this respect as argued below, where we suggest control and direct manipulation of the exchange rate by the central bank.

We elaborate in what follows on these economic policies. The instruments of economic policy summarised above to achieve the objectives, also alluded to above, are discussed in what follows beginning with monetary policy.

7.3 Monetary policy

We examine two dimensions of monetary policy: Interest rate policy and financial stability. we begin, however, with some general observations before we return to the two dimensions.

7.3.1 General observations

The EMU policy arrangements discussed earlier in this book suffer from a number of defects. First, if inflation is induced by a demand shock (if, for example, a higher level of demand pushes up inflation) then a policy to influence aggregate demand, and thereby, it is hoped, inflation may have some validity. But such a policy is powerless to deal with cost inflation or supply shock inflation. A supply shock would lower (raise) output whilst raising (lowering) inflation. The experience with inflation in years such as 2007/08 and 2011, when inflation increased in view of higher oil prices and imported raw materials is very telling. Central banks did not use the rate of interest to contain inflation for the very reason just alluded to, namely the supply shock type of inflation.

Further, the extent to which the domestic interest rate can be changed is circumscribed by exchange rate considerations and are likely to take some time to have any impact on aggregate demand (and then the impact may be rather small). Indeed the British monetary authorities (and others) talk in terms of a two-year lag between the change in interest rates and resulting impact of changes in aggregate demand on the rate of inflation. Interest rates are likely to influence investment expenditure, consumer expenditure, market interest rates and asset prices, expectations and the exchange rate. These changes in turn influence domestic and external demand, and then inflationary pressures. In addition, interest rate changes can also have distributional effects, whether between individuals or between economic regions (see, for example, Arestis and Sawyer, 2002).

Second, changes in interest rates have only a limited impact on aggregate demand. But further in so far as interest rates do have an impact it comes through effects on investment and on the exchange rate. High interest rates have long-term detrimental effects through reducing future productive capacity and through the impact of foreign trade. We have surveyed elsewhere (Arestis and Sawyer, 2003b), and also noted in an earlier chapter of this book, the results of simulations of the effects of monetary policy using macroeconometric models. The survey is based on work undertaken for the ECB, the US Federal Reserve System, and for the Bank of England. The conclusion of that survey is that the effects of interest rate changes on inflation tend to be rather small – typically a 1 percentage point change in interest rates may dampen inflation by 0.2 to 0.3 per cent after two years.

Third, monetary policy is a 'one policy fits all' approach. Within the euro area there is a single central bank discount rate. It is well known that the setting of that single interest rate poses difficulties – the rate, which is appropriate for a country experiencing high demand and perhaps inflationary pressures, is not the same as that appropriate for one facing low demand. Indeed, the impact of interest rate changes is likely to differ markedly across countries. Furthermore, monetary policy may address the average inflation picture but cannot address differences in inflationary experience across the euro area countries.

Fourth, the ECB assessment of the level of economic activity is completely impervious to the behaviour of interest rates. Bibow (2003) puts it aptly: 'Ex ante interest rate policies never seem to conflict with economic growth in ECB policy communications and assessments. Ex post economic developments do not appear to have been related to interest rate developments either' (p. 5). The ECB rationale is that monetary tightening would not pose any risk to economic activity. Such policy keeps inflationary expectations under control, thereby sustaining confidence in price stability, which stimulates economic activity. This is rather surprising in view of the work undertaken on the transmission mechanism in the euro area (ECB 2002d, October), which shows that monetary policy has strong real effects, especially so in 'that investment is a main driving force, with a contribution of more than 80 percent to the total response of gdp after three years' (p. 47) – see, also, Arestis and Sawyer (2003b); Kuttner and Mosser (2002) and our discussion of the DSGE models in chapter 3.

7.3.2 Interest rate policy considerations

Inflation has been relatively low in most industrialised countries and on a global scale for much of the past two decades, and proponents of inflation targeting have claimed the credit for that low inflation. We have argued elsewhere that inflation targeting itself has not been responsible for this low inflation (see, for example, Angeriz and Arestis, 2007a, 2007b, 2008; Arestis and Sawyer, 2008a). Inflation targeting has in effect sought to return to a crude demand reduction approach to the control of inflation, albeit that the instrument chosen (interest rate) was not the most effective one (that is fiscal policy would have been more potent). The cloud on the horizon is to find an alternative and effective way of maintaining low inflation, without having to resort to demand deflation and the associated losses of employment and output (see, for example, Arestis and Sawyer, 2013a).

There is, thus, a need to develop policy instruments to address the issue of inflation, which do not rely on demand deflation and which are effective (as doubt has been cast on the effectiveness of monetary policy as a tool for the control of inflation; see the earlier discussion in this chapter). There is also a need to recognise that interest rates set in pursuit of inflation targeting, have an impact on a range of other significant variables, notably the exchange rate and asset prices. In part, the manner in which interest rates are seen to influence inflation is through the exchange rate and asset prices: higher interest rates are viewed as tending to raise the value of the exchange rate (having downward impact on domestic inflation) and to depress asset prices (thereby generating a wealth effect which tends to lower demand). But these economic variables are clearly important in their own right (rather than merely as a route to inflation) and more significantly interest rates and other changes may feed into price bubbles, whether of the exchange rate or asset prices. It is not a matter of incorporating (or not) asset prices into the targeted measure of inflation for that does not adequately reflect the possible implications of asset price bubbles (and in any event would be limited to assets such as housing). For example, Goodhart (2005a) argues that a focus on domestic variables only in interest rate determination may provide 'a combination of internal price stability and exchange rate instability' (p. 301; see, also, Goodhart, 2005b). In recent times, an important aspect of this can be the influence of low interest rates on asset prices, and whether the stimulus to asset price rises coming from low interest rates can be the spark of setting off a price bubble. The argument of Wicksell (1898), and others, could be seen as one that suggests interest rate policy has an effect on asset price inflation – or at least some subset of asset prices. Asset prices develop a speculative element (meaning here purchase of asset to benefit from expected rise in price, rather than for income stream from asset). It is obvious to say that asset price bubbles have developed – dot.com, house prices, etc. Current arrangements are powerless to deal with those bubbles.

The setting of the interest rate has some clear and obvious implications for the operation of fiscal policy. As indicated above, a total budget deficit relative to GDP of d would lead to a debt ratio of d/g. Let us write $d = d' + rb$ where d' is the primary deficit (that is excluding interest payments), then $b = d/g = (d' + rb)/g$ and hence $d' = (g - r)b$. When the growth rate is greater than (post-tax) rate of interest then there would be a primary deficit, and this would not lead to an unsustainable rise in the debt ratio. When growth rate is below the rate of interest, then a primary surplus would result. The case where $g = r$ is of particular interest, particularly as this would appear a good approximation to the relationship between growth rate and government's cost of borrowing. Pasinetti (1997) remarks that this case

> represents the 'golden rule' of capital accumulation. ... In this case, the public budget can be permanently in deficit and the public debt can thereby increase indefinitely, but national income increases at the same rate (g) so that the D/Y ratio remains constant. Another way of looking at this case is to say that the government budget has a deficit, which is wholly due to interest payments. (p. 163)

The setting of the interest rate equal to the rate of growth of the economy has been discussed earlier (pp. 91/2).

7.3.3 The financial stability dimension

Financial stability has not been at the forefront of monetary policy to say the least. The belief in the efficiency of financial markets prevented a realistic and necessary approach to financial stability (IMF, 2009, 2010). As a result, both the supporters of the New Consensus Macroeconomics framework and policy makers have ignored 'the implications for systemic stability of financial market imperfections, including those stemming from international frictions, moral hazard and other distortions to incentives, such as externalities and herding' (IMF, 2010, p. 7). As a result potential systemic risk was ignored and financial regulation and supervision 'were increasingly light-touch and reliant on self-correcting market forces' (IMF, op. cit., p. 7); and, indeed, in the case of the 'shadow banking' it was completely absent.

The focus of financial stability should be on proper control of the financial sector so that it becomes socially and economically useful to the economy as a whole and to the productive economy in particular. Banks should serve the needs of their customers rather than provide short-term gains for shareholders and huge profits for themselves. In order to achieve these objectives a number of prerequisites should be in place. To begin with, the core function of banking should be restated. This should be to facilitate the allocation and deployment of economic resources over time and place to socially useful purposes. It should also be to maximise long-term financial and social returns under conditions of uncertainty. In order to achieve these objectives a number of reforms should be undertaken. The most important, perhaps, is the separation of commercial banking from investment banking.[1] Commercial banking sits at the moment uncomfortably with the risky activities of the investment banking; and most commercial banks have moved into investment banking in search of quick profits. Separation then should allow investment banks to go bust, if necessary, thereby instilling greater discipline and avoiding moral hazard.

A second reform should be the break-up of banks that are 'too big to fail'. Allowing banks that are big to fail creates moral hazard: banks pursuing high risk activities confident that the public will have to bail them if and when things go wrong. Also banks need to be broken up both to reduce costs and risks to the taxpayer, and also to improve the quality and range of services. A further reform is to tax the financial sector and, also, introduce a financial transactions tax (see, for example, Arestis and Sawyer, 2013b). These would need to take place on a worldwide basis and used to slow financial speculation, one of the main causes of the credit crunch. Better regulation should be introduced. Banks should hold more capital, in the form of leverage and liquidity requirements, particularly in booms when risks are by far greater. This proposed requirement, which forces banks to hold more capital, could push the countries concerned into depression. This can come about since stringent capital requirements may leave the banks with insufficient funds for lending purposes. Due care and attention are, therefore, vital when constructing the relevant new rules. But one aspect is very clear. The 'too big to fail' policy, with national central banks being responsible at the moment, should shift to the ECB; the latter should also be responsible to bail out banks and national governments. In other words, the ECB should become a proper central bank with the lender of last resort function firmly embedded in its functions.

The argument made here is that financial stability should become the central objective of the central bank. Buiter (2008) indicates that 'financial stability means (1) the absence of asset price bubbles; (2) the absence of illiquidity of financial institutions and financial markets that may threaten systemic stability; (3) the absence of insolvency of financial institutions that may threaten systemic stability' (p. 10). It can be noted that the recent Banking Act 2009 in the UK establishes that 'an objective of the Bank (of England) shall be to contribute to protecting and enhancing the stability of the financial systems of the United Kingdom (the 'Financial Stability Objective')'.[2] The Bank will work with other bodies such as the Treasury and the Financial Services Authority (FSA) and will establish a Financial Stability Committee. At present this is placed alongside the monetary stability objective under the heading of inflation targeting. This could be seen a significant step away from the operational independence of the Bank of England and from the single inflationary objective. Our argument here is that the financial stability objective should be the prime objective and the operational independence of the Bank of England should be abandoned.

Current events and the general record on financial crises (see, Laeven and Valencia, 2008, for details of crises over the past three decades and their costs) indicate the substantial costs associated with financial crises and financial instability (which would far outweigh any costs associated with inflation). In terms of the general multiple instruments and multiple objectives framework, it may not be possible to uniquely assign each instrument to a specific objective.

Nevertheless, it may be possible to link an instrument mainly with a specific objective, recognising that coordination in the use of instruments can be advantageous. In this context, the argument is that the main link should be monetary policy, in the sense of monetary and financial stability. However, we have argued above for the policy of seeking to target a specified real rate of interest and to seek to maintain a constant rate of interest. Such a policy may have some beneficial effects on financial stability as opposed to frequent changes in the rate of interest. In the case of lowering interest rates, for example, this can be seen to inflate asset prices with the possibility of setting off an asset price bubble, which at some point will burst. Further, as recent experience suggests, asset price inflation may be inimical to financial stability given the interrelationships between asset price inflation and credit expansion.

Greenspan (2002) put forward one approach to financial stability when considering how to respond to asset price bubbles. He argued that 'the degree of monetary tightening that would be required to contain or offset a bubble of any substantial dimension appears to be so great as to risk an unacceptable amount of collateral damage to the wider economy' (p. 4). But further his general attitude was that policy should be directed towards cleaning up after a crisis rather than seeking to prevent a crisis. He had already argued on another occasion that 'Faced with this uncertainty, the Federal Reserve has focused on policies that would, as I testified before the Congress in 1999, ... mitigate the fallout [of an asset bubble] when it occurs and, hopefully, ease the transition to the next expansion'.[3] The costs (in terms of lost output, unemployment and fiscal costs) as well as the sheer difficulties of propping up the financial system following the financial collapse indicate that this approach should not be one to be applied in the future. An interesting distinction in this context and on the policy score is made by Blinder (2010). It is suggested that there are two types of bubbles. Those associated by relatively little debt finance, where the typical example is 'equity-like bubbles'. Under this type of bubble the recommended policy is to react after the bubble has burst. The second type is the debt-financed bubbles, where early intervention to contain the bubble is proposed. In this context 'supervisory weapons' are recommended rather than monetary policy. The rationale for this recommendation is based on the fact that 'the central bank *does* have weapons to target straight at the bubble – *provided it is also a bank supervisor*' (Blinder, op. cit., p. 2).

The argument here is made more relevant by Goodhart (2007), who suggests that

> [i]n so far, therefore, as the central bank has a prime concern for systemic financial stability, it should want to promote a program of counter-cyclical prudential regulations, where these latter become restrictive during asset price bubbles and relax during asset price downturns. Unfortunately the system of financial regulation is developing in a manner, which will have exactly the reverse proclivity. Under the Basel II accord for financial regulation, this will become more pro-cyclical. (p. 68)

Goodhart (op. cit.) goes on to point out problems with the national adoption of standards different from those set out in Basel II.

There are already in place a variety of regulatory policies, which are intended to develop financial stability, but it could be said that these are often focused on the stability and viability (or otherwise) of individual banking institutions rather than on systemic factors. As D'Arista (2009) argues, in the context of the use of capital requirement,

> As a strategy for ensuring that market forces rather than regulations and quantity controls would determine the volume of bank lending, capital requirements became the rationale for – and poster child of – deregulation. But they have subsequently been seen as its Achilles heel because of their focus on the individual institution rather than the system as a whole. William R. White describes this 'fallacy of composition' as one that can exacerbate a system-wide problem when recommendations for a sale of assets by one institution in a stressful situation could reduce prices and the value of remaining assets, leaving other institutions weaker (White 2007, p. 83). (p. 10)

The argument here is: (i) monetary and financial stability should be adopted as an objective of macroeconomic policy. This is argued in part on the basis of the relative frequency of financial instability and the significant costs associated with financial crisis; (ii) the objective relates to the whole of the financial system, and not as has generally been the case to the banking system. It is now generally recognised that the financial system has evolved and changed such that the banking system has become a (relatively) smaller part of the overall financial system. The key point here is to bring to the forefront a form of monetary and financial policy, which is focused on financial stability. The key elements of such a policy would be tools to influence and control the activities of financial firms as they bear on the issue of financial stability. This firstly suggests that such a policy, financial regulation, has to be comprehensive in its coverage, and this applies to the range of financial institutions, which are covered and also to its international coverage; and presumably with EMU at the level of the ECB. It may further suggest that the policy would need to act in a counter-cyclical manner and to be potentially differentiated. This points away from the capital adequacy ratios of the Basle III system in light of its pro-cyclical nature of operation and the way in which the required capital depends on risk assessment. In contrast an asset based reserve requirement system (see, for example, D'Arista, 2009, Palley, 2004, for proposals) has counter-cyclical features and can apply differential reserve requirements against different classes of assets.

A few comments on the 'Basel III package' are relevant to this discussion. This is actually concerned with bank capital and liquidity standards. The new rulings are being phased in from January 2013 with full implementation achieved only by January 2019. It requires banks to hold equity requirements to 7 per cent of the risk-weighted assets (RWA); liquidity standards include a liquidity coverage ratio, which is a ratio of high quality liquid assets to net cash outflows over a 30-day horizon. These new ratios are lower than they might have been and also they are not to be fully implemented until 2019. This is actually a victory for the banks, which seems to have been a concession to small banks, especially in Germany, in view of their undercapitalisation. A problem concerns the definition of the capital ratio, which is defined in relation to risk-weighted assets, not total assets. An implication of this is that toxic leverage is highly probable: when the RWA is a small proportion of total assets, the exposure of the banking sector to risk would be very high indeed. Clearly, then, Basel III has not managed very well in correcting the mechanism through which the main cause of the 'great recession' emerged; it should not, then, be surprising if another similar crisis were to take place. All in all, and given the key role of Basel III in the global regulatory system, it would appear that financial stability remains unresolved and elusive from the point of view of the 'Basel III package'.

There is an element here of the end of monetary policy, and its replacement by (or incorporation into) financial stability policy. With an objective of financial stability, the central bank would become more like a Central Financial Agency (CFA). It would be responsible for policies, which seek to influence the credit and lending policies of the full range of financial institutions by, for example, assets- based reserve requirements.

Financial stability should entail a new toolkit, which should incorporate both macroprudential and microprudential instruments. Both instruments should be under the banner of the policy makers avoiding rules and employing judgement and thus discretion. The macroprudential toolkit should account for the failures of the system: low levels of liquid assets; inadequate levels of capital with which to absorb losses; too big a financial sector; too leveraged a sector with high risks to the taxpayer and the economy. Thus, macroprudential financial instruments should be able to control the size, leverage, fragility and risk of the financial system. Microprudential instruments relate to the structure and regulation of individual banks. Banks that are 'too big to fail' should be cut down in size; guarantees to retail depositors should be limited to banks with a narrower range of investments; risky banks to taxpayers and economy should face higher capital requirements; large and complex financial institutions can be wound down in an orderly manner; and large banks should not be allowed to combine retail banking with risky investment business. Possibly, combining all the elements just suggested.

Addressing issues of financial stability (or what may be termed the pursuit of macro prudential regulation) clearly requires the development of a range of policy instruments. There are though two other important ingredients in this idea of financial stability as the key objective of the monetary authorities. First, many of the arguments for an independent central bank, based on the 'conservative' (inflation averse) central banker with credibility, weaken substantially. Further with multiple objectives pursued by multiple instruments there is a need for coordination between the macroeconomic authorities (for example, Ministry of Finance, central bank), which is precluded by independence strictly interpreted. Second (and related), monetary policy under inflation targeting was intended to not only target inflation but also reduce the volatility of output and guide output to its 'natural' level. This was summarised in Taylor's rule (Taylor, 1993), where the interest rate was intended to be set based on deviations of inflation from target and output from 'natural' level. The idea of the Phillips curve melds those together – in that constant inflation rate is said to be consistent with zero output gap and a positive output gap would be associated with rising inflation both of which would point towards a higher rate of interest. All these arguments are weakened substantially under the financial stability objective.

We turn our attention next to fiscal policy.

7.4 Fiscal policy

7.4.1 The SGP and fiscal compact are flawed

The general stance of the SGP and the fiscal compact with their requirement of an overall balanced budget and maximum deficit of 3 per cent of GDP is a deeply flawed one. There is no reason to think that a balanced budget position is consistent with high levels of employment (or indeed with any particular level of employment). Furthermore, there is little reason to think that the 3 per cent limit can permit the automatic stabilisers to work, and striving to reach the 3 per cent limit in time of recession is likely to push economies further into recession. The balanced budget requirement does not allow governments to even borrow to fund capital investment projects.

Additional reservations include the separation of the monetary authorities from the fiscal authorities. The decentralisation of the fiscal authorities inevitably makes any effective coordination of fiscal and monetary policy difficult. Since the ECB is instructed to focus on inflation while the fiscal authorities will have a broader range of concerns, there will be considerable grounds for conflict. A serious implication of this is that the SGP is in danger of becoming the 'instability' pact. This suggests a need for the evolution of a body, which would be charged with the coordination of EMU monetary and fiscal policies. In the absence of such a body, tensions will emerge in the real sector when monetary policy and fiscal policy pull in different directions. The SGP in effect resolves these issues by establishing the dominance of the monetary authorities (ECB) over the fiscal authorities (national governments).

As discussed earlier (pp.101–102) The balanced budget requirement over the business cycle was a significant tightening as compared with the Maastricht convergence criteria. The SGP seeks to impose a 'one size (of straightjacket) fits all' fiscal policy – namely that over the course of the cycle national government budgets should be in balance or slight surplus with a maximum deficit of 3 per cent of GDP. It has never been shown (or even argued) that fiscal policy should be uniform across countries. The SGP imposes a fiscal policy, which in the end fits nobody. For, in effect, there is no reason to think that what is in effect a single fiscal policy (balanced budget over the cycle) is appropriate for all.

A balanced budget (on average) means, of course, that current government expenditure will be much less than tax revenue since that tax revenue would also need to cover interest payments on debt and to pay for capital expenditure. In the UK, this has been cast in terms of the so-called 'golden rule' of public finance, which is taken to be that 'over the economic cycle the Government will borrow only to invest and not to fund current expenditure' (Treasury, 1997, p. 1), though capital consumption (depreciation) is regarded as current spending so that it is net capital formation, which can be financed by borrowing. The 'public debt as a proportion of national income will be held over the economic cycle at a stable and prudent level' (Treasury, op. cit., p. 1). Furthermore, 'The fiscal rules focus on the whole of the public sector, because the debts of any part of the public sector could ultimately fall on the taxpayer. Looking at the whole public sector also removes incentives to reclassify activities simply to evade prudent constraints on borrowing' (Treasury, 1997, p. 16). Thus, the use of fiscal policy to regulate aggregate demand in the economy is much reduced, if not entirely removed, especially in the direction of stimulating the economy. It is, thus, argued that 'Discretionary fiscal changes should only be made if they are demonstrably consistent with achievement of the Government's fiscal rules over the economic cycle' (Treasury, op. cit., p. 16).

We argue in the subsection that follows that fiscal policy is by far more important than the latter view suggests.

7.4.2 Fiscal policy is important

Since the forces ensuring that the level of aggregate demand is in line with the productive potential (or full employment) are, at best, weak, there is a requirement for aggregate demand policies. Fiscal policy is a much more potent instrument than interest rate policy for setting the level of demand (Arestis and Sawyer, 2003d, 2010b; Angeriz and Arestis, 2009). The operation of fiscal policy is considered in both a long-term setting and in terms of movements in the fiscal stance in the short term. In the short term, variations in the fiscal stance can be used to offset fluctuations in economic activity arising from, inter alia, variations in private sector aggregate demand. At the extreme this leads to the fine-tuning of fiscal policy. In the longer term, the general fiscal stance can be set to support the level of aggregate demand consistent with high level of economic activity.

For the long term we adopt the approach of Lerner (1943) and Kalecki (1944) and aim to achieve a budget position to achieve a high target level of economic activity, and the appropriate budget deficit is given by equation (1) in chapter 5 the target level of income is labelled as Y^*.

A budget deficit would not be required when there is a high level of private aggregate demand such that investment equals savings at a high level of economic activity (and a surplus would be required when investment exceeds savings at the desired level of economic activity). The budget deficit required to achieve a high level of economic activity can be clearly seen to depend on the propensities to save, invest, import and the ability to export, and these over country and across time. The underlying budget position should then be set in accordance with the perceived underlying values of the propensities to save, invest, import and export (see Sawyer, 2009a, 2009b). This approach to fiscal policy can be said to incorporate a clear rule: set the underlying budget deficit compatible with the desired level of output. But it is clear that the estimation of the relevant budget stance would involve substantial difficulties and disputes. Although whether the latter difficulties are any greater than the estimation of key variables in the current orthodoxy such as the 'equilibrium rate of interest' and the 'non-accelerating inflation rate of unemployment' is an interesting question.

We maintain, therefore, that fiscal policy is paramount both in the short run and in the long run (see, also, Arestis, 2009a; Arestis and Sawyer, 2006e, 2010b); and that it is time for the renaissance of Keynesian fiscal policy (Arestis, 2012a), especially so in view of the strong macroeconomic role of fiscal policy (Arestis, 2012b). We consider the operation of fiscal policy in terms of movements in the fiscal stance in the short run and also in respect of the long-run setting. In the short term, variations in the fiscal stance can be used in conjunction with automatic stabilisers to offset fluctuations in economic activity arising from, *inter alia*, variations in private sector aggregate demand. In the long run, the general fiscal stance should be set to underpin the desired level of output and employment. This approach raises the issue of sustainability of the deficit (see Arestis and Sawyer, 2006e, 2009), which we view as not a significant issue for two basic reasons. First, in this approach, and in the model above, governments borrow because private sector wishes to lend; if there were no potential excess of savings over investment, then there would be no need for a budget deficit. Savings (over and above investment) can only be realised if there is a budget deficit or overseas lending, which absorbs those savings. Second, a total budget deficit of d (relative to GDP) is always sustainable in the sense that the corresponding debt to GDP ratio (b) stabilises at: $b = d/g$ with g as the nominal GDP growth rate. The budget deficit, which is relevant for the level of demand, is the overall budget position rather than the primary deficit (or surplus). To the extent that a budget deficit is required to offset an excess of private savings over investment, then it is the overall budget deficit which is relevant. Bond interest payments are a transfer payment and add to the income of the recipient, which is similar in that respect to other transfer payments (though the propensity to consume out of interest payments is likely to be less than that out of many other transfer payments). In terms of sustainability, then, of a fiscal deficit the condition is generally readily satisfied; this being the requirement of a positive nominal growth rate. Consequently, we may summarise the argument by suggesting that a budget deficit (including interest payments), which bears a constant relationship to GDP, is sustainable. In fact, it leads to a debt/GDP ratio equal to the deficit/GDP ratio divided by the growth of nominal GDP.

Since the forces ensuring that the level of aggregate demand is in line with the productive potential (or full employment) are, at best, weak, there is a requirement for aggregate demand policies. Fiscal policy is a much more potent instrument than interest rate policy for setting the level of demand (see, also, Arestis and Sawyer, 2003d). The operation of fiscal policy is considered both in terms of movements in the fiscal stance in the short term and also in a long-term setting. In the short term, variations in the fiscal stance can be used to offset fluctuations in economic activity arising from, inter alia, variations in private sector aggregate demand. At the extreme this leads to the fine-tuning of fiscal policy. In the longer term, the general fiscal stance can be set to support the level of aggregate demand consistent with high level of economic activity.

A few words on fine-tuning are necessary at this stage. The ultimate in fine-tuning would arise when the budget stance was continuously changed in response to variations in economic activity. This would be comparable to the fine-tuning that is currently attempted by the ECB and other central banks around the world, through interest rate changes, with decisions on interest rates being made on a frequent (for example, monthly) basis, even if the decision is one of no change. The problems of fine-tuning are well known in terms of the various lags involved including those of recognition, decision-making, implementation and effect. However, the automatic stabilisers of fiscal policy already perform part of that task in the sense that a downturn is met by reduced tax and increased expenditure, which modify, but do not eliminate, the degree of fluctuations in economic activity. The tax and expenditure regime could be designed in a manner to increase the extent of stabilisation and a more progressive tax system would enhance the stabilisation properties. But that should be argued for on grounds of equity and income distribution, albeit that there would be the additional benefits for stabilisation.

Automatic stabilisers of the traditional form (that is tax revenues varying through movements in the level of output) are rather useful in this regard and depend on the progressivity of the tax system (and expenditure) and the scale of government. There is a good case for the enhancement of these automatic stabilisers.[4] Although the question remains as to whether a more progressive system, increased scale of government activities or through changes in tax rates triggered by prespecified changes in the level of economic activity should be the ultimate aim (Baunsgaard and Symansky, 2009).

There are other ways by which government policy may be able to influence the level of demand. Interest rate policy is one of those, but we would argue that such a policy is not an effective one as compared with fiscal policy (Arestis and Sawyer, 2003d). Kalecki (1944) addressed the issue of an insufficiency of aggregate demand through 'Three Ways to Full Employment'. The three ways were the use of budget deficits, stimulating consumer expenditure (and hence reducing overall propensity to save) through the redistribution of income and stimulation of investment. These are alternative policy responses to the inadequacy of aggregate demand. This approach is clearly based on the notion that there are no strong (or even weak) market forces, which would push the level of aggregate demand to a level consistent with full employment (or any other desirable level of employment or output). There is a fourth way (which Kalecki, 1944, did not actually explore), namely the promotion of net exports through, for example, exchange rate policies or in the longer-term industrial and regional policies designed to increase international competitiveness. But, of course, promotion of net exports has elements of a 'beggar thy neighbour' policy, and is not a policy, which the majority of countries can successfully pursue.

The effects of a shift in the distribution of income as between wages and profits would depend on whether the economy was in a wage-led or a profit-led regime (Bhadhuri and Marglin, 1990).[5] The stimulation of investment may tend to raise the capital–output ratio, leading to a decline in the rate of profit. In both cases, we would suggest that a demand policy has to take into account the prevailing distribution of income and propensity to invest, and in terms of the coarse tuning approach outlined above the required budget deficit depends on the distribution of income (via its effects on savings and investment behaviour) and on the propensity to invest. However, we would argue that income distribution policies and encouragement or otherwise of investment should not be undertaken for reasons of their effects on aggregate demand but rather assessed on their own terms. For example, there are strong reasons to advocate a less egalitarian distribution of income in social and ethical terms, rather than because such a policy would stimulate demand.

Turning to the promotion of investment, it should be recognised that there are limits to this way of stimulating demand. The basis of the argument is that a higher investment to GDP ratio would lead to capital stock rising relative to output, and as such the rate of profit would tend to fall. The second part of the argument relates to savings. The paradox of thrift and the sense in which more savings may well be in the interests of an individual but not in the collective interest, and that intentions to save more will be frustrated unless matched by investment or budget deficit. One major route by which the average propensity to save could be reduced would be through the re-distribution of income from profits to wages, and from high earners to low earners. Leading up to the financial crisis of the late 2000s and the 'great recession', the average propensity to save by households fell considerably in many countries (the UK, the USA, and Europe, in particular).

Although any precise calculations will always be rather difficult, the essence of the argument here is that savings, investment, net exports and budget deficit should be considered together with the aim of their relationship being consistent with full employment. In the above discussion on fiscal policy, the propensities to save and to invest, as well as the net export position, were rather taken as given with the focus on the use of fiscal policy to ensure a high level of economic activity. It is, therefore, important to set this in a broader context, and to think about potentially additional and relevant economic policy measures that follow from such a broader perspective.[6] It is for this latter reason that we need to discuss next international relations and the role of the exchange rate.

7.5 International relations and exchange rate policy

The level, rate of change and the volatility of the exchange rate have significant effects on the domestic economy both in terms of the level of demand (and hence economic activity) and of inflation. The exchange rate has significant implications for the real standard of living and to some degree the distribution of income, and can be seen as an intermediate rather than final target for economic policy. With regard to the exchange rate, policy concerns would involve the volatility of the exchange rate (in both nominal and real terms) and general level of the real exchange rate. In terms of policy objectives we would argue for the benefits of a stable (real) exchange rate set at a level, which is most conducive for the level of demand. But in an era of market-determined exchange rates and high capital mobility what are the possibilities of achieving a stable exchange rate? Or is it a matter of letting the exchange rate roam where the market determines, and seeking to deal with the consequences?

Changes in the exchange rate affect the domestic economy primarily in terms of the level of demand, and hence economic activity, and of prices. Interest rate could be varied for exchange rate purposes. The effects of exchange rate variations will depend on the extent of pass through. There are several approaches to modelling the exchange rate, but notoriously movements in the exchange rate are difficult (impossible) to predict. It can be readily observed that there is considerable volatility in exchange rates with consequent effects on the current account position. What we can argue, though, is that there are serious difficulties with a floating market-determined exchange rate system. A high real exchange rate contributes to 'imbalances' in the economy through its impact on the domestic composition of output: declines in manufacturing and exports, and increases in services and current account deficit, occur. It is the case that the pass-through effect of a change in the exchange rate, first on import prices and subsequently on the generality of prices, both goods and services, has weakened since the late 1980s (McCarthy, 1999). Consequently, the stronger real exchange rate has had less offsetting effect on domestic prices than in earlier periods.

It follows, then, that the argument, normally used to justify appreciation in the exchange rate, that such a move slows inflation is no longer valid under such circumstances. Also, and as argued above, the impact of interest rate changes may have become more ambiguous. It would appear to be the case that capital movements are based more on equities than on other assets.[7] A change in interest rates then may have the opposite effect on capital movements than otherwise. In any case, the argument sketched above points in the direction of setting a real interest rate broadly in line with the rate of growth. In view of this argument the interest rate could not be varied for exchange rate purposes. It should be recognised, though, that the general global level of interest rates may constrain the domestic rates. Despite the lack of evidence supporting uncovered interest rate parity, the degree to which a country's real interest rate could persistently diverge from real interest rates around the world is difficult. Consequently, it becomes difficult for any single country to secure a stable exchange rate without tightly controlling it. The use of the domestic interest rate does not appear to be an effective instrument, and in any event depends on some co-operation from others since it is the relative interest rate which would be relevant. This suggests that securing a stable exchange rate requires significant intervention along with international co-operation and agreement. Indeed, this is particularly relevant for stability between the major currencies.

These nominal exchange rate fluctuations have also been real exchange rate fluctuations. In a world where exchange rates are set by 'fundamentals' on the trade side, it would be anticipated that exchange rates were rather stable, only evolving as the 'fundamentals' governing trade changed (including the relative demand for imports and exports). The era of flexible exchange rates has also been associated with large current account imbalances. Under a floating exchange rate, the balance of payments of a country must balance (that is change in official reserves zero); nonetheless, there have been major and often persistent imbalances of current accounts and of capital accounts. The capital account positions can be interpreted as permitting capital flows between countries and the re-allocation of capital between countries allowing its more effective use in so far as it flows from low profit to high profit areas. Capital inflows leave a country vulnerable to rapid reversals; namely, a combination of refusal of further capital inflows and the reversal of previous inflows. China, and other countries, has at least for the past decade, run a large and growing current account surplus and hence associated capital outflow and accumulation of dollar denominated assets. The euro area (as other currency unions) has established a fixed exchange rate regime amongst its member countries but has developed current account imbalances between member countries within an overall setting where the euro area is broadly in current account balance.

It can also be observed that the volume of transactions across the foreign exchanges has grown rapidly. The recent rises are also remarkable in that the creation of the euro has reduced the need for foreign exchange transactions between the former currencies of the members of the Economic and Monetary Union. These transactions far exceed (by an order of 50) the volume of international trade, and even making allowance for net capital flows, the volume of transactions look massive and do raise the issue of whether the resources devoted to those transactions are being used in a social useful manner. There have been many debates as to whether the volume of transactions are generating the observed volatility of exchange rates. The global economy is dominated by three or four currencies – the dollar, the euro, the yen and (to a less degree) sterling. But of course much trade and many commodity prices are expressed in dollars. The currencies of many other countries are pegged in one form or another with one of the major currencies. Can there be agreement between major currencies over appropriate exchange rates and agreed intervention? There is the further question of the distribution of deficits and surpluses between countries. If the world were in a position where each country has a current account position, which moved around zero, there would not be a severe problem. In a similar vein, if the countries had a mixture of deficits and surpluses, and the corresponding capital account surpluses and deficits were sustainable and not subject to sudden reversals (for example, through capital flight) there again would be little problem. But the situation that is faced is one where there are severe imbalances in which capital is flowing from countries such as China, Germany and Japan to countries such as the USA, the UK and Spain.

Capital inflows can be viewed to address the twin gaps issue; namely, the shortage of domestic savings relative to investment needs and current account deficit. At what level does a current account deficit become unsustainable is an interesting question. Also to what degree do capital inflows create credit booms and asset price bubbles? Would it be possible to define an upper limit on current account deficits? This may be a principle rather than a numerical value, recognising the difficulties of determining whether a principle held in practice. Let us suppose for a few minutes that some rules could be enunciated on the size of current account deficits (and that may also require some corresponding rules on current account surpluses). The question then is whether there is any way in which such rules could be implemented. The Stability and Growth Pact drew up rules on budget deficits, why not corresponding rules drawn on current account deficits? Indeed, and noting the national accounts identity, a budget deficit rule implies half a current account deficit rule in the sense that for a given difference between savings and investment, budget deficit implies current account deficit. The operation of rules requires co-operation of all countries; if there were limits on deficits there would have to be limits on surpluses (at least the collective surplus). But a country running a current account deficit generally sees advantages in being able to do so in the short run – it enables its citizens to import more than they export and to consume more than they otherwise would be able to do, and it provides additional capital. A country with a current account deficit, which appears to be readily financed (even through portfolio investment that can be readily reversed), would not take kindly to instructions to curb its deficit. Further there is the difficult question of what policy instruments are available. Perhaps limits on capital inflows, which then enforce a limit on current account deficit, might be appropriate; but still there is the question of how the exchange rate would respond to it.

The ability of policy to influence the (nominal) exchange rate may, thus, be doubted. Interest rate policy can be viewed as one way in which the exchange rate could be influenced. The uncovered interest rate parity notion suggests that the rate of change of the nominal exchange rate is equal to the interest rate differential between the rest of the world and country concerned. Casual observation suggests that large movements in an exchange rate (say of the order of 10 per cent per annum or more changes) go alongside relatively small interest rate differentials (say of the order of 1 or 2 percentage points). As the Bank of England (2006) states on its website,

> changes in interest rates can also affect the exchange rate. An unexpected rise in the rate of interest in the UK relative to overseas would give investors a higher return on UK assets relative to their foreign-currency equivalents, tending to make sterling assets more attractive. That should raise the value of sterling, reduce the price of imports, and reduce demand for UK goods and services abroad. However, the impact of interest rates on the exchange rate is, unfortunately, seldom that predictable.

The argument sketched above points in the direction of setting a real interest rate broadly in line with the rate of growth. If that is accepted, then the interest rate could not also be varied for exchange rate purposes. It would though need to be recognised that the general global level of interest rates may constrain the domestic rates. Despite the lack of evidence supporting uncovered interest rate parity, the degree to which a country's real interest rate could persistently diverge from real interest rates around the world can be doubted. It seems rather unlikely that any single country can secure a stable exchange rate without tightly controlling it. The use of the domestic interest rate does not appear to be an effective instrument, and in any event depends on some co-operation from others since it is the relative interest rate, which would be relevant. This suggests that securing a stable exchange rate requires international co-operation and agreement, and this is particularly relevant for stability between the major currencies (dollar, euro, yen and perhaps sterling and yuan).

7.6 Inflation considerations

In view of the importance given to inflation and to the objective of price stability over the recent past, it is important to offer a few comments on the matter. Inflation is a non-monetary phenomenon with a complex of causes, including conflicts of the distribution of income. We take the view that it need not be the focus of economic policy in view of the fact that the causes of inflation vary and also that inflation is not always harmful to growth. In more general terms, the empirical evidence on this issue is actually not very supportive of inflation targeting and the surrounding theoretical model. A critique of inflation targetting is provided above (pp. 84–86).[8]

The control of inflation should be regarded as a side issue unless inflation is exhibiting tendencies to continue to rise and to exceed something of the order of 10 per cent. This argument is based on the evidence that inflation above 10 per cent begins to distort decision-making and that the evidence on the relationship between inflation and growth does not indicate detrimental effects of inflation on growth at rates less than (say) 10 per cent. This is reinforced by the evidence on the relationship between inflation and output, which suggests that it is not necessarily negative for at least single figures (see Ferguson, 2005b, who summarises these arguments; see, also, Ghosh and Phillips, 1998; Fischer, 1993; Bruno and Easterly, 1996; Levine and Renelt, 1994; Khan and Senhadji, 2001). There is, thus, no need to develop policies to tackle inflation unless it reaches high levels. Such approach involves the development of an incomes policy to contain inflation when it reaches unacceptably high rates.

There has not been an effective counter-inflation policy in the EMU, and the ECB has tended to miss its target, albeit by not much (and there have been times such as in 2008 and 2011 when imported inflation has raised its head). We argue that ECB should target financial stability not inflation, so it needs to develop a counter-inflation policy. Also, of course, the major inflation issue in EMU has been differential inflation. Hence there is a need to develop policies (for example, income policies) which can address overall inflation and also inflation across countries. We view inflation as multi-causal and the sources of inflationary pressure varying over time and economy (Arestis and Sawyer, 2005, 2008a). Alternative policies to address inflation are thereby necessary, including the role of incomes policy. In this respect, factors such as the struggle over income shares, the level and rate of change of the level of aggregate demand and cost-push factors emanating notably from the foreign sector (change in import prices and the exchange rate) should be carefully accounted. As a result, a range of policies would be required to address the different sources of inflation.

7.7 Summary and conclusions

We have discussed in this chapter the macroeconomic policies we believe can help to achieve full employment and low inflation. We summarised the objectives of economic policy along with the instruments of economic policy that can achieve these objectives before embarking on a lengthy analysis of them. We began with monetary policy where we concluded that what is important is the financial stability dimension of this policy rather than inflation as in the NCM and ECB economic policy prescriptions. We then moved on to fiscal policy, where we argue that the SGP is flawed and that fiscal policy is a much more potent instrument than interest rate policy; an argument that applies both in the short and in the long run. We also discussed international relations and exchange rate policy to conclude that international co-operation is more appropriate under this heading. Inflation considerations were discussed in the penultimate section where the conclusion is that inflation should only be considered as a side issue in view of the ample evidence and theoretical arguments.

Given the discussion in this chapter but also that of the earlier chapters, the question arises of what the future of the euro might entail: is it likely to collapse? This is the precise aim of the chapter that follows.

8
The Future of the Euro

8.1 Introduction

We discuss the future of the euro in this section, especially in the light of its recent experience. It would seem on the surface that the future of a monetary union encompassing 17 politically independent countries each with their own currencies prior to the union would be much influenced by Optimal Currency Area (OCA) considerations. The formation of the single currency and the euro area provides one of the few occasions on which a change in the scope of a currency area has been actively considered. The other recent cases that come to mind would be the reunification of Germany, and the splintering of Czechoslovakia, the Soviet Union and Yugoslavia. In each of those cases, the political considerations for the currency regime would dominate any OCA-style considerations (we return to the question of the relationship between monetary union and political union in chapter 9). As argued in chapter 2, the OCA considerations had virtually no impact on the decision to introduce a single European currency nor on the conditions governing which countries were to be members. This background is very relevant to the contents of this chapter as suggested in chapter 2.

We proceed in this chapter as follows. We discuss the issues that relate to the future of the euro in section 8.2. We turn our attention to fiscal policy in section 8.3 and to the European Central Bank (ECB) from the point of view of monetary and financial policies in section 8.4. Inflation is discussed in section 8.5 and current account deficits and competitiveness is the focus of chapter 8.6. We summarise and conclude this chapter in section 8.7.

8.2 Way forward

There are two key features of the euro project, which are highly relevant when thinking about its future and whether the euro can continue in anything like its present form and be associated with economic prosperity.

The first is that the euro project is based essentially on the neo-liberal policy framework (which has been outlined earlier in chapter 3; see, also, Arestis and Sawyer, 2006c for a more extensive discussion). This framework has been enshrined in law (most recently in the Treaty of Lisbon) and the neo-liberal ideology has become deeply embedded in the European political elite and the institutions of the European Union.

The second is that the single currency has been widely viewed as the crowning pinnacle of economic integration in removing what could be seen as the final barrier to free trade (different currencies and the associated costs) after the removal of non-tariff barriers under the Single European Act.

The major question here is how these two features of the euro project interact with the operations of the euro and its problems, and more significantly how those two features may prevent changes in the EMU project in order for the EMU to operate to provide economic prosperity across all its member countries. In our view the policy framework within which the EMU operates needs to be drastically changed; but to do so runs into the major obstacles, both political and ideological, of dramatically reforming the economic policy framework. Further, the euro has been a key element of the drive to economic integration that any withdrawal of a country from the euro would be a major defeat for the integration process.

The first feature was embedded in the Treaty of European Union in its various forms and now cemented in the Treaty of Lisbon ('The Treaty on the Functioning of the European Union'). Changes to the Treaty of Lisbon require the unanimous agreement of the 27 member countries, and since the changes required to support the euro involve policies which could be seen as moves towards political integration the possibilities of making those changes is close to zero. This indicates not only the serious weakness of the policy framework, but also that of embedding economic policies into a constitution, which is virtually impossible to change. It is the case, nonetheless, that with the fiscal compact in place now there can be a treaty between a range of countries without amending the Treaty of Lisbon.

It would also have to be recognised that the dominant macroeconomic institutions in the EMU, notably the ECB and the Directorate-General for Economic and Financial Affairs (D-G ECFIN), appear to be fully signed up to the neo-liberal agenda. The D-G ECFIN reports to the EU Commissioner for Economic and Monetary Affairs. In fact, the D-G ECFIN 'strives to improve the economic wellbeing of the citizens of the EU – through policies designed to promote sustainable economic growth, a high level of employment, stable public finances and financial stability. At the present juncture, this means working to ensure that the European economy emerges quickly and strongly from the present deep economic and financial crisis' (available at: http://ec.europa.eu/dgs/economy_finance/index_en.htm – see, also, footnote 5).

With regard to the second feature, it was recognised by some advocates of the euro that there were many ways in which there was insufficient economic integration to support a single currency, but that in the presence of a single currency, integration would continue to a stage, which did support a single currency. The conditions indicated by the Optimal Currency Area (OCA) literature could be seen as the nature of the integration-generating movements in relative prices and permitting factor mobility.

We now advance a range of macroeconomic policies and reforms, which we believe would substantially improve the economic performance and sustainability of the EMU. But we in no way underestimate the political, legal and ideological barriers, which are raised against policy changes along the lines indicated. But it is clear to us that the EMU cannot proceed with its current policy arrangements, and for those who strive for economic integration in the EU must realise that changes are urgently required 'to save the euro'.[1]

8.3 Fiscal policy

Two basic changes in the fiscal policy arrangements in EMU are required. The first is the need for an EMU-level fiscal policy under which the scale of the EMU budget would be greatly increased and the EMU would be able to run budget deficits (or surpluses) to support the level of economic activity within the EMU. The particular concern here is with the euro area, and as such fiscal policy would be limited to EMU members. The scale of such a policy has been variously put at 7½ per cent of GDP (Commission of the European Communities, 1977), 5 per cent (Huffschmid, 2005, chapter 16), 2 to 3 per cent of GDP (Currie, 1997; Goodhart and Smith, 1993). An EMU fiscal policy would, in general, only be able to address EMU-wide 'shocks'. The present crisis could be considered such an EMU-wide shock (though perhaps one on a scale only experienced every several decades), but figures such as those suggested above would not be on a scale to cope with such a shock, unless combined with substantial deficits at the national level.

The second is, in effect, to permit each member country to set its fiscal stance in what it judges to be its own best interests. There have always been concerns of 'spillover' effects, whereby one country's deficit affects the credit ratings and interest rates faced by others. These concerns have been very much overstated. In the absence of a substantial EMU-wide fiscal policy designed to achieve high levels of economic activity, each country has to be free to pursue that objective (if it wishes to do so).

The proposition of 'functional finance' (starting from Lerner, 1943) is that the budget deficit should be set with a view to ensure a high level of economic activity and not tied to any notion of a balanced budget (whether in current budget or total budget terms, whether on an annual basis or over the business cycle). There is the well-known accounting relationship of $(G - T) = (Q - X) + (S - I)$ (where G is government expenditure, T tax revenues, Q imports, X exports plus net income from abroad, S private savings and I private investment). The scale of the budget deficit (or indeed budget surplus) then depends on the size of the current account deficit, private savings and investment at a high level of economic activity. It then follows that the appropriate budget deficit depends on the conditions surrounding the current account (propensities to import, exports) and the net savings position (savings minus investment). For a country with a current account deficit and a tendency for savings to exceed investment would require a large budget deficit, while in contrast for a country with a current account surplus, and investment tending to exceed savings, a budget surplus would be appropriate. This is the basis of the 'one size fits all' problem, which comes with the Stability and Growth Pact (SGP). The shortcomings of the present SGP is that it seeks to impose the same conditions on all countries regardless of their broader economic circumstances and that it is a balanced budget (over the cycle), which is imposed on all. The latter will inevitably lead to deflationary tendencies in many countries without any compensating stimulatory tendencies in other countries.

It should be noted in the context of the SGP rules and fiscal rules in more general terms that they are very difficult if not impossible to enforce. Yet they do exist, and as noted in the *Economist* (14 May 2011, p. 88) there were 80 countries in 2011, which had fiscal rules, with only seven in 1990. Experience clearly shows that enforcement is difficult, if not impossible – see above, and also chapter 5, for relevant SGP enforcement difficulties and failures. In any case, SGP rules did not manage to prevent the recent debt crisis in the EMU. Fiscal rules also entail the serious distributional effects for such rules normally reduced benefits, which hurt severely the low-income groups.

The 'great recession' has raised a host of issues regarding the merits of fiscal policy and worries in certain quarters of debt-financed budget deficits. In the EU/EMU, it has raised another issue, which is concerned with fiscal policy in the environment of a monetary union. We have argued that monetary unions need an active fiscal policy, which is accompanied by fiscal transfers. The reason is simple enough. Regions within the EU/EMU are hit by asymmetric shocks, which can only be contained by interregional transfers, which substitute potentially for capital and labour mobility. The EU/EMU lack such a system, which is desperately needed. In its absence it is conceivable that some member countries may be compelled to exit the euro area.

8.4 European Central Bank: monetary and financial policies

There is a need to make some fundamental changes to the operation of the European Central Bank. The ECB, and the European System of Central Banks (ESCB), have been established as 'independent' entities, with the ECB being the independent central bank. 'Independence' is to be interpreted in a political sense:

> When exercising the powers and carrying out the tasks and duties conferred upon them by the Treaties and the Statute of the ESCB and of the ECB, neither the European Central Bank, nor a national central bank, nor any member of their decision-making bodies shall seek or take instructions from Union institutions, bodies, offices or agencies, from any government of a Member State or from any other body. The Union institutions, bodies, offices or agencies and the governments of the Member States undertake to respect this principle and not to seek to influence the members of the decision-making bodies of the European Central Bank or of the national central banks in the performance of their tasks. (Article 130 of the Treaty establishing the European Community)

It is not 'independent' in an ideological sense, and the ECB has frequently advocated fiscal and other policies, which are formally outside of its remit but which conform to the anti-Keynesian approach of fiscal consolidation, and advocacy of 'flexible labour markets'. For example, writing in December 2009, ECB (2009) argued that

> As regards fiscal policies, the Governing Council (of the ECB) re-emphasises how important it is for governments to develop, communicate and implement ambitious fiscal consolidation strategies in a timely manner. These strategies must be based on realistic output growth assumptions and focus on structural expenditure reforms, not least with a view to coping with the budgetary burden associated with an ageing population. ... With regard to structural reforms, most estimates indicate that the financial crisis has reduced the productive capacity of the euro area economies, and will continue to do so for some time to come. In order to support sustainable growth and employment, labour market flexibility and more effective incentives to work will be needed. Furthermore, policies that enhance competition and innovation are also urgently needed to speed up restructuring and investment and to create new business opportunities. (p. 7)[2]

The 'independence' of a central bank has been based on ideas that politicians are not to be trusted with key elements of macroeconomic policy, particularly in that elected politicians would favour expansionary policies with little regard to the inflationary implications. This view in part has been based on the idea of the Phillips curve and its different shape in the short and long run. There is a short-run trade-off between economic activity and inflation, which is absent in the long run in view of a hypothesised vertical Phillips curve relationship (see Arestis and Sawyer, 2004a; Sawyer, 2010, for a critique of this position). However, the financial crisis has emphasised, to say the least, the need for financial stability as a key objective of macroeconomic policy and of monetary policy. We would argue that the financial stability objective should be a prime objective and the operational independence of the European Central Bank brought to an end. The adoption of financial stability objective would, of course, require the development of a range of policy instruments.[3]

The 'independence' of the ECB would appear to preclude co-operation and coordination between the different bodies responsible for aspects of macroeconomic policies. Yet, in a world of multiple objectives (including high levels of economic activity and employment, financial stability, inflation and so on) there is a need for multiple instruments, which are operated by different authorities, and where there should be some coordination. At present, it is more like subordination with monetary policy taking pride of place and fiscal policy neutered by the lack of EMU fiscal policy and the constraints of the SGP on national budget deficits.

Subnational government can differ from national government with respect to its debt and deficits in that the bonds of the subnational government tier may not be accepted by the central bank as an 'acceptable' financial asset and its debt cannot be monetised, and further lacks any ability to 'print money'. The national government cannot itself 'print money', but through its relationship with the central bank its debt can be monetised, and, *in extremis,* could require the central bank to buy central government bonds in exchange for 'base money'. In effect, through its relationship with the central bank, a national government would never need to default on its own debt, provided that the debt is denominated in the domestic currency. The arrangements within the EMU leave a national member government in the position of a subnational tier in the sense that the ECB can decide whether national debt is 'acceptable' for financial-asset purposes and on what terms. The position needs to be changed such that all financial assets issued by EMU member governments are always acceptable by the ECB.

The key reforms required with regard to the ECB are: (i) a reformulation of the objectives of the ECB to include high and sustainable levels of employment and economic growth and financial stability; (ii) the ECB must be made accountable to the European Parliament, and its statutes changed so that it can clearly be involved in the coordination of fiscal and monetary policies, and indeed that ultimately it can take instructions from other European bodies such as the Economic and Financial Affairs Council (ECOFIN);[4] (iii) the ECB operates with regard to national governments within EMU in the ways in which a national central bank would operate with regard to a national government, and specifically be able to, in effect, monetise the debts of national governments. In effect, the ECB is required to possess the 'lender of last resort' function of the type of all other national central banks.

We comment briefly as a conclusion to this section on recent developments that relate to the independence of the ECB. The 'fiscal compact' for the EMU is now to be embodied in the Treaty on Stability, Coordination and Governance. The fiscal compact is more rigorous in terms of the constraints on budget deficits of the member states in relation to those that were contained in the Stability and Growth Pact and the requirement for a 'structural balanced budget'. The treaty (signed by all the European Union members with the exception of the UK and the Czech Republic) makes no mention of the role of the 'independent' European Central Bank. This is not at all surprising in view of the sacrosanct nature of the current 'most independent' role of the ECB, and also given that 'fiscal consolidation' and calls for 'structural reforms' (which also feature in the Treaty) have been constantly on the agenda promoted by the ECB. But the position of the ECB lies at the heart of the euro crisis through its ambivalence over supporting the fiscal positions of national governments, and in a failure to provide the support to those governments which national central banks generally provide.

Some politicians have begun to question aspects of the current operation of the ECB. During the French Presidential campaign of May 2012, Nicolas Sarkosy 'called for the European Central Bank (ECB) to take a radically different role by lending directly to troubled eurozone states rather than to banks, and by keeping interest rates low' (http://www.bbc.co.uk/news/world-europe-17781224). He was quickly rebuked by a German government spokesman Steffen Seibert who said, 'It is the core belief of the federal government ... that the role and office of the ECB be independent of encouragement and assistance from politics. And that's well known in Paris.' Nicolas Sarkosy's opponent in the run-off election for the Presidency, Francois Hollande called for the ECB's refinancing operations to bypass banks and lend directly to states. He added 'I know that Germany is totally hostile, so this is another topic for discussion' (Interview, Europe 1, 19 April 2012).

The mandate of the ECB should be more akin to the dual mandate of the Federal Reserve with regards to growth and inflation, rather than maintaining the obsessional focus on price stability. This would be a modest small step and could perhaps be achieved by a sufficiently broad interpretation of 'without prejudice to the objective of price stability, the ECSB shall support the general economic policies' of the European Union 'contributing the objectives of economic growth, full employment etc.' (Treaty of Lisbon). However, such a modest change would have little effect. As we have often argued (see, for example, Arestis and Sawyer, 2008a), the current inflation targeting does not deliver, and crucially within the Economic and Monetary Union does not and cannot address inflation differentials between countries, which have contributed to changing relative competitiveness and to the yawning current account imbalances between the countries of EMU. It can further be doubted whether monetary policy itself can have much effect on the pace of economic growth; though the failures to support fiscal policies and financial stability do have considerable damage on economic prosperity.

Major and basic changes in the roles of the ECB are required as argued above. In addition to the changes suggested above, three further changes are relevant. The first change would be to end the independence of the ECB, and to have it integrated with the policy-making arrangements of the Economic and Monetary Union to facilitate the coordination of economic policy-making. The second change should be for a shift away from sole focus on inflation (for which in any event they are not equipped through interest rate policies to influence inflation) and to view the major focus of the activities of the ECB being financial stability. It should be self-evident that financial instability and crisis impose substantial costs (much more than might come from inflation). The third change should be to ensure that the ECB provides support to the fiscal policies being pursued. As we have often argued, this should be a Federal-level fiscal policy with expenditure and tax revenues of the order of 10 or more per cent of GDP with ability to run budget deficits or surpluses as appropriate to the economic conditions. We have also advocated that fiscal policy should not focus on some notion of balanced budget but that it should be used to achieve high levels of aggregate demand, economic activity and employment (whether or not deficits are involved). But in the near term until a Federal fiscal policy is developed, national fiscal policy should be conducted along similar lines. There is always the need for the ECB to give support to the democratically determined fiscal policies by where necessary providing funds and always accepting member governments' debt in open market operations and the provision of funds to the banking system. It should also be mentioned at this point that another important policy consideration is financial stability, an important policy that has been discussed extensively in chapter 5.

We may conclude by suggesting that unless fundamental changes are introduced in terms of the way the ECB functions and the policies pursued by it, no hope is there for the current euro crisis to be resolved satisfactorily. Nor would it provide confidence for the future of the euro area.

8.5 Inflation

The policies on inflation have been, as indicated in chapter 4, at best, a limited success. We have argued that even this has been more by good luck and probably due to globalisation rather than through the efficacy of the policy instrument (Angeriz and Arestis, 2008; Arestis and Sawyer,

2013a). In our view, inflation in the EMU (and elsewhere) is influenced only to a limited extent by domestic policies (Angeriz and Arestis, 2007, 2008; Arestis and Sawyer, 2008a). Although there has been an EMU-level inflation policy operated through the ECB, there are also inflation policies at the national level. To a greater or lesser extent there are national policies on wage and price determination. As seen above, whether for reasons of national policies and/or differences in the price- and wage-setting institutions, differences in national inflation rates have persisted.

Some of the proponents of the euro acknowledged that the conditions to be in place for a successful single currency suggested by the OCA literature were not present (at least to the degree needed; see section 8.2 above). However, and as acknowledged at the same time, the continuing process of integration under a single currency would generate changes in the direction of those conditions. One of the conditions of OCA is price flexibility, understood to mean that the general level of prices in one country could change relative to those in other countries within the currency union where there was a 'shock' to the relative standing of that country. Essentially, changes in the demand or supply position would be compensated by corresponding changes to relative prices. But it turned out that while there was, in a sense, price flexibility between countries it was not in the manner envisaged. As can be seen from Table 2.3 (in chapter 2), over the period 2002–08 inflation in Germany did not increase as rapidly as in Greece, Portugal and Spain (with the exception of 2009 and in the case of Spain and Portugal). Yet Germany was running a current account surplus and Greece, Portugal and Spain deficits. The differences in inflation also had perverse effects in terms of inflation policy.

The continued differences in inflation experience undermine the euro as the competitiveness of the relatively high-inflation countries deteriorate. There is clearly no EU-level policy at present, which can address this issue. One approach would be to assert that the pressures of integration would lead to countries having to achieve similar inflation rates. Even if that is so, similar inflation rates may well be combined with different levels of unemployment. There is then a need for the development of some understanding between EMU member countries on this issue. There is no current policy to address inflation differentials, and the current monetary policy makes it worse (by there being low if not negative (high) real rates of interest in countries with high (low) inflation rate). There is a need for a coordinated approach and common inflation target to be addressed by national policies.

This would not be 'inflation targeting' if that term is understood to mean an inflation objective pursued by an independent central bank through interest rates, but rather a coordinated attempt by the member states of EMU to use their own national policies to achieve a common rate of inflation to avoid the inflation differences. This could take form of using fiscal policy to vary demand – not to be recommended but possible. This could take form of national agreements on incomes and other economic variables. What has to be avoided is competitive devaluation of real exchange rate (between EMU member countries) achieved through super-low inflation.

8.6 Current account deficits and competitiveness

The data in chapter 2 (notably Tables 2.3, 2.4 and 2.5) indicate something of the scale by which relative prices and relative unit labour costs have changed, when the nominal exchange rates of the national currencies of the original EMU member states were locked together, and Table 2.6 indicates the divergent trends in the current account positions. One interpretation of those changes is that they represent the adjustment of real exchange rates between EMU member countries in the face of a combination of inappropriately set nominal exchange rates (back in 1998 for most) and 'shocks'. But this overlooks the prevailing current account deficits when the euro was formed and some tendency for the current account deficits to persist and widen. A country in a fixed exchange rate system, which is in the nature of a currency union for participating countries, in dealing with cumulative differential inflation and current account deficits can endure domestic deflation (to reduce imports and perhaps lower domestic costs) or can devalue its currency. The latter is ruled out by membership of EMU. So it would appear that deflation is the only answer. Before dealing with this proposition, it is important to note that current account imbalances among the EMU member countries were not considered in the process of setting up the euro area (see Arestis and Paúl, 2009, for further details). However, more recently and in view of the 'great recession' a new mechanism for the prevention and correction of macroeconomic imbalances has been proposed (European Council, 2010). Economies with problematic imbalances would be identified along with numerical monitoring. Subsequent inspections would be undertaken to identify the seriousness of the problem and recommendations would be proposed. The latter could include corrective measures to be reviewed by the Council subsequently. Economic sanctions would be applied if necessary within the framework of the revised SGP or the new 'pact for the euro' (see section 8.8 below for further details on the revised SGP and the new 'pact for the euro').

A current account deficit can interact with a budget deficit in the following sense. As is well known from the identity $(X - Q) = (S - I) + (T - G)$, with the symbols as in section 8.3, a current account deficit and a budget deficit will be related for a given net private savings position. Other things being equal (that is net private savings) then a larger current account deficit would be associated with a larger budget deficit (there is no causal link implied). The current account deficits on the scale observed in a number of EMU countries are unlikely to be sustainable as they require continual funding and likely to imply rising external debts. Yet countries are locked into a fixed nominal exchange rate system, where many have experienced a loss of competitiveness and in effect rising real exchange rates. There have to be mechanisms developed for the adjustments of those exchange rates, which would seem to require a coordinated mechanism for the adjustment of the prevailing exchange rates between member countries of the EMU and for the generation of similar rates of inflation. It has also been argued above that the ECB should relate to member governments and to their financial liabilities in a manner similar to the ways in which a national central bank would to a national government. These policy initiatives involve many of the features of a political integration. It is on the latter aspect to which we turn our attention next. Before doing so it is worth noting that another way of regaining the possibility of achieving competitiveness is for the weak countries to reintroduce their national currencies. Such a move would also enable these countries to manage their public debts and avoid bankruptcy since they can under the new circumstances 'print money' and finance budget deficits in the process. However, the latter solution entails the serious problem that the accounts of non-residents are bound to be shifted to non-domestic bank accounts that would lead to an outflow of capital with dramatic adverse implications for the domestic banking sectors. The relevant rescue packages are designed to avoid problems of the type to which we have just referred and also bail out weak countries to prevent them from bankruptcies.

The pattern of current account imbalances poses considerable difficulties for EMU. The presence of trade deficits along with the statistics on the evolution of unit labour costs and prices suggest that many, particularly Mediterranean, countries suffer from a lack of competitiveness and in the context of a single currency area an inability to devalue. The pattern of current account deficits and surpluses implies a corresponding pattern of capital account surpluses (i.e. borrowing) and deficits (i.e. lending). Directly or indirectly capital is flowing from the current account surplus countries to deficit countries, bearing in mind that EMU has an entity close to a balanced current account position. In the era prior to the financial crisis, countries with current account deficits were able to borrow readily from others to fund the deficit, and indeed within the EMU to do so at relatively low rates of interest. As noted above, for those countries with relatively high inflation, real interest rates were particularly low or even negative. The major difficulty with any current account deficit comes from the requirement to continually fund the deficit, and the mounting debts and interest and similar payments on the borrowing. The major challenge now facing EMU is how to correct the pattern of surpluses and deficits, and to put in place policies, which will prevent similar severe imbalances reappearing in the future.

There may be doubts on the effectiveness of devaluation in terms of a nominal exchange rate depreciation leading to a sustained real depreciation and the responsiveness of imports and exports to the changes in prices involved with a devaluation. For a country with its own currency devaluation would clearly be one response to current account deficit. In a single currency area, a combination of slower or negative inflation in the deficit countries and faster inflation in the surplus countries would help to resolve the current account imbalances. However, in EMU this would involve a reversal of the patterns of inflation observed over the past decade and would be a lengthy process to generate the scale of changes in relative competitiveness. Further the process by which a deficit country sought to generate low or negative inflation could well involve demand deflation with the consequent loss of employment and output.

This last point leads us to the major point that a failure to correct the current account imbalances would condemn the deficit countries to many years of slow or negative growth, with spillover effects on to the surplus countries. The survival of the EMU in its present form and membership does depend on an ability to correct these imbalances. The alternative is for some of the deficit countries to leave the euro and reintroduce their national currency, which would then most likely depreciate against the euro, bringing some relief to the deficit. EMU core countries are, however, determined not to allow this procedure. In any case, there are doubts as to how far devaluation (whether through depressing domestic prices within a single currency or through reintroduction of own currency with subsequent depreciation against the euro) could rectify the current account deficits. The productive base of the export industries of the countries concerned may simply lack the capacity and/or markets to be able to expand production and sales sufficiently in the face of devaluation to bring about the necessary changes. The alternative would require a long-term plan to improve competitiveness and build an industrial base. This, however, is a long-term solution and it is short-term ones that are desperately required. In other words, policies to enable the flow of funds from surplus to deficit countries, during the period of reconstruction, are required. How could that be developed is the focus of the chapter that follows. Before turning to chapter 9, though, it is important to comment on recent developments that relate especially to the SGP, namely the fiscal compact. We pursue this avenue immediately in section 8.7.

8.7 The fiscal compact

The Treaty on Stability, Coordination and Governance incorporates the 'fiscal compact' and is an inter-government treaty, not a change to the EU treaties (European Council, 2011a). The fiscal compact requires that tax and spending plans will be checked by the European officials before budgets can be implemented by national governments. There will be automatic actions against those countries that overspend. In effect, the new agreement tightens the rules of the old SGP, which had already been revised in 2005, but to no apparent improvement. The fiscal compact retains the principles of the previous 'fiscal pact' versions but with the added one that breaking of the deficit rules may actually be punished in some way. The limits of the revised and old SGP are, in effect, to balance overall budget over the cycle and limit the national budget deficit in any year to a maximum of 3 per cent of GDP. In place of the previous threat of 0.2 per cent of GDP as a 'fine' (though never implemented even though there were 40 cases where the 3 per cent limit was breached), there is now a change, which is as follows: euro area states' budgets should be balanced or in surplus; this principle will be deemed respected if, as a rule, the annual structural deficit does not exceed 0.5 per cent of gross domestic product; and this is be written into national constitutions. In the case when a euro area member state is in breach of the 3 per cent deficit ceiling, the old SGP ceiling, there will be automatic consequences, including possible sanctions, unless a qualified majority of euro area states is opposed.

The 'fiscal compact' does nothing to address the major problem of the EMU, namely the large current account imbalances, which ranged in 2013 (first quarter) from a surplus of 6 per cent in the case of Germany to a deficit of 1.8 per cent in the case of France (on a quarter to quarter basis). There is also the serious issue of whether existing European institutions can be used to implement what is in effect an intergovernmental treaty. The French and the German governments would like to see the European Commission and the European Court of Justice involved in enforcing and overseeing these new rules. In the words of the European Commission (2011),

> Member States in Excessive Deficit Procedure shall submit to the Commission and the Council for endorsement, an economic partnership programme detailing the necessary structural reforms to ensure an effectively durable correction of excessive deficits. The implementation of the programme, and the yearly budgetary plans consistent with it, will be monitored by the Commission and the Council. (p. 3)

Even so, the implication is that it is by far not a fiscal union arrangement.

Before writing a commitment into a national constitution, it would be worth examining whether a country can ever achieve a 'balanced structural budget'. Some countries may but others not, yet this is being imposed on all. Consider what a balanced structural budget means: at a level of output, which is deemed to be potential (or others such as corresponding to a high level of employment), government revenue and expenditure are in balance. In turn, this implies that private investment equals private savings plus capital inflow (equal to current account deficit); and that this equality holds at potential output and that the equality holds for the intention to invest, intention to save and so on. It is not that the equality holds at some level of output but at a specified level of output. Some neo-liberal economists may believe that savings intentions and investment intentions can be aligned at potential output (or full employment) but where is the evidence?

There is a clear lack of symmetry here. Structural deficits cannot be more than 0.5 per cent but any level of structural surpluses is allowed. Those countries, which have conditions (such as strong net exports, high rates of investment) conducive to budget surpluses, can have such surpluses: those which have conditions requiring budget deficits to sustain demand (net imports, high levels of savings relative to investment) cannot deploy deficits.

The aim of a balanced average ('structural') budget is actually a significant budget surplus when calculations are made (as they should) in real terms; that is, with allowance for the impact of inflation on real value of government debt. But more significantly it would involve a very substantial excess of tax revenue over current government expenditure (excluding interest payments). Further, it makes no allowance for governments to be able to borrow to fund public investment. The profoundly undemocratic nature of this approach is clear – the unelected European Commission can 'request' that the elected national Parliament and government to change its budget (see, for example, European Commission, 2012a). Let us also note the problematic nature of assessment of budgets. The forecast of budget for the year ahead requires forecasts of economic figures such as growth, employment, inflation and so on for that year. The assessment of structural budget position requires estimates of potential output (which have often been subject to revisions many years after the event).

It is clear that the major objections to the fiscal compact, and to the old SGP, is that it seeks to impose without any justification a balanced budget and that it poses restrictions in the use of fiscal policy in the face of economic crises. And as we have argued recently (Arestis and Sawyer, 2011b), and will argue further in chapter 9, proper fiscal union operated without balanced budget requirements is the way forward.

It clearly is the case, then, that the 'fiscal compact' cannot deliver. Neither the governments of the EMU countries nor the European Central Bank (ECB) have committed themselves to doing enough, let alone satisfactorily. The ECB is not prepared to perform the proper role of any central bank, namely the 'lender of last resort' function. EMU governments have not made progress on the 'eurobond' idea, whereby the EMU members would share the troubled economies burden of debt. The adjustment of the EMU country imbalances is imposed entirely on the deficit countries. Strategies that do not account for both creditor and debtor countries cannot succeed. Time and time again in the past, this monolithic approach that avoids including surplus countries in the adjustment process has failed. Keynes (1980) was very clear on this proposition and the need to involve both surplus and deficit countries, but his policies have been ignored. The economic solution proposed for curing persistent imbalances is for the deficit countries to become 'more competitive'; this would help them increase their exports and reduce their imports (see, also, Davidson, 2011). The *New York Times* ('IMF Chief Chastises Policy Makers', August 28, 2011) quote the President of the ECB who suggested at the annual central bankers Jackson Hole August 2011 conference that 'Europe's problems are fundamentally a question of which governments have taken steps to promote growth and become competitive and which have not'; and that 'Greece, Portugal and Ireland, in particular have progressively lost competitiveness vis-à-vis their main trading partners in Europe. Germany is now an example of how big dividends of reform can be if structural adjustment is made a strategic priority and implemented with sufficient patience'.

The markets had been behaving in an encouraging manner in the run-up to the 8/9 December 2011 summit; yields on long-term Italian and Spanish bonds fell – two big euro area countries whose yields had already reached record levels. Since then, yields on the same bonds increased initially and fell again after the ECB's intervention on 21 December 2011, whereby €489.2 billion were injected into the euro-area banking system in the form of bank borrowing. This was undertaken through the Long Term Refinancing Operation (LTRO), one of the ECB mechanisms. There were more than 523 banks involved, encouraged by the policy makers of the region, who borrowed the €489.2 billion in three-year loans, equivalent to 5 per cent of the euro area GDP; actually a much bigger take-up than what had been expected. It is actually the largest amount provided in a single ECB operation so far. However, this amount is not as big as it might appear since the ECB switched funds from shorter-term facilities; in fact it was only about €190 billion the amount of 'fresh' liquidity. The euro and equities also surged as a result. It was expected that the excess liquidity just mentioned would be used to finance purchases of peripheral euro area higher-yielding government debt, thereby helping to ease their debt crisis. Such optimism, however, never materialised!

The initial enthusiasm of the markets soon waned – Italian and Spanish government-bond yields rose and equities as well as the euro retreated. This is not surprising, though, for such measures only help to address the liquidity shortage in the euro area banking sector, but does not provide new loans to the private sector since banks shed assets in an attempt to abide by the new capital rules. There is also the more serious problem that the weak economic performance of most euro area countries would not allow the necessary demand for credit by both business and consumers to materialise. The relevant experience of the period since August 2007 is very telling on this score; it suggests that banks are expected to hoard the cash, especially so in view of the looming refinancing needs in the first quarter of 2012 and also the gloomy expectations for the year 2012 and beyond. In fact, banks in the euro area deposited €452 billion with the ECB by Tuesday 27 December 2011 (*Financial Times*, 29 December, 2011), the week after the LTRO operation. Still it is expected that those countries where the economic difficulties emerged from their troubled banking sector, such as Spain and Ireland, would get some help out of this operation. Interestingly enough, on Wednesday 28 December 2011, €9 billion of six-month Italian bonds were sold at 3.25 per cent, down from the euro area record of 6.5 per cent reached in November 2011. Only for the yield to return to its original level on the same day once news emerged of the €452 billion bank of euro deposits with the ECB. On the 29 December the overall demand for the ten-year Italian bonds was low with the sale raising only €7 billion rather than the targeted €8.5 billion. As a result the interest demanded by investors on these bonds was above the critical 7 per cent level, which is viewed as unsustainable, after the auction. But here again the ECB is not prepared to act as a 'lender of last resort', thereby does not intervene in government bond markets. This would be an illegal act according to the President of the ECB (see, for example, *The Economist*, 17 December 2011).

Two further aspects are worth discussing. The first is the pledge of €200 billion to the IMF by the EMU country-members to deal with the crisis; this amount is clearly not enough but the hope is that other countries outside the euro area would follow. The second is the proposal, discussed at the EU summit of 28/29 June 2012, for the European Stability Mechanism (ESM) to be given a banking licence that would give it access to ECB funding. In addition, banking supervision by the ECB is included. Also important is the long-term proposal to move towards a banking union and a single euro area bank-deposit guarantee scheme. The possibility of introducing common issuance of debt by the euro area, in the form of eurobonds and/or eurobills is included. It is widely recognised that the amounts just referred to would not be enough to cover the borrowing needs of Italy and Spain, if required, over the near future. Clearly the 'fiscal compact' is not promising at all.

Under the current economic circumstances, it is economic policies to promote growth that are vital. The 'fiscal compact' contains nothing of the required economic policies.

8.8 Summary and conclusions

We would argue that the policy framework within which the euro is placed is 'not fit for purpose'. Three aspects of this argument stand out. First, the 'independence' of the ECB precludes the ECB devoting its attention to financial stability and to co-ordinating and co-operating with other macroeconomic institutions in pursuit of other objectives, such as high levels of economic activity. Second, it does not have ways of developing fiscal policy, which would be supportive of high levels of economic activity, recognising that budget deficits are generally required. Third, there are no mechanisms for resolving the pattern of current account deficits and surpluses, which we argue are unsustainable in their present form. Without the ability to vary the exchange rate, countries with current account deficits will be thrown back to deflation. For it is the case that the EMU completely lacks any mechanisms by which countries can resolve their deficit problems.

A further problem which has emerged and been highlighted by the 'great recession' is the dual economic reality in the EMU. This is the northern part of the EMU, where the economies are reviving, with Germany and France at the forefront, especially Germany; and the periphery, mostly southern (Greece and Portugal) but including Ireland, heavily involved in the sovereign-debt crisis. Given the onerous austerity packages imposed on the latter countries, the really interesting question is how long they will be able to withstand the pressures for even more austerity and the undesirable consequences. Fallout is seriously and eminently possible. At the same time, though, no serious attempt is initiated at seriously resolving the dual economic reality. The choice faced by many EMU countries is then the stark one of remaining with the euro and suffering an indefinite future of deflation and high unemployment or in effect leaving the euro.

The economic problems within the euro area have been building since its inception, and have become acute with the onset of the 'great recession'. The faults lie in the neo-liberal design of the euro project, now embedded in the Treaty of Lisbon, and where there is little prospect of serious changes because of the unanimity requirements for change. But without basic and fundamental changes, many (perhaps all) euro area countries face a bleak economic future. Under these circumstances the future of the euro is surely not bright to say the least. This contagious financial crisis is the biggest threat not merely to Europe, but globally. Changes within the euro area are thereby desperately needed.[5] Most important of which is fiscal integration; not the fiscal compact. This is the exact focus of chapter 9 where we examine the importance of economic and political integration.

9
Economic Convergence and/or Political Integration

9.1 Introduction

One might have expected that the formation of the EMU, initially encompassing 12 (and now 17) politically independent countries each with their own currencies prior to them joining the Union, would be considerably influenced by economic convergence and political integration considerations. It is the purpose of this chapter to demonstrate that neither of these considerations had been influential in creating and shaping the EMU and the euro. Indeed to show that in the absence of economic integration political union becomes paramount. Clearly, this is not an argument based on politics but purely on economic grounds that support the importance of developing pan-EMU economic policies, which properly coordinated could potentially drive the union to improved economic development.

We examine these aspects in this chapter. We begin in section 9.2 by looking at monetary unions from a historical perspective in an attempt to draw relevant lessons. We then proceed in section 9.3 to discuss economic convergence before we turn to political integration issues in section 9.4. Constraints on reforms are discussed in section 9.5, while section 9.6 visits recent proposals in EMU towards what is termed fiscal union. Finally, section 9.7 summarises and concludes.

9.2 Monetary unions: historical perspective

We begin by visiting Table 9.1 which describes examples of monetary unions around the world. This table divides monetary unions into a number of categories. Five such examples are shown in Table 9.1. The first example provides a category that includes those monetary unions

Table 9.1 Monetary unions

STILL SURVIVING BUT WITH POLITICAL UNION	
British monetary union between England and Scotland	From 1707
Italian monetary union	From 1861
US Federal Reserve system	From 1913
German unification	From 1990
STILL SURVIVING WITHOUT POLITICAL UNION	
Belgium – Luxembourg union	From 1923
West and Central African CFA Franc Zone[a]	From 1948
Eastern Caribbean Currency Union[b]	From 1983
FAILED ONCE POLITICAL SYSTEM COLLAPSED	
Roman monetary union[c]	286–301
German monetary union	1857–1918
The Soviet system	1917–1993
Yugoslavia	1919–1992
Czechoslovakian Republic	1919–1994
FAILED ONCE ECONOMIC LINKS COLLAPSED	
British monetary union between England and Ireland	1926–1979
TEMPORARY MONETARY UNIONS	
Latin monetary union[d]	1865–1926
Scandinavian currency union[e]	1873–1921
OTHER CURRENCY PEGS	
Gold standard	1870–1931/36
Bretton Woods	1944–1973
European Exchange Rate Mechanism (ERM)	From 1979
Asian currency crisis	1997

[a] CFA: Common Franc Area (Benin, Burkina Faso, Cameroon, Central African Republic, Chad, Congo, Equatorial Guinea, Gabon, Ivory Coast, Mali, Niger, Senegal and Togo); after 1 January 1999 the peg is linked to the Euro.

[b] This Union includes: Anguilla, Antigua and Barbuda, Commonwealth of Dominica, Grenada, Montserrat, St Kitts and Nevis, St Lucia, St Vincent and The Grenadines.

[c] Emperor Diocletian reforms Roman coinage, thereby creating the first single currency union.

[d] This Union included: France, Belgium, Italy and Switzerland; Greece and Bulgaria joined in 1867. The link changed from silver to gold in 1878.

[e] This Union was established between Denmark and Sweden in May 1873 (both almost joined the Latin Union but eventually did not because of the Franco-Prussian War of 1870–1871). Norway joined in October 1875.

Sources: Adapted from The Financial Times (23 March, 1998) and Pentecost (1999).

that still survive but with political union. The political union in the case of this category ensures the success of these monetary unions. The second set of examples is a category that includes unions of small countries that have survived but without political union, but economic convergence with varying degrees of success is in place in the case of these countries. The third category is a good example of those monetary unions where they failed once the political dimension collapsed. No sooner does the political bond disappears, so does the monetary union. The fourth category is the one where once economic links collapsed, the monetary union disappeared. The fifth category contains those cases where although survival for some time took place without political union, they eventually collapsed when they were subjected to severe shocks (in the example of Table 9.1, the suspension of the gold standard at the beginning of the Second World War that led to volatility in real exchange rates, and the inflationary pressures following the cessation of hostilities, were the main causes). A sixth category, other currency pegs, may be portrayed to show examples where the importance of flexibility is evident. The examples cited are particularly pertinent when currency systems bind together economies whose cycles and structures are significantly different; at the end of the day they simply collapse.

The examples of Table 9.1, which are really a short excursion into the history of monetary unions, produce two important lessons. The first is that political union appears to be an extremely important prerequisite for a monetary union to survive. Monetary unions last for some time but eventually they must become a political union to survive. The second is that in the absence of political integration economic convergence is paramount for the survival of a monetary union of a group of independent states.

It clearly follows from these observations on the contents of Table 9.1 that the belief in a market economy to function effectively without government intervention and redistribution would clearly suggest no need for economic policies within the euro area. Clearly, the euro area began with considerable economic disparities. The view that either the disparities would be eliminated through a process of market competition or that such disparities are politically sustainable would lead to the position that there is little requirement for an effective political union. The notion of effective political union clearly implies significant EU-level taxation, social security and public expenditure programmes. We leave open the question as to whether that would entail a formal political union within a federal state. We would argue that the effective operation of a market economy involves government intervention of that form. A common social security system would enhance labour mobility as well as involve elements of redistribution. A substantive fiscal policy would likewise aid economic integration but would involve significant fiscal transfers between regions and between countries. Economic policies throughout the monetary union are thus important not merely by themselves but also coordination of the relevant economic policies (see Arestis, 2012b, on the importance of such a coordination of economic policies).

The current euro area arrangements do not involve mechanisms for the reduction of the disparities of unemployment and GDP per head. The disparities of unemployment inevitably undermine the achievement of high levels of employment across the euro area. When some regions are experiencing low unemployment and high rates of capacity utilisation, others remain with high unemployment. Inflation pressures in the low unemployment regions lead to high interest rates accompanied by policies to slow down the euro area economy. A monetary union involves the imposition of a common currency across a number of nations through the requirement that the common currency is the only legal tender within the nations involved. There is also the obvious requirement for central bank in the monetary union, and in an era of dominance of monetary policy over fiscal policy, that central bank becomes the only effective macroeconomic policy maker. Any requirements for an effective fiscal policy across the monetary union, which would be redistributive across time and space, points in the direction of the emergence of a fiscal authority at the level of the monetary union. Further requirements, such as measures to enhance trade or for a common social security system to enhance labour mobility, again point in the direction of policies being exercised at the level of the monetary union. It could be argued that it is feasible that such policies can be introduced through the construction of institutions at the level of the monetary union without formal political union. But in a number of respects if there were to be fiscal policy, social security policy etc., at the level of the monetary union, it comes close to being a political union. We would suggest, though, that a monetary union requires considerable central government to operate fiscal and social security policies across the euro area.

Clearly, then, the historical perspective of monetary unions discussed in this section points towards a political union, where economic policies and close coordination of them, is absolutely necessary for a successful monetary union. The second conclusion reached from our discussion of Table 9.1 is that of economic convergence, which we discuss in the section that follows.

9.3 Economic convergence

Although the importance of economic convergence in our discussion above is concerned with small states, the argument can easily be generalised. It might be expected that any monetary union encompassing a number of politically independent countries, each with their own currencies prior to the union, would be much influenced by Optimal Currency Area (OCA) considerations. As discussed in chapter 2, OCA considerations had virtually no impact on the decision to introduce the single euro currency, nor on the conditions governing which countries were to be members either. It ought to be noted, though, that the single currency was preceded by the Single European Act that created a single market, which involved more than just free trade in that it sought to bring in common standards for goods and services, reduction of 'invisible' trade barriers, and legal mobility of capital, adding to the free movement of labour which had been enshrined since the original Treaty of Rome. There were also, of course, the Maastricht criteria as explored in chapter 2, but they related to convergence in nominal variables at a particular point in time, and made no reference to convergence in real variables (whether in terms of levels such as GDP per head or rates of change and position within the business cycle). Nor was there any reference to what could be termed structural economic convergence in terms of institutional and organisational arrangement.

It would be desirable for a single currency to be used in an economic area within which there is openness of goods markets and mobility of factors of production (labour, capital) as the mobility of factors is seen as one way in which adjustment is made to differences in economic performance. Further, member economies should share similar inflationary tendencies since a common currency imposes a common inflation rate. The Single European Act of 1986 and the implementation of the single European market by the end of 1992 were steps in seeking to ensure the mobility of goods and services and of capital within the EU. But it is well known that effective labour mobility within the EU remains low, especially by comparison with the US, despite the large differences in real wages and unemployment rates across the EU. Although not specifically linked with the single currency, there has been considerable labour mobility since 2004 with the accession of new member countries. Perhaps three points need to be made about this. First, the operation of national social security systems rather than EU-wide inhibits labour mobility, for example, a person moving from one country to another is not immediately entitled to benefits in the country to which they are moving. Second, when movement of labour is termed migration, then the social consequences of labour mobility need to be considered, and the possible hostility of host economies and the losses of skilled labour to the departure countries. Third, the 'model' underlying labour mobility (particularly in the OCA) is that labour moves from low-wage areas to high-wage areas, and from areas of high unemployment to ones of low unemployment; the effects then of labour mobility are intended to be to restore some form of labour market equilibrium, with a tendency towards the equalisation of wages; wages in previously high-wage areas would tend to fall.

Price flexibility (in terms of relative prices across countries) appears to have remained low. The differences in labour market institutions, notably over wage determination, mean that there are different inflationary tendencies and different responses to economic shocks. The convergence criteria ensured a convergence of inflation rates, which is not the same as convergence of inflationary mechanisms and tendencies. Indeed, similar rates of inflation across the euro area countries in 1998 (the relevant year for the application of the convergence criteria) were accompanied by widely differing rates of unemployment from around 4 per cent in the case of Austria and the Netherlands to 17 per cent in the case of Spain (and the difference in unemployment between regions was much more marked – from 3 per cent in the Oberösterreich region of Austria to 32 per cent in the Andulucia region of Spain and nearly 37 per cent in Reunion, France; these figures refer to 1997). The calculated output gap, as a sign of the stage of the business cycle, varied (according to the OECD, 1999, measure) from over +2 per cent in Ireland to –2 per cent in Italy (and there was a slight widening of the differences in 1999). Fiscal transfers are hardly in evidence and there is no possibility of the EU budget operating as a stabiliser. There is currently no mechanism for the operation of an EU level fiscal policy that could have stabilising effects (as an automatic stabiliser) over time. Nor is there a mechanism, which could have any significant redistributive element across economic regions.

The optimists would tend to believe that the continuing effects of the single European market and the existence of the euro will lead to further integration between the national economies. This integration could then be reflected in some convergence between national business cycles and (perhaps) some reduction in the extent of asymmetric shocks that impact on some countries but not on others. There could, in the fullness of time, be increased mobility of labour. But there seems little prospects of EU-wide measures such as a common social security policy, which would enhance the mobility of labour. In any case, it is clear and the 'great recession' has demonstrated it all vividly; namely that since the introduction of the euro in January 1999, there is no evidence that economic convergence has taken place or is in sight of materialising. In any case, it would appear to be the case that labour mobility has increased (within the EU rather than the EMU and not so much as a consequence of the single currency). In addition, the intra-EMU trade has increased, which in turn is supposed to aid the integration of business cycles.

This brief discussion, combined with the relevant discussion in chapters 4 and 8, indicates to us that OCA considerations appear to have played little role in the formation of the euro area. Further, if the OCA literature is correct, then the euro area would appear not to be an Optimal Currency Area, indeed it is far from optimal. Some of the departures of the euro area from an OCA arise from policy decisions (notably the absence of a EU fiscal policy) whereas others (notably the lack of labour mobility) are more deeply embedded and some attempts have been made to address them (for example. the development of transferability of qualifications between countries). But to say that the euro area is not optimal is not the same as saying that the euro area is not better than the continuation of national currencies. However, we would argue that it is still the case that the criteria proposed by the OCA literature still have some relevance in judging whether the introduction of the euro is an improvement. The point remains that the OCA requirements have been ignored in terms of the Economic and Monetary Union.

9.4 Political integration

A relevant question is the extent to which the recent changes at both the EMU and the EU levels, especially so since the eruption of the 'great recession' in August 2007 and the subsequent euro area debt crisis, move closer to a de facto political integration. To begin with the absence of bailout mechanisms should be noted for it left the euro area completely unarmed to deal with the debt crisis when it was erupted. A series of ad hoc measures have been initiated and introduced as we discuss in what follows. It should also be noted that regulation and supervision of the EMU financial system was grossly inadequate. We consider all the aspects just touched upon in the rest of this section and in section 9.5.

The European Commission called on 26 May 2010, and pledged on 8 June 2010, for new taxes to be imposed on all the continent's banks – but nothing has materialised yet. The levies would form a set of national funds, managed by national governments but under the aegis of a network of 'bank resolution funds' that could be used to disburse emergency money in case of a financial crisis. It is thereby the banks not the taxpayers that would bear the cost of such a crisis. This is a different arrangement from the proposed 'European Financial Stability Facility' (EFSF), formed on 1 July 2010 and endowed with a €250 billion fund, which was raised to €440 billion at a relevant meeting on 11 March 2011, and confirmed at another meeting of the European Commission on 25 March 2011. This was initially intended to be a temporary arrangement with an operational life of three years. However, on 17 December 2010 European leaders at a summit in Brussels agreed to make a treaty change so that EFSF functions until 2013. It will then be replaced by the European Stability Mechanism (ESM) to help member indebted states when in acute cash flow difficulties; ESM will then become permanent. It was also decided at the meeting of 11 March 2011, confirmed on 25 March 2011, that the new permanent bailout mechanism should be able to lend up to €500 billion through increased guarantees from triple-A states and paid-in capital from those states with weaker balance sheets – in a subsequent meeting of the European finance ministers it was agreed to €700 billion capital, of which €80 billion would actually be paid in; the rest would be 'callable' capital.[1] This facility aims to reassure financial markets and help out euro-area member states struggling to issue sovereign debt and faced with banking troubles. In terms of the funding arrangements of both the EFSF and ESM, however, the relevant decision has been postponed until later. This was due essentially to the German negotiators who bowed at the last minute to domestic political pressure and persistently proposed a reduction of their contribution to the bailout mechanism. Under the deal reached on 25 March 2011, euro area and other governments will have to pay their share of capital over five years, instead of the four years initially agreed.[2] The rate of interest on new loans from this facility is expected to be lower by up to 1 per cent than previously.

The key element is the creation of a permanent liquidity facility under the aegis of the ESM. This would be available as a means of crisis resolution if there is a risk to the stability of the euro area as a whole. The crucial difference between the EFSF and ESM is that the credits of the latter would be more senior to those of private investors. This will reduce the risk to the budget of the creditor nations, since it is expected that by 2013 European banks should be in a better position to absorb losses. The ESM will not come into force before 2014. All the changes of the 'grand bargain' had to be ratified by the parliaments of the EU's member states and they were by the time the whole package was eventually confirmed.[3] These new measures reduce the cost of bailing out countries in trouble but increase it for those who have been, or potentially could be, in need of a bailout. They do not address the issue of high sovereign debt, which had appeared to have been the focus of the whole exercise. Still, the exercise has been turned into a political game, one of what should have been an exercise to sort out the economic crisis. In this sense, it would not be surprising if the European leg of the 'great recession' is not contained any sooner.

It should be stressed that all these arrangements had not been envisaged by the creators of the EMU. For it is the case that one of the 'pillars' of the EMU and the euro was the 'no bailout, no exit and no default' clause. The sovereign debt crisis simply changed that principle significantly, at least in terms of the 'bailout' part of the clause. Still the agreed funds mentioned above should not be used to purchase government debt in the open market. They should be used to buy the debt from struggling governments. But there is a condition attached. This is that the struggling governments should agree to implement significant austerity measures. Yet it all amounts to an increase to the level of debt in the countries concerned. This is justified on the premise that the new mechanism helps the countries involved in that the loan conditions are much better than the ones replaced. But the debt of the countries involved piles up, thereby creating another serious danger, the possibility of default. This, however, entails a further danger in view of the high exposure of a number of European banks to weak countries' debt.[4] This may very well explain that despite the alleged seriousness of the European debt crisis, default has not been seriously considered yet. Indeed, it might not happen to the extent that support continues to be forthcoming. The weak country debt would continue to grow so long as support is forthcoming until the debt is all accumulated in, and held, by the official sector. Under these conditions the official sector will be the last holder of the assets that take the full loss. The taxpayer will carry the burden yet again, rather than the original bondholder. The ECB is trying very hard to avoid this problem. While helping the troubled countries, at the same time it attempts to sell debt to avoid excess liquidity in the market – the ECB does not undertake 'Quantitative Easing'. This is not always possible, though. It is not infrequent to find that since May 2010 when this operation started that that the ECB failed in its attempt to neutralise fully the effect on liquidity of purchasing government bonds.

Further relevant developments, discussed in chapter 5 (section 5.5), and we briefly comment on them in this paragraph, that will come into effect in 2013, include common fiscal and economic policies. One dimension of these policies may very well be dubbed as 'a reformed Stability and Growth Pact'. This includes close monitoring on government spending, pension schemes, and limits on wage increases in the public sector. There is also a further commitment for country-members to close the gap between their current debt levels and the EU's debt limit of 60 per cent of GDP. This is, of course, in addition to the financial penalties of countries that do not conform with the budget deficit of 3 per cent. The debt to GDP limit should be achieved by member countries initiating a 5 per cent per year reduction until the 60 per cent target is met. If a member country fails to close the gap between its debt level and the 60 per cent limit of GDP, by 5 percentage points per year, it will be subject to a fine of 0.2 per cent of its GDP. The fine would be automatic, unless a majority of the council opposed it. The agreement does also allow for pension reforms to be offset in national accounts and private indebtedness to be taken into consideration before a country is fined. Furthermore, governments must not spend more each year than their medium-term economic growth rate. All these measures, however, amount to deficit- and debt-tightening until the same rules as prior to the 'great recession' are achieved. But those rules failed since they lacked credible enforcement. So that for the same reasons its predecessors failed in the past (see, for example, Arestis, 2010; also Arestis and Sawyer, 2006a, 2006c), the current proposals are bound to fail again. This is actually the third attempt at a revised SGP. It clearly follows that what is needed is a plan for reform not a pact that has shown to have been so unsuccessful in the past. Such a plan should be based on effective economic governance, with firm roots on economic convergence. The coordination of economic policies is vital. Consequently the current, similar with previous, proposals are bound to fail again without such different and more secured foundations. An important missing dimension of the 'grand bargain' in relation to the 'great recession' is the lack of pan-European policies to let banks fail safely, thereby forcing losses on creditors rather than on taxpayers.

There is also the competitiveness pact, what has been labelled as the 'pact for the euro', or 'euro-plus pact' (European Council, 2011b). This is concerned with boosting the growth potential along with a common corporate tax base in the region. It covers a number of areas: improving competitiveness, through higher productivity and better alignment of wages and productivity; boosting employment through flexibility and tax reforms; improving public finances; reinforcing financial stability through legislation on banking and regular bank stress tests; and introducing a financial transaction tax. The 'pact for the euro' is, in principle, a framework for economic policy coordination in a number of macroeconomic policies. But it is far from it in that no indication of such an objective is evident in the 'pact for the euro'. It should be noted that these arrangements are not merely for the EMU members. They would equally apply for the non-EMU members of the EU, if they chose to participate in the 'pact for the euro'.

On 23 July 2010, the results of the Committee of European Banking Supervisors (CEBS) bank stress tests were published. The exercise was repeated in July 2011 and subsequently with similar results. These tests subjected banks in Europe to 'unlikely but plausible scenarios', and were designed to ascertain whether banks had enough capital to avoid default in crisis; also the setting of reasonable capital targets a better lending environment would follow. Like the 2009 US similar bank stress tests, the European results revealed a clean bill of health and a resilient banking system.[5] However, in view of the results, interesting questions arise. The most important is perhaps the question of no provision for the possibility of sovereign default. A further question is the extent to which the safety margin of capital ('core' capital to asset ratio with a threshold of 6 per cent) that banks were required to hold should have been higher. Consequently, was the threshold ratio sufficiently stressful? Indeed, a number of banks perceived as weak, managed to pass the test – including five of the six Greek banks tested. There is also the argument that the 'core' capital, defined as equity, retained earnings and various types of hybrid debt instruments (which have the characteristics of equity but also of bonds) is not suitable. The relevant argument is that if 'core' capital had been defined as equity and retained earnings, the real risk-absorbing elements, a number of banks would not have passed the test. Still there is the question of whether the institutions left out were unimportant enough. Indeed, there are institutions whose financial health is not entirely clear and yet left out of the test. In any case, these tests complement the establishment of the EFSF and the recent financial supervisory framework within Europe. We may note in passing that CEBS is due to become the European Banking Authority (EBA).[6]

These recent changes, which are by far stricter than previously, do not form in any way a step forward towards a de facto political integration. One implication is that the agreement to strengthen the euro area, the 'reformed Stability and Growth Pact' together with the 'euro-plus pact', focussing on broader macroeconomic reforms imply that future economic decisions will be taken collectively by the 17 euro-area states – not separately as in the past. Still they rely on the supply side of the EMU economy, neglecting the role and importance of aggregate demand. They also need to be applied to all member countries in a consistent way. For example, in the case of imbalances within the euro area countries both deficit and surplus members should be involved in the rebalancing, not merely to deficit countries as it is in the current versions. This type of policies failed in the past and they will fail again in the future. There is nothing in the revised proposals to suggest that they will not fail. When it comes to conflicts between national governments and the European Commission, the latter loses. This reinforces our main point. For it is clear that all these developments lack the important dimension of integration. It clearly follows that future steps to closer integration are absolutely necessary. For otherwise there is a serious risk of gradual unravelling of what little has been achieved. It is true, of course, that some integration is in place within the EU/EMU, which is difficult to break. It is, nonetheless, too weak to function satisfactorily as we have demonstrated in this book. Clearly, further integration is vital.

An interesting proposal comes from the then President of the ECB in a speech (Trichet, 2011a) where he argues for an EU Finance Ministry. The suggestion is that

> In this Union of tomorrow, or of the day after tomorrow, would it be too bold, in the economic field, with a single market, a single currency and a single central bank, to envisage a ministry of finance of the Union? Not necessarily a ministry of finance that administers a large federal budget. But a ministry of finance that would exert direct responsibilities in at least three domains: first, the surveillance of both fiscal policies and competitiveness policies, as well as the direct responsibilities mentioned earlier as regards countries in a 'second stage' inside the euro area; second, all the typical responsibilities of the executive branches as regards the union's integrated financial sector, so as to accompany the full integration of financial services; and third, the representation of the union confederation in international financial institutions. (p. 7)

The president concludes by clarifying to suggest that 'I think that [eventually] a confederation of sovereign states of a new type, with new institutions to manage the interdependence of today and tomorrow, would be fully in line with such a heroism of reason' (Trichet, op. cit., p. 8; see, also, Trichet, 2011b). This proposal may be seen as a step towards a closer integration of national budgetary policies and enforcement of controls over spending and borrowing within the EU. Such a suggestion, though, is by far short of providing a true and closer integration that would provide policies to be able to tackle the kind of problems the EU/EMU area has faced at the time of the 'great recession'.

Another proposal which would in effect be a step along the road to political integration would be the introduction of eurobonds. This is the arrangement whereby the member states of the EMU would be able to borrow in bonds issued by an EMU debt agency. It would be guaranteed by all the EMU countries, thereby underwritten by the most creditworthy ones, presumably Germany in particular. We have argued (Arestis and Sawyer, 2011a) that there are some basic questions to be resolved on this issue. A major one is in terms of who guarantees them. Would it be the EMU member governments collectively in some sense? Or would it all rely on one or two EMU countries and would this be acceptable to them? Further, what conditions would be imposed on member governments who sought to make use of the funds raised by the bonds with the need to avoid the imposition of fiscal consolidation by another route? In any case, would such conditions be met by the members of the EMU? The experience with the Stability and Growth Pact does not inspire confidence on this front; especially when we remind us of the past performance of the two main EMU members, namely Germany and France in the context of the SGP experience. Ultimately, eurobonds should involve some form of governance and, thus, political integration. EMU would need tax-raising powers to be able to service the bonds, and there would have to be EMU fiscal and financial policies. There is no suitable institution at the moment to undertake this responsibility. Political integration that would provide common fiscal and financial policies throughout the EMU not only would it guarantee the successful introduction, implementation and performance of the eurobonds, but would also aid the viability of the euro as a healthy currency, and the EMU as a strong economy.

9.5 Constraints on reforms

In our view the policy framework within which the EMU operates needs to be drastically changed, but to do so runs into the major obstacles, political and ideological, to changing the policy framework. Further, the euro has been a key element of the drive to economic integration that any withdrawal of a country from the euro would be a major defeat for the integration process.

The first feature was embedded in the Treaty of European Union in its various forms and now cemented in the Treaty of Lisbon ('The Treaty on the Functioning of the European Union'). Changes to the Treaty of Lisbon require the unanimous agreement of the 28 member countries, and since the changes required to support the euro involve policies, which could be seen as moves towards political integration, the possibilities of making those changes is close to zero. This indicates not only the serious weakness of the policy framework, but also that of embedding economic policies into a constitution, which is virtually impossible to change. It would also have to be recognised that the dominant macroeconomic institutions in the EMU, notably the ECB and the Directorate-General of Economics and Finance, appear to be fully signed up to the neo-liberal agenda.

With regard to the second feature, it was recognised by some advocates of the euro, that there were many ways in which there was insufficient economic integration to support a single currency, but that in the presence of a single currency, integration would continue to a stage, which did support a single currency. The conditions indicated by the Optimal Currency Area (OCA) literature could be seen as the nature of the integration-generating movements in relative prices and permitting factor mobility.

We have argued above, section 9.4, and elsewhere (Arestis et al., 2003; Arestis and Sawyer, 2006a, 2006d, 2006e) that in the absence of economic integration monetary unions without political integration did not in general have a good record of long-term survival. It is true, though, that those monetary unions involving very small countries, for example Eastern Caribbean Currency Union, which covers a total population of half a million, had a better survival rate. It can also be argued that a monetary union has one feature of political integration in the sense that it is governments, which determine what is treated as legal tender and accepted as payment of taxes. In this sense, the need for a significant EMU fiscal policy is paramount. The implementation of such a policy does require that the levels of tax revenues and of public expenditure, which come within the scope of EMU fiscal policy, and the balance between them (that is, the budget deficit/surplus) is settled at the EMU level. It is though also remarkable how little attention has been paid by the EMU to the promotion of economic integration, which would promote convergence of economic conditions between the member countries, whether with respect to unemployment, positions in the business cycle or common inflationary and changes in competitiveness experience.

The necessary reforms of EMU would require a new set of monetary and fiscal policies within which policies supported achievement of high levels of economic activity, the coordination of policies and policy objectives of full employment. The development of a substantial EMU budget (a manifold increase over the scale of the present EU budget) and the ability of EMU to operate its own fiscal policy with the full support of the ECB are likely further requirements. Policies would also be required to ensure similar inflationary experience across member countries, and to raise the competitiveness of the 'periphery' countries.

9.6 The dangers of pseudo-fiscal union in the EMU

In view of what we have argued in this chapter, indeed in the whole book, that a currency union such as the Economic and Monetary Union (EMU) would need to be accompanied by what could be termed a fiscal union (see, for example, Arestis et al., 2001), we should welcome the recently proposed moves in EMU towards what is termed fiscal union. Unfortunately, we have to argue of the dangers of the proposed fiscal union rather than welcome it. The fiscal union, which we would view as required, would be one where there are substantial tax raising powers at the EMU level, say of the order of 10 per cent of EMU GDP (compare this with the Federal government in the USA raises taxes of the order of 20 per cent of GDP). This fiscal union would involve a significant amount of fiscal transfer from richer countries to poorer countries: a proportional tax regime would raise absolutely more money in richer countries than in poorer countries, and a progressive one also relatively more. Provided that public expenditure did not exactly match tax revenue in a particular region, but rather was to some degree related to population size and to need, there would be transfer of resources from rich to poor. Another key element of fiscal union would be the ability of the relevant Federal authority (Ministry of Finance) to operate a fiscal policy with deficits and surpluses as appropriate for the state of the economy. Further it would require the support of the European Central Bank in the operation of fiscal policy and willingness to buy where the bonds issued by that Federal authority.

The type of fiscal union currently under discussion is rather different. It does not involve any EMU level tax raising powers nor the ability of EMU itself to run budget deficits (or surpluses). Fiscal policy remains with the national governments but subject to severe constraints and monitoring, all summarised under the 'fiscal compact', as discussed above.

The pledge of €200 billion to the IMF by the EMU country-members to deal with the crisis – this amount is clearly not enough but the hope is that other countries outside the euro area would follow. Further, the European Stability Mechanism (ESM) is accelerated into entry as soon as it is ratified by 90 per cent of the member states with capital commitments to it. The objective is now for the ESM to come into operation once it has been approved by the relevant national parliaments. The increase in addition to the €500 billion already planned for the ESM, was examined in March 2012 but no changes were decided. It is widely recognised that the amounts just referred to would not be enough to cover the borrowing needs of Italy and Spain, if required, over the near future.

Now that the 'fiscal compact' has been signed (1 March 2012) by all EU members, with the exception of the UK and the Czech Republic, and the further details that became available subsequently (European Union, 2012), do not provide any hope at all. The treaty will now have to be ratified by individual parliaments and, in the case of Ireland, by a referendum. It is now renamed as the treaty on Stability, Coordination and Governance. It requires that tax and spending plans will be checked by the European officials before national governments intervene. There will be automatic actions against those countries that overspend. In effect the fiscal compact retains the principles of the previous 'fiscal pact' versions but with the added one that breaking the deficit rules may actually be punished in some way. The limits of the revised and old SGP are in effect to balance overall budget over the cycle and limit the national budget deficit in any year to a maximum of 3 per cent of GDP. In place of the previous threat of 0.2 per cent of GDP as a 'fine' (though never implemented even though there were 40 cases where the 3 per cent limit was breached), there is now a change, which is as follows: euro area states' budgets should be balanced or in surplus; this principle will be deemed respected if, as a rule, the annual structural deficit does not exceed 0.5 per cent of gross domestic product, unless the ratio of government debt to GDP is significantly below 60 per cent in which case the annual structural deficit should not exceed 1 per cent; and this is to be written into national constitutions. In the case when a euro area member state is in breach of the 3 per cent deficit ceiling, the old SGP ceiling, there will be automatic consequences, including possible sanctions, unless a qualified majority of euro area states is opposed.

There is also the problem in this context, which is that it is really unbelievable to mandate in terms of the EMU countries' constitutions notions that are so vague in terms of their calculations, like 'structural deficits', 'output gap'; and 'potential GDP'. Its predecessor, the Stability and Growth Pact, did not work and there is absolutely no reason the Fiscal Pact will work for it is not very different in any case.

The ECB continued to support Italian bonds so that Italy is not cut off the financial markets. In the first three months of 2012, Italy had €300 billion of maturing debt. Unless this debt was rolled over in financial markets, no troika could cover these sums of money. The method applied could be more effective if the ECB were to announce a ceiling on bond yields or a floor on bond prices. In the case of Switzerland, for example, the mere announcement of such a scheme by the Swiss central bank had the desired effect without any real purchases. Further, the ECB was happy to salvage the financial system with the mere promise that governments would do their best to control budget deficits and public debts. Thus, the ECB provided three-year financing to 500 banks in the EU with loans that nearly hit €0.5 trillion. The ECB extended this package by another €530 billion with 800 banks involved (it costs them only 1 per cent per annum on a three-year loan deal) – banks had actually hoped for €1 trillion in the new round. Italian and Spanish banks dominated the take-up, which accounted for almost half of the funds on offer – half of the 800 banks were German. This kind of money may have prevented the meltdown of the EU financial system. However, it has done nothing to get the economy out of the recession. The reason is simply that banks do not trust each other and therefore prefer to park all this liquidity with the ECB. Interestingly enough, funds of €452bn after the first round (see *Financial Times*, 27 December 2011), and €777bn after the second round, were deposited with the ECB following the two operations referred to above. Furthermore, ECB's financing operation has failed to boost bank lending to the real economy. Data released by the ECB showed that, despite injecting €1 trillion in long-term liquidity to the euro area banks, loans to non-financial firms fell by €3bn during February. Corporate lending grew by just 0.4 per cent, lower than the growth recorded in November and December 2011.

Returning to our discussion of the policy rules now proposed for a fiscal union, two major problems are in place. First, they are likely to operate in a destabilising manner. Attempts to balance a government budget with no regard to the economic circumstances would involve raising tax rates and cutting public expenditure in the face of economic slowdown, thereby exacerbating the slowdown. The rules may be modified to allow for the position of the business cycle (that is focus on the so-called structural budget position). This would though exclude the use of discretionary policy measures, which would be deemed to increase the structural budget deficit. It would also face difficulties of calculating the structural budget position (assuming that a structural budget position is a well-defined concept; see Sawyer, 2012).

Second, there is the presumption that the desirable budget position for every country in every year is that of a balanced budget. A major element of the euro crisis arises from the pattern of current account imbalances amongst EMU member countries, and the lack of the means for countries to resolve those imbalances, and yet the external borrowing required to fund the current account deficits is not available. The imposition of the same budget position in all countries requires that the sum of net private savings (savings minus investment) plus current account deficit are the same. It is possible that such a requirement can accommodate large differences in current account deficits provided that there are corresponding large differences in net private savings. But it is more likely that the differences in current account deficits cannot be so accommodated.

The aim of a balanced average ('structural') budget is actually a significant budget surplus when calculations are made (as they should) in real terms; that is with allowance for the impact of inflation on real value of government debt. But more significantly it would involve a very substantial excess of tax revenue over current government expenditure (excluding interest payments). Further, it makes no allowance for governments to be able to borrow to fund public investment. The profoundly undemocratic nature of this approach is clear: the unelected European Commission can 'request' that the elected national Parliament and government to change its budget. Let us also note the problematic nature of assessment of budgets. The forecast of budget for the year ahead requires forecasts of growth, employment, inflation etc. for that year. The assessment of structural budget position requires estimates of potential output, which have often been subject to revisions many years after the event.

It is clear that the major objections to the old SGP, the new fiscal compact, and the proposed fiscal union, as discussed in this section, are that they seek to impose without any justification a balanced budget and that they pose restrictions in the use of fiscal policy in the face of economic crises. And as we have argued recently, proper fiscal union is the only way forward (Arestis and Sawyer, 2011c).

9.7 Summary and conclusions

The creation of a monetary union obviously creates a union-level monetary policy. It is widely recognised that monetary policy imposes a single policy applying across a diverse set of economic regions. A particular monetary policy may be appropriate for the position of some economies but not for others given their position in the business cycle and the responsiveness of their economies to monetary policy, and the monetary policy is more likely to favour the politically strongest (even when operated by an 'independent' central bank). Further, monetary policy is constructed to deal with demand induced inflation with interest rates raised (lowered) in response to inflation (actual or expected) above (below) the target rate, though we would doubt the effectiveness of monetary policy to significantly influence aggregate demand. But monetary policy cannot deal with other forms of inflation (for example, cost-push inflation) nor with situations in which there is high (or rising) inflation combined with low (or falling) levels of economic activity. The monetary union requires a further set of policy instruments including fiscal policy. This could only be possible within an EMU that enjoys political integration.

In this book we have raised the question as to whether a sustainable monetary union requires a considerable degree of political integration (and perhaps political union). We would strongly suggest that fiscal policy and a social security system operating at the level of the monetary union is required. The diversity of economic performance, institutional arrangements and beliefs on economic policy and the operation of market economies are all important difficulties in the construction and operation of a monetary union. Political integration is an important dimension to all these problems as this chapter has hopefully elaborated.

We have previously argued (Arestis et al., 2003; Arestis and Sawyer, 2006a, 2006c, 2006d) that in the absence of economic integration, monetary unions without political integration would not have a good chance of long-term survival. It is true, though, that those monetary unions that involve very small countries, for example Eastern Caribbean Currency Union, which covers a total population of half a million, have a better survival possibility. It can also be argued that a monetary union has one feature of political integration in the sense that it is governments which determine what is treated as legal tender and accepted as payment of taxes. In this sense, and as we have argued in this book, the need for a significant EMU fiscal policy is of paramount importance.

The implementation of such a policy does require that the levels of tax revenues and of public expenditure, which come within the scope of EMU fiscal policy, and the balance between them (that is, the budget deficit/surplus), is settled at the EMU level. It is though also remarkable how little attention has been paid by the EMU to the promotion of economic integration. This would encourage convergence of economic conditions between the member countries, whether with respect to unemployment, positions in the business cycle or common inflationary and changes in competitiveness experiences. Whether the latter or any other fundamental change is forthcoming, it is unfortunately a very sad expectation. It should also be clear that cosmetic measures as currently proposed will not save the euro. It is undoubtedly the case that the euro experiment is going through a severe test.

The overall conclusion, then, of the whole of this book is to suggest, very strongly indeed, for a political integration, especially so in view of the fact that economic integration within the EMU/EU is completely absent.

Notes

1 Introduction

1. In some respects the global financial crisis could be dated 2007–09, and it became the 'great recession' subsequently. Then a further banking and sovereign crisis became evident in 2011 and onwards, and in many respects the latter crisis was a continuation of the initial crisis, but the latter had a clear 'euro area' dimension.
2. Since not all of the EU states have joined the euro, the ESCB could not be used as the monetary authority of the euro area. The activities of the European Central Bank are at the heart of the European System of Central Banks (ESCB), along with the national central banks of the 27 European Union member states. Since not all 27 member states have adopted the euro as their currency, the term Eurosystem is used to describe the ECB and the national central banks of those Member States that have adopted the euro, currently 17.
3. Available at: http://european-council.europa.eu/media/639235/st00tscg26_en12.pdf.
4. The European Union, of course, has a budget but it is relatively small (near 1 per cent of all the EU countries' GDP) and deficits cannot be operated.

2 The Launch of the Euro and Economic Performance

1. The global financial crisis could be seen as first in evidence during 2007, particularly in August/September 2007, gathering pace during 2008, reaching full intensity in September/October 2008, and turning into a true 'great recession'. The financial crisis continues (up to the time of writing in mid-2013) with banks and financial institutions continuing to be in some difficulties, and the economic slowdown, rising unemployment following the financial crisis continue.
2. For an extensive discussion on the degree to which initial member countries met the convergence criteria, see Arestis, Brown and Sawyer (2001, chapter 3).
3. The relevant information is available at: http://ec.europa.eu/economy_finance/euro/adoption/who_can_join/index_en.htm (accessed March 2012).
4. The Treaty was signed on 2 March 2012 by all of the 27 member states of the European Union except the Czech Republic and the United Kingdom. The treaty entered into force on 1 January 2013.
5. Denote trade deficit (as proportion of GDP) by $(m - x)$, foreign debt, D, to GDP, Y, ratio as $d = D/Y$, then $dd/dt = (m - x) + d(i - g)$ where $(m - x)$ is the difference between imports (m) and exports (x, as percentage of GDP), i is rate of interest on foreign debt, and g is the growth rate of GDP (both in real terms, or both in nominal terms). The debt to GDP ratio will then tend to rise, though is can be seen that there are circumstances in which it would not, for example, g much greater than i, or d itself positive.

6. It should be noted that HICP, as reported in the quote of the text, is the Harmonised Index of Consumer Prices. This is the index used in the EMU for the 'official' definition of inflation.
7. The OCA literature starts from Mundell (1961), McKinnon (1963) and Kenen (1969); for reviews see, for example, Baldwin and Wyplosz (2009, chapter 11).

3 The Economic and Monetary Union Model: Theoretical Underpinnings of Macroeconomic Policy

1. See Meyer (2001) for an introduction to the NCM model. Woodford (2003) for a very detailed elaboration of the model albeit using the term neo-Wicksellian, and the Bank of England (2005) for a model along NCM lines in the context of building a macroeconomic model; Arestis (2007) contains a range of papers on the NCM. For a critique of the NCM, see Arestis, (2009) and Arestis and Sawyer (2008a, 2008b).
2. It is interesting to note in this context that in 1971–74 US deficit reductions led to the recession of the 1970s that began at the end of 1973. US deficit reductions in 1977–80 were followed by the recession of the 1980s. US deficit reductions in 1987–89 had similar effects.
3. The explicit non-appearance of nominal money in the model is justified on the assumption that the central bank allows the money stock to be what is necessary to achieve the desired real rate of interest. Money is thereby a residual (see Woodford, 2008, for example).
4. We discuss these issues at length in Arestis and Sawyer (2003a, 2003b, 2003c).
5. A brief indication of the models of the ECB is given in ECB (2008, pp. 36–7); see also Fagan and Morgan (2005) and Smets and Wouters (2003).
6. The reference to Solans (2000) is from a speech by Eugenio Domingo Solans, Member of the Governing Council and the Executive Board of the European Central Bank, at the Fourth Annual Conference of Banco Central de Chile, Santiago de Chile, 1st December 2000. Obtainable from http://www.ecb.int/press/key/date/2000/html/sp001201_1.en.html.
7. The quote in the text is from a speech by Jürgen Stark, Member of the Executive Board of the ECB Conference on inflation targeting, Magyar Nemzeti Bank (MNB) Budapest, 19 January 2007. Obtainable from http://www.ecb.int/press/key/date/2007/html/sp070119.en.html.
8. Hofman (2008) offers evidence for the period 1999(1Q) to 2006(3Q) to suggest that although in the early years of the ECB the predictive ability of money-based forecasts was high, it has, nonetheless, deteriorated substantially since then. Still, the predictive ability of M3 improves when the ECB's internal M3 series, corrected for the effects of portfolio shifts, are utilized.

4 Monetary Policy in the Economic and Monetary Union

1. HICP includes the prices of the following items, suitably weighted: goods, food, non-energy industrial goods, energy services, housing services, transport, communication, recreation and personal services, and miscellaneous (ECB,

2004c, p. 52). This is the so-called 'headline' HICP. When food and energy prices are subtracted, the notion of 'core' HICP emerges.

2. Interestingly enough, that review concerned itself only with the mandate of price stability, the ECB's primary objective. The subsidiary objective of the ECB, to 'support the general economic policies in the Community', and the interaction of monetary policy with other policies, essentially fiscal and wages policy, both were completely ignored by the review.
3. It ought to be noted, though, that the inflation rate in the euro area has generally been above the 2 per cent level for more or less the whole of the ECB's life as indicated in chapter 2.
4. Covered bonds are securities that usually attract top triple-A ratings. They are also a major source of mortgage finance in Europe.
5. A critical role for the Bank of England is provided, which is to be developed (it is planned that the governor of the Bank of England would join as number two to the president of the ECB; the latter would chair the new body). If such a role were eventually to be offered to the governor of the Bank of England, it would be implicit recognition of the importance of the UK's financial role in Europe and to both the UK economy and to that of Europe. It is the case that the City of London is the largest financial centre in Europe. In fact, new and more recent research by the think-tank Z/Yen Group, and reported in the *Financial Times* ('London Stays Top of Finance League', 19 March 2012), clearly shows that London is the leading 'global financial centre', followed by New York and Hong Kong.
6. In the case of New Zealand, the Governor of the Reserve Bank of New Zealand cannot be dismissed for failing to meet the policy targets but can be dismissed for what is deemed inadequate performance in pursuit of the inflation and other targets: see http://www.rbnz.govt.nz/monpol/about/2851362.html.
7. Strictly speaking, the minutes of the ECB monthly meetings will be published seventeen years after the relevant meetings.

5 Fiscal Policy in the Economic and Monetary Union

1. One may ask, of course, why 'a maximum deficit of 3 per cent of GDP', and not a higher one. See below for a possible answer to this question.
2. The change in the debt ratio is given by

   $\frac{d}{dt}(\frac{B}{Y}) = \frac{1}{Y}\frac{dB}{dt} - \frac{B}{Y^2}\frac{dY}{dt} = \frac{1}{Y}D - \frac{B}{Y}\frac{1}{Y}\frac{dY}{dt}$ where Y is the level of income since

   the change in debt is equal to the deficit (including interest payments) and the debt ratio is stable when the change in ratio is zero which would imply $d - bg = 0$ and hence $b = d/g$.
3. The US had an 8.6 per cent of GDP budget deficit (and 70 per cent of debt to GDP, of which 54 per cent is in foreign hands) and China's infrastructural plan implied a 7 per cent deficit to GDP (*Economist*, November 2008).

4. Full details on the EERP can be found on: http://ec.europa.eu/economy_finance/publications/publication13504_en.pdf.
5. Interestingly enough, a number of Asian and Latin American countries managed to avoid the most serious aspects of the crisis: their precautionary measures after the 1997 Asian crisis helped (build-up of large foreign reserves; reduced exposure to foreign borrowing); and tighter controls over their banking systems, especially so in some of the Latin American countries.
6. The Fed has used the term 'credit easing', more akin to the Bank of England's 'quantitative easing', but different from the ECB's 'enhanced credit support', or 'liquidity enhancing' policy, in its approach to non-standard policy-making in the context of the recent financial crisis.
7. In the EMU the focus is on the banking sector; the decision to purchase covered bonds outright by the ECB is with the specific aim to support the covered bond market, which is the major source of support of finance for the EMU banks.
8. We may note in passing the enormous exposure of a number of EMU banks to Central and Eastern European (CEE) countries. BIS (various issues) data show that 90 per cent of loans to CEE come from EMU banks (Austria, for example, is exposed to CEE by about 80 per cent of its GDP; the Netherlands by 66 per cent of GDP). Clearly, this exposure provides risks to the current state of the EMU.
9. It should be noted that the €700 billionn fund is not really substantial in that the 'callable' capital entails the real danger of some countries not being able to honour their commitments.
10. The EFSF/ESM will comprise of all the seventeen EMU-member states, plus a number of EE, but not EMU, members. The latter include Denmark, Poland, Latvia, Lithuania, Bulgaria and Rumania, which have pledged to join the EFSF/ESM arrangements.
11. In the meantime, the EFSF is in the process of issuing the 'eurobond', a sovereign responsibility of the EMU. This is an important development in that it is the first time that a bond issue is undertaken by an institution on behalf of the EMU as one entity. There is, however, great controversy over this issue (see, for example, Arestis and Sawyer, 2011).

6 Labour Markets, Employment Policies and the Single Currency

1. Available at: http://www.ecb.europa.eu/press/key/date/2012/html/sp120224.en.html (accessed 20 March 2012).
2. The relevant web site is: http://ec.europa.eu/social/home.jsp?langId=en.
3. The relevant web page on the European Employment Strategy is: http://ec.europa.eu/social/main.jsp?langId=en&catId=101 (accessed 29 July 2012).
4. The employment protection legislation is defined broadly and covers all types of employment protection measures resulting from legislation, court rulings, collective bargaining or customary practices. The OECD (1999)

study considered a set of 22 indicators, summarised in an overall indicator on the basis of a four-step procedure (pp. 115–18).

7 Macroeconomic Policies for Full Employment and Low Inflation

1. The US experience is very telling on this score. The 1933 Glass–Steagall Act, which separated banks as suggested in the text, produced a period until 1999, when the 1933 Act was repealed, of financial stability during which no financial crisis took place, let alone of the type of the late 1920s and August 2007 (see, for example, Arestis and Karakitsos, 2011, 2012).
2. See http://www.opsi.gov.uk/acts/acts2009/ukpga_20090001_en_1.
3. Committee on Banking and Financial Services, US House of Representatives, 22 July 1999.
4. It should be noted, though, that automatic stabilisers can change. Creel and Saraceno (2008), argue that the automatic stabilisers in the EU countries have diminished recently.
5. For some empirical work on this issue see Stockhammer et al. (2009).
6. It is interesting to note that empirical evidence (Eggertson, 2006) suggests that under fiscal and monetary policy coordination, fiscal multipliers are higher than when no policy coordination prevails (even bigger than the Keynesian ones). This is possible so long as the fiscal and monetary authority have a common objective, for example maximization of social welfare. Eggertsson (2006) utilising a calibrated model, not dissimilar in substance to the NCM type of macroeconomic model (see, for example, Arestis, 2007), concludes that under fiscal and monetary policy coordination fiscal multipliers are higher than when no policy coordination prevails. Indeed, they are bigger than those found in the traditional Keynesian literature (see, also, Arestis, 2012a, 2012b).
7. A report in the *Financial Times* (Fund Management section, 16 January 2006) makes the point that between a third and a half of institutional investors in Northern Europe, Australia and the UK, turn to the equity market from other asset markets. Under such circumstances, changes in the rate of interest would have ambiguous effects. For example, a rise in interest rates might reduce rather than encourage inward capital movements. The effect of interest rate changes on the exchange rate may have become rather ambiguous.
8. Further references include Angeriz and Arestis (2007a, 2007b, 2008), as well as Arestis and Sawyer (2004a).

8 The Future of the Euro

1. See, also, Chadha et al. (2012) for a different analysis of the problematic nature of the euro-area model. Chadha et al. (op. cit.) suggest that euro-area policy makers 'not only concentrate on the necessary reforms for a currency union but also offer to put the victims of the battle into intensive care' (p. 79).

2. Similar statements are made by the Governor of the ECB at the press conference after the monthly meetings of the Governing Council of the ECB (see, for example, Trichet, 2011b).
3. We elaborate further on the importance of financial stability in chapter 7 of this book (see, also, Arestis and Sawyer, 2012).
4. The ECOFIN is a 'configuration of the Council of the European Union ... and is composed of the Economics and Finance Ministers of the 27 European Union member states, as well as Budget Ministers when budgetary issues are discussed'. The tasks of the ECOFIN are: 'economic policy coordination, economic surveillance, monitoring of Member States' budgetary policy and public finances, the euro (legal, practical and international aspects), financial markets and capital movements and economic relations with third countries. It also prepares and adopts every year, together with the European Parliament, the budget of the European Union which is about €100 bn' (both quotes are available at: http://en.wikipedia.org/wiki/Economic_and_Financial_Affairs_Council).
5. Other contributors recognise the importance of euro area changes. Different proposals have been suggested. A most recent one is by Chadha et al. (2012), who suggest the 'reset option' whereby member countries of the EMU can temporarily leave the euro area but remain members of the EU with the 'ongoing objective' to return to the EMU at some future point in time.

9 Economic Convergence and/or Political Integration

1. It should be noted that the €700 billion fund is not really substantial in that the 'callable' capital entails the real danger of some countries not being able to honour their commitments.
2. The EFSF/ESM will comprise of all 17 of the EMU member states, plus a number of EE, but not EMU, members. The latter include Denmark, Poland, Latvia, Lithuania, Bulgaria and Rumania, which have pledged to join the EFSF/ESM arrangements.
3. In the meantime, the EFSF is in the process of issuing the 'euro bond', a sovereign responsibility of the EMU. This is an important development in that it is the first time that a bond issue is undertaken by an institution on behalf of the EMU as one entity. The first issue took place on the 25 January 2011 as part of its mission to provide liquidity to countries whose financial markets face serious difficulties.
4. It is interesting to note that 'As of 31 December 2009, banks headquartered in the euro area accounted for almost two-thirds (62%) of all internationally active banks' exposures to the residents of the euro area countries facing market pressures (Greece, Ireland, Portugal and Spain). French and German banks were particularly exposed to the residents of Greece, Ireland, Portugal and Spain. Together, they had $727 billion of exposures to Spain, $402 billion to Ireland, $244 billion to Portugal and $206 billion to Greece. At the end of 2009, they had $958 billion of combined exposures ($493 billion and $465 billion, respectively) to the residents of these countries. This amounted to 61% of all reported euro area banks' exposures to those economies' (BIS, 2010a, pp. 18–19). It clearly is the case that France and

Germany have a strong interest in rescuing the weak countries to avoid possible bankruptcies and/or a dramatic fall in the value of these countries' sovereign debt.

5. In the European case 91 banks, with seven of them failing the stress test, were included in the sample. In the US 19 banks were included and ten failed the stress test. Apparently, the more stringent and earlier US stress test has not helped in terms of its objective to boost bank lending, which continues to contract under tight conditions.
6. An important international development that affects the EU/EMU members and their banking sectors is the Basel III standards (BIS, 2010b). The main purpose of Basel III is to enhance banks' capital requirements to make them safer and avoid the problems of the 'great recession'. The EU intends to modify Basel III standards in an attempt to allow banks to count for more in their total capital. This would relax Basel III regulations and relax EMU's grip on banks when the opposite should be forthcoming.

References

Allington, N.F.B., Kattuman, P. and Waldmann, F.A. (2005), 'One Market, One Money, One Price?', *International Journal of Central Banking*, 1(3), 73–115.

Amable, B. (2003), *The Diversity of Modern Capitalism*, Oxford: Oxford University Press.

Angeloni, I., Kashyap, A., Mojon, B. and Terlizzese, D. (2003), 'The Output Composition Puzzle: A Difference in the Monetary Transmission Mechanism in the Euro area and the US', *European Central Bank Working Paper Series* No. 268, September, Frankfurt: European Central Bank.

Angeriz, A. and Arestis, P. (2007a), 'Monetary Policy in the UK', *Cambridge Journal of Economics*, 31(6), 863–884.

Angeriz, A. and Arestis, P. (2007b), 'Assessing the Performance of Inflation Targeting Lite Countries', *World Economy*, 30(11), 1–25.

Angeriz, A. and Arestis, P. (2008), 'Assessing Inflation Targeting Through Intervention Analysis', *Oxford Economic Papers*, 60(2), 293–317.

Angeriz, A. and Arestis, P. (2009), 'The Consensus View on Interest Rates and Fiscal Policy: Reality or Innocent Fraud?', *Journal of Post Keynesian Economics*, 31(4), 567–86.

Arestis, P. (2007), 'What is the New Consensus in Macroeconomics?', in P. Arestis (ed.), *Is There a New Consensus in Macroeconomics*, Houndmills, Basingstoke: Palgrave Macmillan.

Arestis, P. (2009a), 'Fiscal Policy within the NCM Framework', in J. Creel and M. Sawyer (eds), *Current Thinking on Fiscal Policy*, Houndmills, Basingstoke: Palgrave Macmillan.

Arestis, P. (2009b), 'New Consensus Macroeconomics: A Critical Appraisal', in E. Hein, T. Niechoj and E. Stockhammer (eds), *Macroeconomic Policies on Shaky Foundations – Whither Mainstream Economics?*, Marburg: Metropolis, pp. 165–86.

Arestis, P. (2010), 'Interview with Philip Arestis', *Intervention. European Journal of Economics and Economic Policies*, 7(2), 231–6.

Arestis, P. (2012a), 'Fiscal Policy: Time for the Renaissance of Keynesianism', in G. Chaloupek and M. Marterbauer (eds), *75 Jahre General Theory, Employment, Interest and Money*, Wirtschaftswissenschaftliache Tagungen der AK-Wien, Band 17.

Arestis, P. (2012b), 'Fiscal Policy: A Strong Macroeconomic Role', *Review of Keynesian Economics*, Inaugural Issue, 1(1), 93–108.

Arestis, P. and Biefang-Frisancho Mariscal, I. (2000), 'Capital Stock, Unemployment and Wages in the UK and Germany', *Scottish Journal of Political Economy*, 47(5), 487–503.

Arestis, P., Biefang-Frisancho Mariscal, I., Brown, A. and Sawyer, M. (2003), 'Asymmetries of Demand for Money Functions Amongst EMU Countries', *Investigación Económica*, LXII(245), 1–23.

Arestis, P. and Chortareas, G. (2006), 'Monetary Policy in the Euro Area', *Journal of Post Keynesian Economics*, 28(3), 371–94.

Arestis, P., Brown, A. and Sawyer, M. (2001), *The Euro: Evolution and Prospects*, Cheltenham: Edward Elgar Publishing.

Arestis, P., Ferrari, F. Fernando de Paula, L. F. and Sawyer. M. (2003), 'The Euro and the EMU: Lessons for Mercusor', in P. Arestis and L. Fernando de Paula (eds), *Monetary Union in South America: Lessons from EMU*, Cheltenham: Edward Elgar Publishing Limited.

Arestis, P., Fontana, G. and Sawyer, M. (2013), 'The Dysfunctional Nature of the Economic and Monetary Union', in Dagmar Schieck (ed.), *The European Union's Economic and Social Model – Still Viable in a Global Crisis?*, Farnham: Ashgate.

Arestis, P. and Karakitsos, E. (2011), 'An Analysis of the Causes of the 'Great Recession' and Some Policy Implications', in T. Niechoj, Ö. Onaran, E. Stockhammer, A. Truger and T. van Treeck (eds), *Stabilising an Unequal Economy? Public Debt, Financial Regulation, and Income Distribution*, Marburg: Metropolis-Verlag.

Arestis, P. and Karakitsos, E. (2012), 'Economic Policy Implications of the 'Great Recession'', in H. Herr, T. Niechoj, C. Thomasberger, A. Truger, and T. van Treeck (eds), *From Crisis to Growth? The Challenge of Imbalances and Debt*, Marburg: Metropolis-Verlag.

Arestis, P., McCauley, K. and Sawyer, M. (2001), 'An Alternative Stability and Growth Pact for the European Union', *Cambridge Journal of Economics*, 25(1), 113–30.

Arestis, P. and Paúl, J. (2009), 'Déficits en cuenta Corriente en la Unión Económica y Monetaria europea y crisis Financiera Internacional', *Ola Financiera*, September–October.

Arestis, P. and Sawyer, M. (2002), 'The Bank of England Macroeconomic Model: Its Nature and Implications', *Journal of Post Keynesian Economics*, 24(4), 529–45.

Arestis, P. and Sawyer, M. (2003a), 'Macroeconomic Policies of the Economic and Monetary Union: Theoretical Underpinnings and Challenges', *International Papers in Political Economy*, 10(1), 1–54.

Arestis, P. and Sawyer, M. (2003b), 'On the Effectiveness of Monetary and Fiscal Policy', *Review of Social Economics*, 62(4), 441–63.

Arestis, P. and Sawyer, M. (2003c), 'Does the Stock of Money Have Any Significance?', *Banca Nazionale Del Lavoro Quarterly Review*, LVI(225), pp. 113–36.

Arestis, P. and Sawyer, M. (2003d), 'Reinventing Fiscal Policy', *Journal of Post Keynesian Economics*, 26(1), 4–25.

Arestis, P. and Sawyer, M. (2004a), 'Can Monetary Policy Affect the Real Economy?, *European Review of Economics and Finance*, 3(3), 9–32.

Arestis, P. and Sawyer, M, (2004b), 'On Fiscal Policy and Budget Deficits', *Intervention, Journal of Economics*, 1(2), 65–78.

Arestis, P. and Sawyer, M. (2005), 'The Nature and Role of Monetary Policy When Money is Endogenous', *Cambridge Journal of Economics*, 29(6), 959–74.

Arestis, P. and Sawyer, M. (2006a), 'Macroeconomic Policy and the European Constitution', in P. Arestis and M. Sawyer (eds), *Alternative Perspectives on Economic Policies in the European Union*, Basingstoke: Palgrave, pp. 1–36.

Arestis, P. and Sawyer, M. (2006b), 'The Nature and Role of Monetary Policy When Money is Endogenous', *Cambridge Journal of Economics*, 30(6), 847–60.

Arestis, P. and Sawyer, M. (2006c), 'Alternatives for the Policy Framework of the Euro', in W. Mitchell, J. Muysken and T.V. Veen (eds), *Growth and Cohesion in the European Union: The Impact of Macroeconomic Policy*, Cheltenham: Edward Elgar Publishing Limited.

Arestis, P. and Sawyer, M. (2006d), 'Reflections on the Experience of the Euro: Lessons for the Americas', in M. Vernengo (ed.), *Monetary Integration and Dollarization: No Panacea*, Cheltenham: Edward Elgar Publishing Limited.

Arestis, P. and Sawyer, M. (2006e), 'Fiscal Policy Matters', *Public Finance*, 54(3–4), 133–53.

Arestis, P. and Sawyer, M.C. (2008a), 'A Critical Reconsideration of the Foundations of Monetary Policy in the New Consensus Macroeconomics Framework', *Cambridge Journal of Economics*, 32(5), 761–779.

Arestis, P. and Sawyer, M. (2008b), 'New Consensus Macroeconomics and Inflation Targeting: Keynesian Critique', *Economia e Società*, vol. 17, Special Issue, pp. 631–55.

Arestis, P. and Sawyer, M. (2008c), 'Are the European Central Bank and Bank of England Macroeconomic Models Consistent with the New Consensus in Macroeconomics?', *Ekonomia*, 11(2), 51–68.

Arestis, P. and Sawyer, M. (2009), 'Path Dependency and Demand–Supply Interactions in Macroeconomic Analysis', in P. Arestis and M. Sawyer (eds), *Path Dependency and Macroeconomics*, Annual edition of International Papers in Political Economy, Houndmills, Basingstoke: Palgrave Macmillan, pp. 1–36.

Arestis, P. and Sawyer, M. (2010a), '21st Century Keynesian Economic Policy', in P. Arestis and M. Sawyer (eds), *21st Century Keynesian Economics*, Annual Edition of International Papers in Political Economy, Basingstoke: Palgrave Macmillan, pp. 81–119.

Arestis, P. and Sawyer, M. (2010b), 'The Return of Fiscal Policy', *Journal of Post Keynesian Economics*, 32(3), 327–46.

Arestis, P. and Sawyer, M. (2010c), 'What Monetary Policy After the Crisis?', *Review of Political Economy*, 22(4), 499–515.

Arestis, P. and Sawyer, M (2011a), 'Eurobonds Will Need a Form of Political Union: Letter to the Editor', *Financial Times*, 18 August.

Arestis, P. and Sawyer, M. (2011b), 'Ideas on Fiscal Union Welcome but Inadequate: Letter to the Editor', *Financial Times*, 6 December.

Arestis, P. and Sawyer, M. (2012a), 'Can the Euro Survive After the European Crisis?', in P. Arestis and M. Sawyer (eds), *The Euro Crisis*, Annual Edition of International Papers in Political Economy, Houndmills, Basingstoke: Palgrave Macmillan, pp. 1–34.

Arestis, P. and Sawyer, M. (2012b), 'Economic Policies of 'New Economics', *International Review of Applied Economics*, 26(2), 147–60.

Arestis, P. and Sawyer, M. (eds) (2012c), *The Euro Crisis*, Annual Edition of International Papers in Political Economy, Houndmills, Basingstoke: Palgrave Macmillan.

Arestis, P. and Sawyer, M. (2013a), 'Moving from Inflation Targeting to Prices and Incomes Policy', *Panoeconomicus*, LX(1), 1–17.

Arestis, P. and Sawyer, M. (2013b), 'The Financial Transactions Tax: Its Potential and Feasibility', Annual Edition of *International Papers in Political Economy*, Houndmills, Basingstoke: Palgrave Macmillan, pp. 87–121.

Baccaro, L. and Rei, D. (2006), 'Institutions and Unemployment in OECD Countries: A Panel Data Analysis', in W. Mitchell, J. Muysken and T. van Veen (eds), *Growth and Cohesion in the European Union*, Cheltenham: Edward Elgar Publishing Limited.

Baker, D., Glyn, A., Howell, D. and Schmitt, J (2002), 'Labour Market Institutions and Unemployment: A Critical Assessment of the Cross-Country Evidence', Working Paper 2002-17, Center for Economic Policy Analysis, New School University, New York: USA.

Baker, D., Glyn, A., Howell, D and Schmitt, J. (2004), 'Unemployment and Labor Market Institutions: The Failure of the Empirical Case for Deregulation', *Report to the International Labour Organization*, Working Paper No 43, Statistical Development and Analysis Unit, November. Geneva: International Labour Office.

Baker, D., Glyn, A., Howell, D and Schmitt, J. (2005), 'Labor Market Institutions and Unemployment: A Critical Assessment of the Cross–country Evidence', Chapter 3 in D. Howell (ed.), *Fighting Unemployment: The Limits of Free Market Orthodoxy*, New York: Oxford University Press.

Bayoumi, T. and Eichengreen, B. (1998), 'Exchange Rate Volatility and Intervention: Implications of the Theory of Optimum Currency Areas', *Journal of International Economics*, 45, 191–209.

Bhaduri, A. and Marglin, S. (1990), 'Unemployment and the Real Wage: The Economic Basis for Contesting Political Ideologies', *Cambridge Journal of Economics*, 14(3), 375–93.

Ball, L. and Sheridan, N. (2003), 'Does Inflation Targeting Matter?', *NBER Working Paper Series*, No. 9577, Cambridge, MA: National Bureau of Economic Research.

Baldwin, R. and Wyplosz, C. (2009), *The Economics of European Integration*, 3rd edition, London: McGraw Hill.

Bank of England (2006), 'From interest rates to inflation'. Available at: http://www.bankofengland.co.uk/monetarypolicy/how.htm.

Bank of International Settlements (BIS) (2002), *Annual Report*, Basel: Switzerland.

Bank of International Settlements (BIS) (2010a), 'International Banking and Financial Market Developments', *Quarterly Review*, June, Basel: Switzerland.

Bank of International Settlements (BIS), (2010b), *The Group of Governors and Heads of Supervision Reach Agreement on Basel Committee Capital and Liquidity Reform Packages*. Available at: http://www.bis.org/press/p100726/annex.pdf.

Baunsgaard, T. and Symansky, S. (2009), 'Automatic Fiscal Stabilizers,' IMF Staff Position Note SPN/09/23, Washington, DC: International Monetary Fund.

Bibow, J. (2002), 'The Monetary Policies of the European Central Bank and the Euro's (Mal-) Performance: A Stability Oriented Assessment', *International Review of Applied Economics*, 16(1), 31–50.

Bibow, J. (2003), 'Is Europe Doomed to Stagnation? An Analysis of the Current Crisis and Recommendations for Reforming Macroeconomic Policymaking in Euroland', *Working Papers Series,* No. 379, Levy Economics Institute of Bard College (May).

Blanchard, O. (2006a): *Adjustment Within the Euro: The Difficult Case of Portugal,* available at: http://econ-www.mit.edu/faculty/download_pdf.php?id=1295.

Blinder, A. (1987), *Hard Heads, Soft Hearts,* Reading, MA: Addison-Wesley.

Blinder, A.S. (2010), 'Commentary: Rethinking Moneatry Policy in Light of the Crisis', *Federal Reserve Bank of Kansas City Annual Conference,* 28 August, Jackson Hole, Wyoming.

Brand, N., Burniaux, J.-M. and Duval, R. (2005), 'Assessing the OECD Jobs Strategy: Past Dimensions and Reforms', *Working Paper, ECO/WKP16,* Paris: OECD.

Bruno, M. and Easterly, W. (1996), 'Inflation and Growth: In Search of a Stable Relationship', *Federal Reserve Bank of St. Louis Review,* 78(3), 139–46.

Buiter, W.H. (2008), 'Central Banks and Financial Crises'. Paper presented to the Federal Reserve Bank of Kansas City Symposium on *Maintaining Stability in a Changing Financial System,* Jackson Hole, Wyoming, 21–3 August 2008. Obtainable from: http://www.kc.frb.org/publicat/sympos/2008/Buiter.09.06.08.pdf.

Buiter, W. Corsetti, G. and Roubini, N. (1993), 'Excessive Deficits: Sense and Nonsense in the Treaty of Maastricht', *Economic Policy,* 16, 58–90.

Buti, M., Franco, D. and Ongena, H. (1997), *Budgetary Policies During Recessions: Retrospective Application of the 'Stability and Growth Pact' to the Post-War Period,* Brussels: European Commission.

Centre for European Policy Studies (CEPS) (2005), 'EMU at Risk', *Seventh Annual Report,* CEPS Macroeconomic Policy Group, Brussels: Centre for European Policy Studies.

Chadha, J.S., Dempster, M.A.H. and Pickford, D. (2012), *The Euro in Danger: Reform and Reset,* Cambridge: Searching Finance Ltd.

Coats, D. (2006), *Who's Afraid of Labour Market Flexibility?,* London: Work Foundation.

Commission of the European Communities (1977), *Report of the Study Group on the Role of Public Finances in European Integration,* chaired by Sir Donald MacDougall, Economic and Financial Series No. A13 (Brussels, 1977).

Commission of the European Communities (2004), *COM(2006) 322 Final,* Brussels, 22 June.

Council of the European Union (2002), *Council Recommendation of 21 June 2002 on the Broad Guidelines of the Economic Policies of the Member States and the Community,* Brussels.

Council of the European Union, (2005), 'Presidency conclusions', European Council, Brussels, 22 and 23 March 2005 Document 7619/1/05 REV 1.

Creel, J. and Saraceno, F. (2009), 'Automatic Stabilisation, Discretionary Policy and the Stability Pact', in J. Creel and M. Sawyer (eds), *Current Thinking on Fiscal Policy,* Basingstoke: Palgrave Macmillan.

Currie, D. (1997), *The Pros and Cons of EMU,* July, London: HM Treasury (Published originally by the Economist Intelligence Unit, January 1997).

D'Arista, J. (2009), 'Setting an Agenda for Monetary Reform', Political Economy Research Institute, University of Massachusetts, Amherst, *Working Paper Series*, No. 190.
Davidson, P. (2011), 'The Keynes Solution for Preventing Global Imbalances'. Paper given at the 15th Conference of the Research Network Macroeconomics and Macroeconomic Policies, entitled *From Crisis to Growth? The Challenge of Imbalances, Debt and Limited Resources*, Berlin, Germany, 28–9 October.
De Grauwe, P. and Costa Storti, C. (2005), 'Is Monetary Policy in the Eurozone Les Effective than in the US?', *CESifo Working Paper No. 1606*, November.
De Haan, J., Berger, H. and Jensen, D.-J. (2003), 'The End of the Stability and Growth Pact?', *CESifo Working Paper Series*, No. 1093, December.
Dow, S.C. (1986), 'The Capital Account and Regional Balance of Payments', *Urban Studies*, 23(3), 173–84.
Duisenberg, W.F. (1999), 'Economic and Monetary Union in Europe: the Challenges Ahead', in *New Challenges for Monetary Policy*, proceedings of A Symposium Sponsored by the Federal Reserve Bank of Kansas City, Jackson Hole, Wyoming, 26–8 August, pp. 185–94.
Duisenberg, W.F. (2001), 'Introductory Statement, and Questions and Answers', *ECB Press Conference*, Frankfurt, Germany, 6 December.
Duisenberg, W.F. (2002), *Testimony to the European Parliament*, October, Brussels: Belgium.
Duisenberg, W.F. (2003a), 'Introductory Statement, and Questions and Answers', *ECB Press Conference*, 8 May, Frankfurt, Germany.
Duisenberg, W.F. (2003b), 'Introductory Statement, and Questions and Answers', *ECB Press Conference*, 5 June, Frankfurt, Germany.
Duisenberg, W.F. (2003c), 'Monetary and Fiscal Policy in the Euro Area', *Introduction, International Monetary Conference*, Berlin, 3 June.
Duisenberg, W.F. (2003d), 'Changing Fortunes: Financing World Growth', *The 2003 Spruce Meadows Round Table*, Calgary, 5 September.
Eggerston, G. B. (2006), 'Fiscal Multipliers and Policy Coordination', *Federal Reserve Bank of New York Staff Reports*, No. 241, New York: Federal Reserve Bank of New York.
Eichengreen, B. (1997), 'Is Europe an Optimum Currency Area', in B. Eichengreen, *European Monetary Unification: Theory, Practice and Analysis*, Cambridge, MA: MIT Press.
Eurobarometer (2006), *Public Opinion of the European Union*, Standard Barometer 65, Spring.
European Central Bank (ECB) (1999), 'The Institutional Framework of the European System of Central Banks', *Monthly Bulletin*, July, Frankfurt, Germany, pp. 55–63.
European Central Bank (ECB) (2001a), *Monthly Bulletin*, January, Frankfurt, Germany.
European Central Bank (ECB) (2001b), *Monthly Bulletin*, March, Frankfurt, Germany.
European Central Bank (ECB) (2001c), *Monthly Bulletin*, April, Frankfurt, Germany.
European Central Bank (ECB) (2001d), *Monthly Bulletin*, May, Frankfurt, Germany.

European Central Bank (ECB) (2001e), *Monthly Bulletin*, June, Frankfurt, Germany.
European Central Bank (ECB) (2001f), *Monthly Bulletin*, October, Frankfurt, Germany.
European Central Bank (ECB) (2001g), *Monthly Bulletin*, November, Frankfurt, Germany.
European Central Bank (ECB) (2001h), *Monthly Bulletin*, December, Frankfurt, Germany.
European Central Bank (ECB) (2002a), *Monthly Bulletin*, January, Frankfurt, Germany.
European Central Bank (ECB) (2002b), *Monthly Bulletin*, April, Frankfurt, Germany.
European Central Bank (ECB) (2002c), *Monthly Bulletin*, May, Frankfurt, Germany.
European Central Bank (ECB) (2002d), *Monthly Bulletin*, October, Frankfurt, Germany.
European Central Bank (ECB) (2002e), *Monthly Bulletin*, December, Frankfurt, Germany.
European Central Bank (ECB) (2003a), 'The Relationship Between Monetary Policy and Fiscal Policies in the Euro Area', *Monthly Bulletin*, February, Frankfurt, Germany, pp. 37–49.
European Central Bank (ECB) (2003b), *Monthly Bulletin*, March, Frankfurt, Germany.
European Central Bank (ECB) (2003c), 'The Need for Comprehensive Reforms to Cope with Population Ageing', *Monthly Bulletin*, April, pp. 39–51, Frankfurt, Germany.
European Central Bank (ECB) (2003d), *Monthly Bulletin*, May, Frankfurt, Germany.
European Central Bank (ECB) (2003e), *Monthly Bulletin*, June, Frankfurt, Germany.
European Central Bank (ECB) (2003f), *Monthly Bulletin*, July, Frankfurt, Germany.
European Central Bank (ECB) (2003g), *Monthly Bulletin*, August, Frankfurt, Germany.
European Central Bank (ECB) (2003h), *Monthly Bulletin*, September, Frankfurt, Germany.
European Central Bank (ECB) (2004a), *Monthly Bulletin*, June, Frankfurt, Germany.
European Central Bank (ECB) (2004b), *Monthly Bulletin*, October, Frankfurt, Germany.
European Central Bank (ECB) (2004c), *The Monetary Policy of the ECB*, Frankfurt: European Central Bank.
European Central Bank (ECB) (2005a), *Monthly Bulletin*, March, Frankfurt, Germany.
European Central Bank (ECB) (2005b), 'The Reform of the Stability and Growth Pact', *Monthly Bulletin*, August, Frankfurt, Germany, pp. 59–73.
European Central Bank (ECB) (2008), *European Central Bank: The First Ten Years, 1998–2008*, Monthly Bulletin 10th Anniversary of the ECB, Frankfurt, Germany.

European Central Bank (ECB) (2009), *Monthly Bulletin*, December, Frankfurt, European Central Bank.
European Central Bank (ECB) (2009), *Monthly Bulletin*, December, Frankfurt, European Central Bank.
European Central Bank (ECB) (2011), *Monthly Bulletin*, October, Frankfurt: European Central Bank.
European Commission (MacDougall Report) (1977), *Report of the Study Group on the Role of Public Finance in European Integration*. Brussels: European Commission.
European Commission (2000), *Public Finances in EMU*, Brussels: European Commission.
European Commission (2003a), 'Flash Estimates for the First Quarter of 2003', website http://europa.eu.int, May.
European Commission (2003b), *Public Finances in the EMU*, European Commission: Brussels.
European Commission (2004), *Facing the Challenge: The Lisbon Strategy for Growth and Employment*, Report from the High Level Group chaired by Wim Kok, Brussels
European Commission (2006), 'Introduction of the euro in the New Member states: Analytical Report', *Flash Eurobarometer 183*, Brussels.
European Commission (2008), 'EMU@10 Successes and challenges after ten years of Economic and Monetary Union', European Economy 2.
European Commission (2011), 'A Single Market for Intellectual Property Rights Boosting Creativity and Innovation to Provide Economic Growth, High Quality Jobs and First Class Products and Services in Europe', *COM(2011) 287*, Brussels, 24 May.
European Commission (2012a), 'The Second Economic Adjustment Programme for Greece', *European Economy*, Occasional Papers 94, March.
European Commission (2012b), *Directorate-General for Employment, Social Affairs and Inclusion Employment and Social Developments in Europe 2012*, Luxembourg: Publications Office of the European Union.
European Convention (2002), 'Economic Governance', *Working Group IV, Working Document 19*, 7 October, European Commission: Brussels.
European Convention (2003a), *Draft Constitution*, Volume 1, 26 May, Brussels: European Commission.
European Convention (2003b), *Draft Constitution*, Volume 2, 26 May, Brussels: European Commission.
European Council (2010), *Strengthening Economic Governance in the EU*, Report of the Task Force to the European Council, Brussels, 21 October.
European Council (2011a), 'Statement by the Euro Area Heads of State or Government', Brussels, 9 December. Available at: http://consilium.europa.eu/uedocs/cms_data/docs/pressdata/en/ec/126658.pdf.
European Council (2011b), 'Conclusions', Brussels, 20 April. Available at: http://www.consilium.europa.eu/uedocs/cms_data/docs/pressdata/en/ec/120296.pdf.
European Union (2010), 'Council Decision of 21 October 2010 on Guidelines for the Employment Policies of the Member States (2010/707/EU)', *Official Journal of the European Union*, 24 November.

European Union (2012), *Treaty on Stability, Coordination and Governance in the Economic and Monetary Union*, Brussels: European Union.

Fagan, G. and Morgan, J. (2005), *Econometric Models of the Euro-Area Central Banks*, Cheltenham: Edward Elgar Publishing Limited.

Feldstein, M. (1997), 'The Political Economy of the European Economic and Monetary Union: Political Sources of an Economic Liability', *Journal of Economic Perspectives*, 11(4), 23–42.

Ferguson, R. (2005a), 'Monetary Credibility, Inflation, and Economic Growth'. Speech at the Cato Institute 23rd Annual Monetary Conference on *Monetary Institutions and Economic Development*, Washington, DC, 3 November.

Ferguson, R. (2005b), 'Safeguarding Good Policy Practice' in *Reflections on Monetary Policy 25 Years after October 1979, Federal Reserve Bank of St. Louis Review*, March/April 2005, *87*(2, Part 2), 293–8.

Fertig, M. and Schmidt, C.M. (2002), 'Mobility within Europe – What Do We (Still Not) Know?', *IZA Discussion Paper*, No. 447, March.

Fischer, S. (1993), 'The Role of Macroeconomic Factors in Growth',' *Journal of Monetary Economics*, 32(3), 458–512.

Fitoussi, J.-P. and Creel, J. (2002), *How to Reform the European Central Bank*, London: Centre for European Reform.

Frankel, J. and Rose, A. (1997), 'Is EMU More Justifiable Ex Post Than Ex Ante?', *European Economic Review*, 41(3–5), 753–60.

Frankel, J.A. and Rose, A. K. (1998), The Endogeneity of the Optimum Currency Area Criteria, *Economic Journal*, 108(449), 1009–25.

Friedman, M. (1968), 'The Role of Monetary Policy', *American Economic Review*, 58(1), 1–17.

Forder, J. (2000), 'The Theory of Credibility: Confusions, Limitations, and Dangers', *International Papers in Political Economy*, 7(2), 1–40.

Forder, J. (2003), 'Central Bank Independence: Economic Theory, Evidence, and Political Legitimacy', mimeo, Balliol College, Oxford University, UK.

George, E. (2000), 'Future of Central Banking – Speech by The Rt Hon Eddie George, Governor', 27 August. Available at: http://www.bankofengland.co.uk/publications/Pages/speeches/2000/speech96.aspx.

Ghosh, A. and Phillips, S. (1998), 'Warning: Inflation May be Harmful to Your Growth', *IMF Staff Papers*, 45(4), 672–710.

Glyn, A., Howell, D. and Schmitt (2006), 'Labor Market Reforms: The Evidence Does not Tell the Orthodox Tale', *The Challenge Magazine*, 49(2), 5–22.

Goodhart, C.A.E. (2005a), 'Safeguarding Good Policy Practice' in *Reflections on Monetary Policy 25 Years after October 1979, Federal Reserve Bank of St Louis Review*, March/April 2005, *87*(2, Part 2), 298–302.

Goodhart, C.A.E. (2005b), 'The Experience of Inflation Targeting since 1993', in P. Arestis, M. Baddeley and J. McCombie (eds), *The New Monetary Policy*, Cheltenham: Edward Elgar.

Goodhart, C.A.E. (2007), 'Whatever Became of the Monetary Aggregates?', The Peston Lecture delivered in honour of Maurice, Lord Peston, Queen Mary, University of London, 28 February.

Goodhart, C.A.E. (2008), 'The Continuing Muddles of Monetary Theory: A Steadfast Refusal to Face Facts', Paper presented to the 12th Conference

'Macroeconomic Policies on Shaky Foundations – Wither Mainstream Economics' of the Research Network, *Macroeconomics and Macroeconomic Policies* (RMM), 31 October–1 November.
Goodhart, C.A.E. and Smith, S. (1993), *Stabilization*, European Economy, Reports and Studies No. 5/1993, *The Economics of Community Public Finance*, pp. 417–55.
Grahl, J. (2006), 'Labour Market Policies in the European Union', in P. Arestis and M. Sawyer (eds), *Alternative Perspectives on Economic Policies in the European Union*, Houndmills, Basingstoke: Palgrave Macmillan.
Greenspan, A. (2002), 'Opening Remarks', in *Rethinking Stabilization Policy*, Kansas: Federal Reserve Bank of Kansas City, pp. 1–10.
Hayo, B. (2006), 'Is European Monetary Policy Appropriate for the EMU Member Countries? A Counterfactual Analysis', *Marburg Papers on Economics*, no. 10–2006.
Hein, E. and Mundt, M. (2012), 'Financialisation and the Requirements and Potentials for Wage-Led Recovery – A Review Focussing on the G20', *ILO Conditions of Work and Employment Series No. 37*, Geneva: ILO.
Hermann, C. (2009), 'The European Social Models: Contours of the Discussion', in M. Frangakis, C. Hermann, J. Huffschmid and K. Lóránt (eds), *Privatisation Against the European Social Model*, Basingstoke: Palgrave Macmillan, pp. 77-92,
Higgins, M. and Klitgaard, T. (1998), 'Viewing the Current Account Deficit as a Capital Flow', *Current Issues in Economics and Finance*, Federal Reserve Bank of New York, 4(13), 1–6.
HM Treasury (2003), *EMU and Trade*, London: HMSO.
Huffschmid, J. (ed.) (2005), *Economic Policy for a Social Europe A Critique of Neo-Liberalism and Proposals for Alternatives*, Houndmills, Basingstoke: Palgrave Macmillan.
IMF (2005), *World Economic Outlook*, Washington, DC: International Monetary Fund.
IMF (2006), *World Economic Outlook*, Washington, DC: International Monetary Fund.
IMF (2009), *World Economic Outlook*, October, Washington, DC: International Monetary Fund.
IMF (2010), 'Central Banking Lessons from the Crisis', *Monetary and Capital Markets Department, 27 May 2010*, Washington, DC: International Monetary Fund.
Issing, O. (2002), 'ECB Watchers Conference: Monetary Policy and the Role of the Price Stability Definition', Panel Speech, Milan, 10 June 2002. Obtainable from: http://www.ecb.int/press/key/date/2002/html/sp020610.en.html.
Issing, O. (2003), 'Evaluation of the ECB's Monetary Policy Strategy', *ECB Press Conference and Press Seminar*, Frankfurt, Germany, 8 May.
Kalecki, M. (1944), 'Three Ways to Full Employment', in Oxford University Institute of Statistics, *The Economics of Full Employment*, Oxford: Blackwell, pp. 39–58,.
Kenen, P. (1969), 'The Theory of Optimum Currency Areas: an Eclectic View', in R. Mundell, and A. Swoboda (eds), *Monetary Problems of the International Economy*, Chicago: University of Chicago Press.

Keynes, J.M. (1936), *The General Theory of Employment, Interest and Money*, London: Macmillan.

Keynes, J.M. (1980), 'Activities, 1940–1946: Shaping the Post-War World: The Clearing Union', *Collected Writings Vol. 25*, London: Macmillan.

Khan, M.S. and Senhadji, A.S. (2001), 'Threshold Effects in the Relationship between Inflation and Growth', *IMF Staff Papers*, 48(1), 1–21.

Kleinknecht, A. and Naastepad, C.W.M. (2005), 'The Netherlands: Failure of a Neo–classical Policy Agenda', *European Planning Studies*, 13(8), 1193–203.

Kleinknecht, A., Oostendorp, R.M., Pradhan, M.P. and Naastepad, C.W.M. (2006), 'Flexible Labor, Firm Performance and the Dutch Job Creation Miracle', *International Review of Applied Economics*, 20(2), 171–87.

Kuttner, K. and Mosser, P. (2002), 'The Monetary Transmission Mechanism: Some Answers and Further Questions', *Economic Policy Review*, New York: Federal Reserve Bank of New York.

Kydland, F. and Prescott, E.C. (1977), 'Rules Rather than Discretion: The Inconsistency of Optimal Plans', *Journal of Political Economy*, 85(3), 473–92.

Lavoie, M. and Seccareccia, M. (1999), 'Interest Rate – Fair', in P.A. O'Hara (ed.), *Encyclopedia of Political Economy*, London: Routledge, pp. 543–45.

Laeven, L. and Valencia, F. (2008), 'Systemic Banking Crises: A New Database', *IMF Working Paper WP/2008/0224*, Washington, DC: International Monetary Fund.

Layard, R., S., Nickell, S. and Jackman, R. (1991), *Unemployment: Macroeconomic Performance and the Labour Market*, Oxford: Oxford University Press.

Lehndorff, S. (ed.) (2012), *A Triumph of Failed Ideas of the European Models of Capitalism in the Crisis*, European Trade Union Institute (ETUI) D/2012/10.574/01.

Lerner, A. (1943), 'Functional Finance and the Federal Debt', *Social Research*, February, 38–51.

Levine, R. and Renelt, D. (1992), 'A Sensitivity Analysis of Cross–Country Growth Regressions', *American Economic Review*, 82(3), 942–63.

McCarthy, J. (1999), 'Pass-through of Exchange Rates and Import Prices to Domestic Inflation in Some Industrialised Economies', BIS Working Papers, No. 79, November, Basel: Bank for International Settlements, Monetary and Economic Department.

McKinnon, R.I. (1963), 'Optimum Currency Areas', *American Economic Review*, 53(4), 717–25.

Meade, E.E. and Sheets, N.D. (2001), 'Regional Influences on US Monetary Policy: Some Implications for Europe', *Discussion Paper No. 523*, London: Centre for Economic Performance, LSE.

Mundell, R.A. (1961), 'A Theory of Optimal Currency Areas', *American Economic Review*, 53(1), 657–64.

Nordhaus, W. (1973), 'The Effects of Inflation on the Distribution of Economic Welfare', *Journal of Money, Credit, and Banking*, 5(4), 465–504.

OECD (2009), *Economic Outlook*, May, Paris.

OECD (2012), *Economic Policy Reforms 2012: Going for Growth, OECD Publishing.* http://dx.doi.org/10.1787/growth-2012-en.

Palley, T. (2001), 'The Role of Institutions and Policies in Creating High European Unemployment: The Evidence', *Working Paper Series*, No. 336, Levy Economics Institute of Bard College (August).

Palley, T.I. (2004), 'Asset-based Reserve Requirements: Reasserting Domestic Monetary Control in an Era of Financial Innovation and Instability', *Review of Political Economy*, 16(1), 43–58.

Pasinetti, L. (1981), *Structural Change and Economic Growth*, Cambridge: Cambridge University Press

Pasinetti, L. (1997), 'The Social 'Burden' of High Interest Rates' in P. Arestis, G. Palma and M. Sawyer (eds), *Capital Controversy, Post-Keynesian Economics and the History of Economics: Essays in honour of Geoff Harcourt*, London: Routledge, pp. 161–8.

Pentecost, E.J. (1999), 'Monetary Unions in Nineteenth Century Europe: An Historical Perspective and Lessons for EMU in the Twenty-first Century', in S. Daniel, P. Arestis and J. Grahl (eds), *The History and Practice of Economics, Essays in Honour of B. Corry and M. Peston*, vol. 2, Cheltenham: Edward Elgar Publishers.

Rogoff, K. (1985), 'The Optimal Degree of Commitment to an Intermediate Monetary Target', *Journal of International Economics*, 35(1), 151–67.

Santos Silva, J. M. C. and Tenreyro, Silvana (2010a), 'Currency Unions in Prospect and Retrospect', *Centre for Economic Performance, Discussion Paper No. 986*, June.

Santos Silva, J. M. C. and Tenreyro, Silvana (2010b), 'Has the Euro Increased Trade? Short Answer: No', *CentrePiece*, Autumn. Available at: http://personal.lse.ac.uk/TENREYRO/euro.pdf.

Sawyer, M. (1997), 'On budget deficits and capital expenditure', *Working Paper Series* 208, Levy Economics Institute of Bard College.

Sawyer, M. (2002), 'The NAIRU, Aggregate Demand and Investment', *Metroeconomica*, 53(1), 66–94.

Sawyer, M. (2007), 'The Foundations of Monetary Policy in the New Consensus Framework: A Partial Critique', in P. Arestis (ed.), *Is There a New Consensus in Macroeconomics*, Houndmills, Basingstoke: Palgrave Macmillan.

Sawyer, M. (2009a), 'Fiscal and Interest Rate Policies in the 'New Consensus Framework': A Different Perspective', *Journal of Post Keynesian Economics*, 31(4), 549–65.

Sawyer, M. (2009b), 'The Continuing Relevance of Fiscal Policy', in J. Creel and M. Sawyer (eds), *Current Thinking on Fiscal Policy*, Basingstoke: Palgrave.

Sawyer, M. (2009c), 'Interest Rates and Inflation: What are the Links?', *Intervention. European Journal of Economics and Economic Policies*, 6(1), 81–96.

Sawyer, M. (2010), 'Phillips Curve, Independence of Central Banks and Inflation Targeting', in G. Fontana, J. McCombie and M. Sawyer (eds), *Macroeconomics, Finance and Money, Essays in Honour of Philip Arestis*, Houndmills, Basingstoke: Palgrave Macmillan.

Sawyer, M. (2012), 'The Contradictions of Balanced Structural Government Budgets', in H. Herr, T. Niechoj, C. Thomasberger, A Truger, and T.l van Treeck (eds), *From Crisis to Growth? The Challenge of Imbalances and Debt*, Marburg: Metropolis Verlag.

Stiglitz, J. (2003), 'Too Important for Bankers: Central Banks' Ruthless Pursuit of Price Stability Holds Back Economic Growth and Boosts Unemployment', *The Guardian*, 10 June.

Stockhammer, E., Onaran, O and Ederer, S. (2009), 'Functional Income Distribution and Aggregate Demand in the Euro Area', *Cambridge Journal of Economics*, 33(1), 139–59.

Svensson, L.E.O. (2003), 'How Should the Eurosystem Reform Its Monetary Strategy'. Briefing paper for the Committee on Economic and Monetary Affairs of the European Parliament. Available at http://www.princeton.edu/~svensson.

Taylor, J.B. (1993), 'Discretion Versus Policy Rules in Practice', *Carnegie–Rochester Conference Series on Public Policy*, December, 195–214.

Taylor, J.B. (2008), 'The Financial Crisis and the Policy Responses: An Empirical Analysis of What Went Wrong', mimeo, November.

Thirlwall, A.P. (1980), 'Regional Problems are "Balance of Payments Problems" ', *Regional Studies*, vol. 14, 419–25.

Treasury (1997), *Pre Budget Report*, Cmnd. 3804, London: HMSO.

Treasury (1998), *Pre Budget Report*, Cmnd. 3804, London: HMSO.

Treasury (2003), *Fiscal Stabilization and EMU*, Available at http://www.hm-treasury.gov.uk.

Trichet, J.-C. (2004), 'Introductory Statement, and Questions and Answers', *ECB Press Conference*, Frankfurt, Germany, 5 February.

Trichet, J.-C. (2005), 'Introductory Statement, and Questions and Answers', *ECB Press Conference*, Frankfurt, Germany, March–December.

Trichet, J.-C. (2006), 'Introductory Statement with Q&A', *Press Conference 6 July 2006*, Frankfurt am Main: European Central Bank.

Trichet, J.-C. (2008), 'Introductory Statement with Q&A', *Press Conference 4 December 2008*, Frankfurt au Main: European Central Bank.

Trichet, J.-C. (2011a), 'Building Europe, Building Institutions', Speech on receiving the Karlspreis, 2011 in Aachen, 2 June 2011. Available at: http://www.ecb.int/press/key/date/2011/html/sp110602.en.html.

Trichet, J.-C. (2011b), 'Introductory Statement to the Press Conference (with Q&A)', Frankfurt am Main, 9 June. Available at: http://www.ecb.int/press/pressconf/2011/html/is110609.en.html.

Tridico, P. (2012), 'Financial Crisis and Global Imbalance: Its Labour Market Origins and the Aftermath', *Cambridge Journal of Economics*, 36(1), 17–42.

United Nations Conference on Trade and Development (UNCTAD) (2005), *Trade and Developments Report, 2005*, New York: United Nations.

White, W.R. (2007), 'The Need for a Larger Policy Horizon: A Less Orthodox Approach, in J.J. Teunisson and A.A. Akkerman (eds), *Global Imbalances and Developing Countries: Remedies for a Failing International Financial System*, The Hague: Forum on Debt and Development (FONDA).

Van Veen, T. (2006), 'Institutions and the Labour Market: Examining the Benefits', in W. Mitchell, J. Muysken and T. van Veen (eds), *Growth and Cohesion in the European Union*, Cheltenham: Edward Elgar Publishing Limited.

Vergeer, R. and Kleinknecht, A. (2010), 'The Impact of Labor Market Deregulation on Productivity: A Panel Data Analysis of 19 OECD Countries (1960–2004)', *Journal of Post Keynesian Economics*, 33(2), 371–407.

Vieira, C. and Vieira, I. (2012), 'Assessing the Endogeneity of OCA Conditions in EMU', *Manchester School*, 10(5), 77–91.

Wicksell, K. (1898), *Geldzins und Güterpreise*, Frankfurt: Verlag Gustav Fischer. English Translation in R.F. Kahn (1965), *Interest and Prices*, New York: Kelley.

Whyman, P.B., Baimbridge, M and Mullen, A. (2012), *The Political Economy of the European Social Model*, London: Routledge.

Woodford, M. (2008), 'How Important is Money in the Conduct of Monetary Policy?', *Journal of Money, Credit and Banking*, 40(8), 1561–98.

Index

Page numbers in *italics* refer to references in the Notes section.

The manufacturer's authorised representative in the EU is Springer
Nature Customer Service Centre GmbH, Europaplatz 3, 69115 Heidelberg,
Germany. If you have any concerns regarding our products, please
contact ProductSafety@springernature.com

Printed and bound by CPI Group (UK) Ltd, Croydon, CR0 4YY
10/10/2026
02231219-0005